Apprenticeship in Critical Ethnographic Practice

THE LEWIS HENRY MORGAN LECTURES / 1993

Presented at
The University of Rochester
Rochester, New York

APPRENTICESHIP

in Critical Ethnographic Practice

JEAN LAVE   FOREWORD BY *Thomas P. Gibson*

The University of Chicago Press   CHICAGO AND LONDON

Jean Lave is an anthropologist, now professor emerita at the
University of California, Berkeley. She taught at UC Irvine from
1966 through 1988 and UC Berkeley from 1989 to 2006, and
continues to teach in the Berkeley geography department. She
is the author of *Cognition in Practice: Mind, Mathematics, and
Culture in Everyday Life* (1988); coauthor of *Situated Learning:
Legitimate Peripheral Participation* (1991) and *Understanding
Practice* (1993); and coeditor of *History in Person: Enduring
Struggles, Contentious Practice, Intimate Identities* (2000).

The University of Chicago Press, Chicago 60637
The University of Chicago Press, Ltd., London
© 2011 by The University of Chicago
All rights reserved. Published 2011.
Printed in the United States of America

20 19 18 17 16 15 14 13 12 11   1 2 3 4 5

ISBN-13: 978-0-226-47071-9 (cloth)
ISBN-13: 0-226-47072-6 (paper)
ISBN-10: 0-226-47071-7 (cloth)
ISBN-10: 0-226-47072-5 (paper)

Library of Congress Cataloging-in-Publication Data

Lave, Jean.
    Apprenticeship in critical ethnographic practice / Jean
Lave ; foreword by Thomas P. Gibson.
        p.   cm. — (The Lewis Henry Morgan lectures ; 1993)
    Includes bibliographical references and index.
    ISBN-13: 978-0-226-47071-9 (hardcover : alk. paper)
    ISBN-13: 978-0-226-47072-6 (pbk. : alk. paper)
    ISBN-10: 0-226-47071-7 (hardcover : alk. paper)
    ISBN-10: 0-226-47072-5 (pbk. : alk. paper)   1. Vai
(African people—Social life and customs.   2. Gola (African
people)—Social life and customs.   3. Tailors—Liberia—
Apprentices.   4. Ethnology—Liberia.   I. Title.   II. Series:
Lewis Henry Morgan lectures ; 1993.
DT630.5.V2L38 2011
331.25'922089963—dc22
                                    2010028189

♻ This paper meets the requirements of ANSI/NISO
Z39.48-1992 (Permanence of Paper).

This book is dedicated to
the tailors and their apprentices
in Happy Corner

CONTENTS

FOREWORD

This volume is based on the Lewis Henry Morgan Lectures that Professor Jean Lave delivered at the University of Rochester in 1993. They were the thirty-first in a series initiated by Meyer Fortes in 1963. The lectures were originally conceived in 1961 by Bernard Cohen, who was then chair of the Department of Anthropology and Sociology. They were organized and edited by Alfred Harris from 1963 until 1993 and by Anthony Carter until 2007, when I took over the responsibility for doing so. This is my first opportunity to write a foreword to a published set of lectures, and I do so with great pleasure.

In this book, Jean Lave intertwines an analysis of Vai and Gola tailors' apprenticeship and everyday mathematical practice in Liberia in the 1970s with a detailed account of the process of carrying out that research. Together they pose questions for apprentice ethnographers: What is critical ethnographic practice? What does it mean to move from a commonsense vernacular theoretical problematic to a relational theoretical perspective? What does that do to our understanding of apprenticeship? She develops the thesis that in critical, relational theoretical terms, we are all apprentices to our own changing practice.

The book project has a long history. Professor Lave's original lectures were organized as a theoretical and methodological meditation on a series of ethnographic investigations she had carried out in West Africa between 1973 and 1978. They were intended to challenge the assumptions and methods of cross-cultural research on education, learning, and cognition. The central contention of these theories was that "formal education processes were supposed to enhance the application of general, abstract, higher cognitive skills, resulting in flexible, problem-solving capabilities." These learned skills could then be "transferred" to all manner of particular social contexts, unlike the concrete sorts of skills acquired through "traditional" forms of learning, which could not be transferred. Experiments compared "schooled" to "non-schooled" subjects. Professor Lave decided that the place to begin a comparative investigation was to replace that residual term "non-schooled" with a specific, local, complex educational practice—thus her study of tailors' apprenticeship in Monrovia.

The Liberian project concluded with a theoretical commitment to the situated character of all learning and with a sense that to go deeper required a nuanced inquiry into everyday life in other places. This led to a separate research project on the way "just plain folks" in Orange County, California, engaged with dilemmas of quantity, interwoven with a theoretical perspective in which social practice was front and center. The results of this research were published in 1988 in the highly influential book *Cognition in Practice: Mind, Mathematics and Culture in Everyday Life.*[1]

By the time Professor Lave returned to her West African material in preparation for delivering the Lewis Henry Morgan Lectures in 1993, she was thus operating within a theoretical framework that was far more sophisticated than the one she had set out with twenty years before. As it turned out, her lectures marked just one more milestone in her journey toward the development of what she now calls critical ethnographic practice. The current book is structured as a series of contemporary commentaries on earlier phases in the development of her understanding both of learning in Monrovia, and of developments in the field of cultural anthropology as a whole over the last fifty years.

Publications by previous Morgan lecturers play a central part in her argument, especially those delivered by Meyer Fortes in 1963, Margery Wolf in 1983, Marilyn Strathern in 1989, Jane Guyer in 1997, and Caroline Bledsoe in 1999.[2] As one of the manuscript reviewers commented, "like Guyer and Strathern, Lave compels us and challenges us to re-think and to re-do pretty much everything we have been doing as social analysts so far."

On the one hand, Lave's narrative provides a concrete example of the form of analysis she advocates. It shows how her developing understanding of a particular field site, Monrovian tailors in the 1970s, has been intertwined with her developing understanding of a relational theory of practice. This tradition is itself composed of a number of disparate strands, including the theory of praxis first outlined by Karl Marx in the 1840s; the work of Henri LeFebvre on the production of space; the work of Stuart Hall, Paul Willis, and others at the Centre for Contemporary Cultural Studies at Birmingham; and the theory of Critical Social Psychology associated with Klaus Holzkamp in Berlin and Ole Dreier in Copenhagen. Her book provides an informative account of how scholars in a number of fields have combined and modified these approaches to suit the needs of their own empirical research, and what anthropologists can learn from them.

On the other hand, her narrative provides an ethical and political model for anyone using ethnographic methods in the qualitative social sciences. She demonstrates with the Liberian research how fieldwork, as a long and improvised process, deeply shapes and is shaped by the sometimes subtle but always crucial political-ethical qualities of comparative research. The book moves from the social-political implications of uncritical theorizing, to the limited shifts involved in critical inquiry from within vernacular positivist theory, and then pushes further to demonstrate the effects on theoretical/empirical practice of adopting a relational theoretical problematic.

In the final chapter, Lave sums up what has been learned by following the process of producing the ethnographic research in Liberia about tailors' apprenticeship on the one hand and exploring apprenticeship in critical ethnographic practice on the other: "Reading each with respect to the other has changed how I have come to understand each one. This process treats them not as identical, but considers each as produced in and through the other—research on apprenticeship, research as apprenticeship." As Professor Lave develops her argument through the course of this book, she provides readers with the opportunity to observe this process as she experienced it over the last several decades, and perhaps with the inspiration to integrate a similar process into their own theoretical/empirical work.

Thomas P. Gibson, Editor
The Lewis Henry Morgan Lectures

Notes

1. Cambridge University Press, 1988.

2. Published versions of these lectures appeared under the following titles: Meyer Fortes, *Kinship and the Social Order: The Legacy of Lewis Henry Morgan* (Chicago: Aldine, 1969); Margery Wolf, *A Thrice-Told Tale: Feminism, Postmodernism, and Ethnographic Responsibility* (Stanford University Press, 1992); Marilyn Strathern, *After Nature: English Kinship in the Late Twentieth Century* (Cambridge University Press, 1992); Jane I. Guyer, *Marginal Gains: Monetary Transactions in Atlantic Africa* (University of Chicago Press, 2004); Caroline Bledsoe, *Contingent Lives: Fertility, Time, and Aging in West Africa* (University of Chicago Press, 2002).

ACKNOWLEDGMENTS

These acknowledgments, before anything else, must include my thanks to the tailors in Happy Corner who allowed me to participate in their working/learning lives over long periods of time and were unfailingly kind and patient in doing so. If I was engaged over years of fieldwork in and with situated learning, the tailors responded with a great deal of situated instruction. Most especially I wish to thank Gbelly Larjeh, generous friend and insightful participant in life in the tailors' alley and in that process of instruction. I have not returned to Liberia since the alley was destroyed shortly before the devastating civil war in the 1980s. There are no words adequate to acknowledge that destruction or what the tailors have endured, but on the last day of working on this book I learned of a new beginning: somehow Happy Corner is back, tailors once again at work there. I am glad and thankful for their return.

One reason that no one should take thirty years to write a book is because it is impossible to offer acknowledgments that rise to the level of the generous, specific, labor-intensive, and creative contributions of colleagues, friends, family, and institutions who have helped to make this project what it has become. For their many intellectual contributions, practical help, and enduring support, I owe them an overwhelming debt. Part of the reason it has taken so long to reach this moment is that I have written other books and papers that have kept getting in the way of finishing this one. The acknowledgments in every paper and book I have written since the 1970s ought to be collected and reproduced here, testifying to those many contributions along the way.

There was a beginning to the research and to the book project, which created lasting relations that have wound in and out of my life and work all these years: It began at the University of California, Irvine, in close and inspiring collaboration with Mike Cole and the group of students and colleagues in

Program B in the School of Social Sciences. Our families spent time in Monrovia together. The sense of family connection laid down in those years has endured and been renewed. Michael Butler, an early and long-term friend, is the brilliant visionary behind the Farm School at UC Irvine, intensely unorthodox in his ways of making deep mathematical knowledge available to children and others. Rogers Hall, a graduate student in the Department of Information and Computer Sciences at Irvine when we met, later became the best of colleagues at the University of California, Berkeley.

Two other enduring friendships from this period also stand out. I've known Ray McDermott since the early 1970s. We have read together, taught seminars together in northern California and in Japan and Denmark, and finally produced a paper together (see the acknowledgments to Lave and McDermott 2002). Dorothy Holland is a social practice theorist and the most versatile and skilled ethnographer I've ever known. She inspired our School of American Research seminar and coedited book, *History in Person* (2001). We have talked each other into many adventures (intellectual and otherwise) over the years. Our collaboration and friendship took root in the early days at Irvine.

Other collaborators and friends from both Irvine days and Berkeley have been sources of inspiration, shared intellectual labor, and situated instruction at different moments and in diverse ways. My thanks to Barbara Rogoff, Carol Stack, Nadine Fernandez, Shawn Parkhurst, and Carol Page for their lasting impact on my life and work.

My research on apprenticeship has always seemed to provide the medium for my struggle to change. The process of learning and coming to inhabit the problematic of social practice theory is a major reason this book has been incubating so long. That process challenged what I initially understood about the tailors' apprenticeship and its theoretical conception—again, and again, and again; the Adult Math Project and the seminal work of Olivia de la Rocha and Michael Murtaugh changed my understanding of everyday math practices. *Cognition in Practice* (Lave 1988), with its cover painting by friend and colleague Liisa Malkki, was intended as a prologue to the present book (see its acknowledgments). But its publication ushered in another intense period of change through collective work, reading, and debate at the Institute for Research on Learning in 1987–88, with Penny Eckert, Etienne Wenger, Paul Duguid, Lucy Suchman, and others at Xerox PARC (see the acknowledgments to Lave and Wenger 1991). Paul, Etienne, and I went on to form a reading group with Martin Packer in Berkeley that met on Thursday nights for several years to work on Marxist theory. Martin and I taught a two-year seminar at Berkeley, "Everyday Life and Learning," which blew our Sunday afternoons and transformed our understanding of theories of learning.

Weaving through these years and efforts were the work and collaboration of Danish critical social psychologist Ole Dreier, extraordinary scholar, theorist, colleague, and friend. The centrality of his work in the improvement of mine cannot be overstated. We shared colleagues in Denmark, especially Steinar Kvale and Uffe Juul Jensen at Aarhus University, and students, some of whom spent time in Berkeley and all of whom now hold professorships— Erik Axel, Carsten Osterlund, and Klaus Nielsen. While teaching at Copenhagen University in 2000, I was fortunate to spend time with colleagues old and new, including among the former Seth Chaiklin and Mariane Hedegaard, and among the latter Morten Nissen (and his amazing dad), Tove Borg, Bente Elkjaer, Line Lerche Moerk, Charlotte Hojholt, Hysse Forchhammer—whose painting graces the cover of *History in Person* (Holland and Lave 2001)—Niels Jacobsen, and Tone Saugstad. I thank each of them for their colleagueship and friendship.

Through this entire project I have benefited from the constructive critical reading of a small group of scholars whom I think of as my personal editorial board. Some of them have read virtually everything I've worked on over many years: they include Paul Duguid, Ole Dreier, Ray McDermott, Gillian Hart, and Rebecca Lave. People who love you enough to help you do what you want to do—and to do it better than you could without them—are priceless. I have indeed been fortunate. Gill and Ole finished their most recent books before I finished this one (Hart 2002; Dreier 2008). I can only offer a grateful echo of their kind acknowledgment of the pleasures of years of conversation about our projects and social practice theory.

One very difficult aspect of taking thirty years to work on a book is that over such a long period family, colleagues, and friends die. This is an appropriate moment to remember Don Bunker, who went with me to Liberia in 1975 and would have returned in 1976 but for his sudden and premature death. Allan Pred, cultural geographer at UC Berkeley, social practice theorist, and blithe spirit, died in 2007. Charles Lave, my sometime husband and always an extraordinarily loyal friend and colleague, was the statistical guru for Program B and the Liberia gang. He died in 2008. Steinar Kvale, my first and longtime Danish colleague, also died in 2008. Michael Kearney, anthropologist, social theorist, and political activist, died in 2009. Michael was a person of profound integrity and political commitment who fought for indigenous migrant labor rights in Mexico and the United States. He read an early draft of my manuscript, and we also talked about it shortly before he died. Mathematician Josie "H. J." Reed died this year. My sister, Anne Carter

Underhill, died in 1997; my mother, Elizabeth Carter, in 2005; and my father, Herbert Carter, in 2007. I don't think my getting the tailors' book done was anyone's dying wish, but I know they would have been happy to see it, and I wish I had had the pleasure of giving it to them.

The project was supported early on by research grants from the Office of Education, the Foundation for Child Development, and the National Institutes of Health. The analysis of the arithmetic data received support from the Institute for Comparative Human Development at the Rockefeller University. Without the sustained support of the Spencer Foundation I could not have carried out the research in Liberia over five years. In the 1970s, they supported social scientists with a wide variety of interests, whose research, whatever its focus, might have implications for education. This policy recruited me into the work I have done ever since, and enriched the world with perspectives on education that would never have emerged otherwise. As the first Spencer Foundation Senior Fellow (1989–95), I was able to follow that vision in establishing the PhD program in Social and Cultural Studies in Education at UC Berkeley. I hereby send them this, the long-overdue final report on the Liberian research in the 1970s—with deep gratitude for their support.

The Lewis Henry Morgan Lecture Series was established in 1963 by the anthropology department at the University of Rochester. I am grateful to Tony Carter for inviting me to give the Morgan Lectures in 1993 on my research on Vai and Gola tailors' apprenticeship and its implications for comparative research on education and learning. The Morgan Lecture Series has been situated in anthropology, but with that point of departure secured has also encouraged the exploration of interdisciplinary boundaries. In this commitment I see recognition of the achievements and influence of the founding lecturer, Meyer Fortes, given his ethnographic research in West Africa on, among other things, Tallensi childhood and education and his interest in relations between anthropology and psychology. Whether directly or indirectly related, the work of a number of Morgan lecturers has found its way into my book, often without my realizing that we shared this particular connection. In addition to Meyer Fortes (1963), I want especially to thank Margery Wolf (1983), Jane Guyer (1997), and Caroline Bledsoe (1999).

Over the years, a number of graduate student research assistants have worked on the tailors' project; first Mary Elizabeth Brenner, whose dissertation and subsequent research focused on mathematical practices in Vai school classrooms (she is now professor of education at UC Santa Barbara). Some years later Mia Fuller (now professor of Italian studies, UC Berkeley) worked through available materials on Vai and Gola history. At the University of Chicago Press, Executive Editor T. David Brent's welcome of the book was heartwarming, as he forbore mentioning it was a couple of decades late. Along with three anonymous reviewers at the University of Chicago Press, he and Tom Gibson, Morgan Lecture Series editor, provided careful, critical suggestions for revising the manuscript. I thank them very much for stirring up what has turned out to be a serious rethinking of the book. Helen Verran and Bill Maurer deserve special credit for this last undertaking. As I've pursued revisions, Paul Duguid, Jim Ferguson, Amanda Lashaw, Gill Hart, and Rebecca Lave have given thoughtful and careful readings of chapter drafts. Sheila Cole and William Taufic have generously let me use their photographs of the tailors' alley in the 1970s. Teo Ballve, graduate student in geography at Berkeley, and Laura Avey at the University of Chicago Press, along with Carlisle Rex-Waller, copy editor extraordinaire, have helped press the manuscript into final shape. Darin Jensen's skill as geography department cartographer is infused in the maps. Thanks, one and all.

1 Introduction: Apprenticeship and Critical Practice

Overview

The title of this book sums up its several concerns. The book is about apprenticeship—that of Vai and Gola tailors in Liberia in the 1970s, my own, and by extension, yours. It explores the tailors' practices of apprenticeship. It explores my ethnographic inquiry, which unfolded over five years, furnishing an example for apprentice ethnographers of a long process of sustained and changing ethnographic work. "Long process" and "changing practice" are certainly terms that may evoke a notion of "critical ethnographic practice," but still, this may sound more strenuous than critical.

Critical ethnographic practice? My ethnographic project on tailors' apprenticeship began with an impulsive three-week field trip to Monrovia, Liberia, in 1973, spurred by discussions with colleagues about how to address the cultural shortcomings of cross-cultural psychological research practice.[1] The political and ethical implications of cross-cultural psychological experimentation were egregious, although for the most part their multilayered ethnocentrism went unnoticed and unaddressed. A detailed account of tailors' apprenticeship, a local example of informal education, was intended to challenge Western psychologists' claims about divisions between modes of education and modes of thought, as well as their assumptions about the unmatched superiority of schooling for fostering general cognitive power. How was I to proceed? It seemed likely that the only way to be heard by psychologists was to speak to them in the language of psychological experiments. I thought that well-formed experiments, based on close ethnographic work, might demonstrate the ethnocentric distortions inherent in the cross-cultural psychological enterprise and plead the case for robust cultural guidelines for cross-cultural experimentation.

The project was intended to be critical of the work of others, but critical ethnography is not only an objection *to* something. The term "critical ethnographic practice" here refers to the craft of ethnographic inquiry integral to a historical-materialist theoretical stance. This stance is rooted in a Marxist theory of praxis—forged through the work of many, as in all theoretical traditions, into a contemporary relational theory of practice. Within this perspective, critical ethnographic practice is part of its logic of inquiry.

Part of critical ethnographic practice is an ongoing commitment to rethinking and redoing one's work as ethnographer and activist. The question is how to become over the long term an apprentice to one's own changing practice. It takes practice to come to inhabit a critical ethnographer's craft. Most anthropologists would say that this transformation principally takes place during the course of fieldwork. This may sound as if "critical ethnographic practice" is dedicated to empirical investigation, as if fieldwork is foremost in shaping anthropological identities. Fieldwork is widely and correctly viewed as a rite of passage in anthropology and it is deeply empirical, but critical ethnographic practice is just as deeply a matter of theoretical formation. In my view, the ethnographic account of the tailors' apprenticeship is also an account of the theoretical unfolding of the project. (That makes apprentice ethnographers and apprentice social theorists one and the same.) The ethnographic project in Liberia didn't stand still theoretically. It began to move from one theoretical—ontological, epistemological and political/ethical—stance to another, which of course changed the direction of field inquiries, which further changed theoretical concerns, and so on.

I've come to call the theoretical stance, or "problematic," toward which the project moved "social practice theory." One assumption underlying social practice theory (and thus this conception of critical ethnographic research) is that theoretical and empirical endeavors are mutually constitutive and cannot be separated—social practice theory is a theory of relations.[2] So research on learning (through apprenticeship) and research as learning (through critical ethnographic practice) are each and together empirical/theoretical practices. It is difficult to address these relations—unless you do so as they are produced. That concern helps to explain why I focus on the process of research on the tailors' apprenticeship throughout the book, for this makes it possible to address critical ethnographic practice, in practice.

Becoming an apprentice to one's own changing practice? Briefly, I made four additional field trips to Liberia between 1973 and 1978. On the second visit to Monrovia, I spent six months in Happy Corner, the tailors' alley, trying to grasp the lineaments of apprenticeship. I spent the following two summers comparing math used by tailors whose tailoring experience and schooling varied. Surprising and puzzling results from these learning transfer experiments led to one more summer of field research focused on differences between experimental and everyday math practices in the tailor shops. For good and for ill, a comparative theory that divided "formal" from "informal" education furnished an agenda of expectations and explanations that shaped my research questions throughout the project. I finished a book manuscript called *Sowing Knowledge* in 1981, worked on half a dozen other versions of that manuscript over the next twelve years (some arguably titled with better puns), gave the Lewis Henry Morgan Lectures on this material in 1993, and worked on several other versions after that. I was critical from the beginning of conventional assumptions about education and learning transfer, but the more I worked on the project, the more clearly I could see that most of my fieldwork in Liberia was predicated on those very assumptions. Clearly something further was required. As I worked through the implications of my last field trip to Liberia in 1978, looking at everyday math in the tailor shops, I began to consider seriously the possibility that learning, knowledgeability, skillfulness, whatever else they might be, are always only part of ongoing social arrangements and relations. From this it followed that the meaning of tailoring must come from its partial relations in the tailors' lives more broadly. What relations? How? A retrospective eye certainly makes it easier to call attention to the tensions and uneven movement between empirical and theoretical work as different lines of questions, different aspects of the tailors' practices, and understandings of those questions and practices unfolded. In the long run, this process led me from a vernacular commonsense problematic to a relational one, from one to another set of assumptions about the world and how we know it, and to different ways of exploring and investigating participation in social life.

Given the existence of different problematics, we can hardly turn to the ethnography of tailors' apprenticeship without first addressing anthropological debates about ethnography, its place in anthropology, its political-ethical commitments and relations with broad questions about theory and practice—looking for guidance about whether and how to change theoretical problematics through ethnographic labor. Later sections of this chapter will address several kinds of historical framing of the tailors' project, first by considering the intellectual ambience that shaped it in the 1970s in the work of anthropologists and cross-cultural psychologists. We'll consider historical relations between craft apprenticeship as an exemplar of "informal education" and other kinds of labor and learning in Western commonplace wisdom. We'll then turn to a quite different history of craft practices with respect to Vai and Gola tailors. Finally, we'll address the long trajectory of the book and the trajectories of its changing parts.

Ethnographic Practices

Some of the predilections that inform this book also shaped a seminar on ethnographic research that I taught for many years as a way for apprentice ethnographers to learn by doing. Each student engaged in a modest ethnographic project, from start to finish, over the course of a year. The seminar was a place to learn by finding field sites, research problems, developing field notes, lines of inquiry, writing, discussing, making analytic arguments and mistakes. It was not exclusively a fieldwork course, nor was it an ethnographic writing course (a distinction dear to historical and theoretical debates about ethnography).[3] Cerwonka and Malkki explore field research similarly, not by talking about how to do it, but instead by following Cerwonka's day-to-day practice, "that process," Malkki says, is "the critical theoretical practice of ethnography . . . typically long, often meandering, inescapably social, and temporally situated" (Cerwonka and Malkki 2007, 177). The present book follows such a process over the five-year project with the tailors.

ETHNOGRAPHY IN DEBATE

Ethnographic practice in anthropology has been reconceived several times over in its little more than a century of existence, first from Sir James Frazer's *Golden Bough*, whose genre stands for the whole until about 1920, to structural-functional anthropology from roughly 1920 to 1980. Then a line between old and new ethnography in the 1980s, styled as "postmodern," rejected in a "crisis of representation" an earlier "modernist" practice of ethnography. The novel discussions of the 1980s included Clifford and Marcus 1986, Rabinow 1986, and Geertz 1988 and were mounted from the borders of anthropology with a cultural/literary version of cultural studies (Tyler and Marcus 1990, 129).

Given their differences, is it possible to set periods of ethnographic fashion beside one another in a way that allows consideration of what they have in common? Strathern set herself this difficult task in her Frazer Lecture in 1986, casting the differences between genres of ethnography as a pair of relations: between the ethnographer and the social world she studies and between the ethnographer and her audience (1990, 91). This double relation breaks out of simple empirical/theoretical and fieldwork/writing dichotomies to see the anthropologist as a mediator between two social worlds, facing problems of "how to manipulate familiar ideas and concepts to convey alien ones" (101). Malinowski has been widely credited with inventing the central anthropological tradition of long-term fieldwork, whose mission was to explain how an apparently bizarre culture (to readers) was common and ordinary (to the objects of study). Strathern contends that Malinowski's role as emblem of an epoch and a genre of ethnographic practice could not be explained as a matter of founding fatherhood, for his supposedly novel research practices—"holism, synchrony, intensive fieldwork, and the rest"—were in fact in place many years previously. Rather, she argues,

> it lay in how he wrote, and specifically the organization of text. This implemented the kinds of relationships between writer, reader and subject matter that were to dominate anthropology, British and beyond, for the next sixty years.... What must be laid to Malinowski's door ... is the proclamation of the kinds of spaces that had to be made to convey the "new" analytical ideas. It was because this contextualisation was novel that the ideas themselves came to appear novel and that other scholars who might have been regarded as former exponents of them were rendered invisible. Its power for anthropologists lay in the parallel between the framework of the monograph and the framework of the field experience. (97–98)

What sort of framework? Strathern suggests that

> once that context had been created in the separation of the culture of those to whom [Malinowski] was speaking from the culture of those about whom he was speaking ... the audience was required to connive in its distance from the anthropologist's subject matter. Meanwhile the anthropologist moved between the two. His proximity to the culture he was studying became his distance from the one he was addressing, and vice versa. This, *tout court*, is how the modern(ist) fieldworker has imagined him- or herself ever since. (103)

What about fieldwork in relation to the production of written ethnographies? Strathern agrees with Clifford 1986 that "the fieldwork experience *was reconstructed in the monographs* in such a way as to become an organising device for the monograph as such" (1990, 98; emphasis hers).[4]

A major effect of the 1980s "crisis of representation" was to shift attention to ethnographic monographs as the site of the productive labor of anthropologists and to minimize the role played by fieldwork. Clifford's view of the relationship between fieldwork and the production of a monograph portrays fieldwork as a sort of amorphous object, "experience," or "quality of experience" to be made something of in the production of a text (1986, 162). He and similarly minded colleagues did not inquire into how fieldwork "made a new kind of persuasive fiction possible." Thus "ethnographic comprehension (a coherent position of sympathy and hermeneutic engagement) is better seen as a creation of ethnographic *writing* than as a consistent quality of ethnographic *experience*" (quoted in Strathern 1990, 98n23; emphasis Clifford's).[5]

This certainly asserts a change in the relationship of the anthropologist to the object of study, though reducing fieldwork to "experience" seems to strip it of its complexities and reciprocal effects on the production of ethnographic texts. There was also a concern in the 1980s "to expose the figure of the fieldworker who was the register of the otherness of cultures." As Strathern puts it, "Clifford tackles the authority which anthropologists claimed this gave their writings: the fieldworker who came back from another society spoke for it in a determining way which now appears repugnant. Whether or not anthropologists ever did claim such authority is beside the point. It is the kind of book they wrote which is exposed" (1990, 109).

What about the anthropologist and his audience? If deep in the bones of modernist anthropology was a commitment to separate the context of a (holistic) culture from that of the author/anthropologist and his audience, the prescriptions of the '80s challenged this as well:

> The postmodern mood is to make deliberate play with context. It is said to blur boundaries, destroy the dichotomizing frame, juxtapose voices, so that the multiple product, the monograph jointly authored, becomes conceivable. . . . A new relationship between writer, reader, and subject matter is contemplated. Decoding the exotic ("making sense") will no longer do; postmodernism requires the reader to interact with exotica in itself. (Strathern 1990, 111)[6]

At a distance of several decades (and from a point of view more in tune with recent reworking of ethnographic relations), the 1980s movement appears vulnerable to several critical worries, not least because of the habit of its proponents to collapse the entire discipline into their vision of ethnography.[7] This is tantamount to saying that only one theoretical problematic is appropriate to the discipline as a whole. No wonder this view has led to considerable controversy, much of it couched in terms that obscure and reject, if only by remaining silent, other relations that constitute ethnography, including the ethnographer's concerns as theorist and political activist. The critique of ethnography in the 1980s failed to register deep theoretical differences inhabited by different anthropologists. Further, placing empirical fieldwork offstage left relatively untouched a commonsense empiricism around that "fieldwork experience." Its place in the writers' program remained unattended. This oversight has been recognized and regretted by Marcus (e.g., Faubion and Marcus 2009, 2n2; see also Westbrook 2008, 10–11; Comaroff and Comaroff 2003).

The 1980s movement to refashion ethnographic practice proposed that, to avoid conventional claims to ethnographic authority and as a matter of creative freedom from conventional representations of "the other," anthropologists should engage in new, experimental ways of writing ethnography.[8] Gupta and Ferguson (1992), among others, found this solution inadequate:

> Power does not enter the anthropological picture only at the moment of representation, for the cultural distinctiveness that the anthropologist attempts to represent has always already been produced within a field of power relations. There is thus a politics of otherness that is not reducible to a politics of representation. . . . The issue of otherness itself is not really addressed by the devices of polyphonic textual construction. (As reprinted in Robben and Sluka 2007, 344)

Strathern commented in passing that the 1980s moment opened up a new audience and thus a new relationship between anthropologist and text as informants who were formerly only objects of study became readers as well. But it seems to me there was a much stronger shift toward narrowing the audience in a process that might be called professional involution—because the motive for ethnographic work and the focus for ethnographic critique was the practice of writing ethnography itself.[9] Other reasons for ethnographic inquiry, impelled by or focused on social movements, for instance, were not at the center of critical concerns. Strathern, among others, has pointed out that feminist anthropology was generated in a different set of relations in/with the world beyond the practice of anthropology. It is sometimes transdisciplinary or plays with contexts and different voices—but if it is successful, it is precisely because it is anchored in "the relationship . . . between scholarship (genre) and the feminist movement (life)" (1990, 118).[10]

Over time the 1980s critique of ethnographic practice has lost its critical political edge (Willis and Trondman 2000, 10). Today's proponents still reject any sort of political commitment, which of course is itself a political stance. For instance, Westbrook (2008, 11) derides the "preachy," "thought-clouding" "moralizing stance" of ethnography focused on "the margins, where other folks are either inarticulate, outside society's interest, or even oppressed," and suggests "a style for the intellectual, cheerfulness in good times and sangfroid in bad, in lieu of the moral earnestness or facile irony that are so ubiquitous" (5).

Given these problems, and no doubt partly in reaction to them, a different vision of ethnographic practice has significantly captured new energy and new questions since the turn of the twenty-first century. It began with acknowledgment of complex global changes in political-economic conditions of social and cultural life, politics, and ethnographic research (e.g., Gupta and Ferguson 1997; Comaroff and Comaroff 2003; Hart 2002; Willis and Trondman 2000). These challenges have produced a broadly shared, sometimes literal manifesto for ethnographic practice. Rather than trying to command a unified center for a single theoretical problematic for anthropology, this movement has embraced diversity.

One of the conveners of a pivotal conference on ethnographic practice in 2002 introduced the project in the new journal *Ethnography*, describing the conference and the journal as multinational, multidisciplinary, and intent on reflecting differences in the theory and practice of ethnographic research: "Modern, neomodern, and postmodern; positivist, interpretive and analytic; phenomenological, interactionist and historical; theory-driven and narrative-oriented; local, multi-sited, and global" (Wacquant 2003, 6). The participants began with a relatively simple statement that ethnography is "social research based on the close-up, on-the-ground observation of people and institutions in real time and space, in which the investigator embeds herself near (or within) the phenomenon so as to detect how and why agents on the scene act, think and feel the way they do" (5).

Willis and Trondman, the founding editors of *Ethnography*, propose in their opening manifesto several distinguishing features of ethnography, beginning with the role of theory, "as pre-cursor, medium and outcome of ethnographic study and writing" (2000, 7). They cite the centrality of culture—always indeterminate in relation to economic and social conditions, but nonetheless always moored in historical and cultural life (8).[11] They identify a critical focus on the "operations and results of unequal power. . . . Important too, is the ethnographic and theoretical tracing of responses to power and of how the interests and views of the powerful are often finally secured within processes and practices which may seem to oppose dominant interests" (10). They further point to cultural policy and cultural politics as important facets of ethnographic practice. Their vision of the practice of ethnography emphasizes theoretically forged politics, a critical pursuit of questions of unequal power, and the centrality of culture in its multiple social relations and mutual entailments. Further, it makes salient relations between theory and practice.

Gupta and Ferguson helped define this "moment" in debates over ethnography by arguing that it was the field, and fieldwork, central to the discipline of anthropology, that had been left unexamined in the '80s debate.

Fieldwork defines the discipline and its boundaries, is at the core of professional socialization and training, and is central to its intellectual principles and professional practices (1997, 1–3). Arguing that "ethnography's great strength has always been its explicit and well-developed sense of location" (35), they raised multiple scopes of spatial issues to theoretical, political and practical urgency.[12] They also offered a short list of what constitutes the power of ethnographic work. They admire ethnographic practice in part because it counters Western ethnocentrism. In their view, moreover, "fieldwork's stress on the taken-for-granted social routines, informal knowledge, and embodied practices can yield understanding that cannot be obtained through" other methods (36). In this way, finally, "fieldwork reveals that a self-conscious shifting of social and geographical location can be an extraordinarily valuable methodology for understanding social and cultural life, both through the discovery of phenomena that would otherwise remain invisible and through the acquisition of new perspectives on things we thought we already understood" (36–37).

Since the beginning of the twenty-first century, anthropologists have raised many questions about the feasibility of fieldwork-based research in a changing, radically interconnected world. The locatedness of social phenomena has become deeply problematic, given the historical commitments of anthropologists to "a powerful form of knowledge production that is (or can be) as deeply empirical as research gets" (Malkki 2007, 170), that is, to locally focused research into the complex global entailments and relations of everyday practice (Willis and Trondman 2000, 9; Gupta and Ferguson 1997, 36; Law 2004, 13).

What, then, is an anthropologist to do with the rapid, sprawling, entangled, and close relations between everyone and everything, via, among other things, instant forms of communication and new media (Hannerz 2004; from the 2000 Lewis Henry Morgan Lectures)? Given extraordinarily extensive economic, political, social, and cultural relations, effects, and consequences, Comaroff and Comaroff argue for "ethnography on an awkward scale": "It demands an ethnography that, once orientated to particular sites and grounded issues, is pursued on multiple dimensions and scales" (2003, 169).

The Comaroffs' focus on ethnographic practice leads to several closely interrelated points: a recognition that there is always a "prior conceptual scaffolding" to ethnographic work and so "a dialectic of the concept and the concrete"; a commitment to locate crucial issues in place as the focus of field research, so that ethnography "takes off *not* from theory or from a meta-narrative, but from the situated effects of seeing and listening" (2003, 164). Ethnographic practice, then, involves mapping the phenomenal landscape, following locally the workings of multiple relevant dimensions and scales "from their densest intersections to wherever else they may lead" (168).[13]

As I read these debates about what ethnography should be and how it has been envisioned at different times, several themes are notable because they are repeatedly mentioned but rarely analyzed. Four key points stand out with respect to what we might mean by apprenticeship in critical ethnographic practice.

First, different approaches to ethnography frequently invoke terms like "critique" and "critical" understood in commonsense terms—as in being critical of certain practices, or having a commitment to ethical/political ethnographic practice, or undertaking ethnographic practice critical of social injustice, or insisting on the importance of exploring unequal social power (Willis and Trondman 2000, 9–10). Critical ethnography certainly is engaged in social criticism and an integral concern for social justice. Malkki, for one, says that critical ethnographic practice is "knitted into the very backbone of anthropology" (Cerwonka and Malkki 2007, 166).[14] But critical ethnography has other entailments and layers of meaning as well. It involves a relational, historical worldview and metaphysics that question a number of commonsense understandings. It envisions ethnographic research as a long struggle to illuminate social life, challenge commonplace theories and their political implications, and change theoretical practice in the process.[15] This book pursues a more ample consideration of what we mean by critical ethnographic practice.

Second, participants in the various visions of ethnographic practice considered above assume wildly different relations between empirical and theoretical facets of inquiry. I have pointed to one view that we would do well to give up theory altogether on grounds that the world exists only in our interpretations of it.[16] Another suggests that, while neither grand theory for its own sake nor raw empiricism will do, theory and practice cannot be separated (see, e.g., Becker 2000, 257). Others maintain that ethnographic work begins with "data gathering," followed by "data analysis" that leads eventually to "theory,"[17] moving from particularities to generalities, from the concrete to the abstract. Still others insist instead that theoretical commitments are always a precursor to empirical inquiry.

Relations between "theory" and "practice" are conceived differently in various theoretical problematics, and those problematics differ in ways that make them mutually contradictory. They cannot be rolled into some grand eclectic compromise, and they matter profoundly for what it means to be an ethnographer. One thing all apprentice ethnographers do is find their way into one theoretical/empirical problematic or another. This book is intended to show such a process of apprenticeship. It documents a transition from a commonplace, commonsense stance toward a problematic for relational (social practice) theory through the process of research on tailors' apprenticeship in Liberia.[18]

This brings us to the third issue raised by the debates over ethnography. I mentioned earlier regrets from proponents of the reflexive turn of the 1980s for their inattention to ethnographic fieldwork.[19] How might we characterize commonsense ethnographic practice? Murphy provides a succinct description:

> The paradigm of functional positivism that has been regnant in all social sciences for most of the 20th century . . . still provides the intellectual framework of much of our profession. This older model of society—as a network of causally and functionally related empirical entities forming natural systems—was implicitly based on a belief in the autonomy and objectivity of the scientific observers who collect these nuggets of fact. This so-called objectivity, in turn, derived from the assumption that we, as subjects, can squat in remote villages with our notebooks and study the natives as objects. It was an innocent creed, but it bespoke an underlying imperialism of attitude. (1990, 332–33)

One often encounters comments, dropped into discussions of ethnographic methods without much elaboration or specification, that there used to be, and in fact still is, a kind of "innocent creed" of vernacular positivism in the broad, general, ordinary practice of anthropology. If so, where does it lie? Who are its exemplars and proponents? Some anthropologists argue that Marxism is dead, others that feminist anthropologies are marginal, and (if Murphy is right in his assessment) that "postmodernism, along with the new interpretive and reflexive anthropologies . . . despite their success, . . . remain[s] the domain of a small . . . minority" (1990, 332). If these scholars are right, theoretical stances other than a commonsense problematic are marked exceptions to usual anthropological practice (see Comaroff and Comaroff 2003). Perhaps there *is* a central "there" there to anthropology, if only by default. Yet I also sometimes hear an impatient response to concerns with ways in which positivist assumptions inform ethnographic work today—"we dealt with that stuff decades ago and have moved on." Colson (1985) points instead to the notion that the discipline of anthropology has moved from an early period of consensus, not past it, but into a period of huge variety in theory and practice, a view reflected in the *Ethnography* manifesto. So again, why the assumptions of a positivist core? Malkki points to several sources of our sense of our own practice, including the historical place of (humanistic) anthropology with respect to more unblushingly positivist neighboring social science and professional disciplines, the positivist inclinations of some granting agencies, and the aggressively scientistic monotone of university human subjects boards.

I wonder if our semiautomatic concern comes not so much from a functionalist past (or present) relativist/positivist "core" but rather from our experience as students and teachers. I would argue that positivist, often dualist epistemological frameworks are the commonsense, and common, ways of understanding the world that virtually all of us bring with us into whatever transformative trajectories of theoretical/empirical practice we come to inhabit as ethnographers.[20] Maybe we are right in guessing that the majority of anthropologists take such an approach, some of the time or all of the time. Who knows? But maybe we are also recognizing that each new generation of students brings commonplace assumptions with them—sometimes to reject and transform them, sometimes not.[21] Why make this observation here? Apprentices in ethnographic practice have to start somewhere (theoretically speaking). Whether sophisticated social theorists remember or not, at some point they had to make a break from naturalized, uncritical, commonsense conceptions of the world to the theoretical position they now espouse. The book is about such a transformative process. And though the ethnographic project began in the 1970s, I believe it still addresses the commonsense theoretical condition of the world we live in and the assumptions apprentice ethnographers bring into ethnographic practice today. The theoretical focus of the tailors' project, pro and con, should make dramatically clear what its techniques and commitments are by the time we're done.

Finally, as anthropologists we don't often think about the processes by which we come to embody and inhabit a theoretical/empirical stance. Many of us take fieldwork as the central formative experience in "becoming an anthropologist" but few pursue questions of how the apprentice ethnographer comes to *inhabit* a theoretical problematic. As Malkki puts it: "Anthropological fieldwork is not usually a straightforward matter of working. It is also a matter of living. Ethnographic research practice is a way of being in the world" (Cerwonka and Malkki 2007, 178; see also, e.g., Law 2004, 10). How do you come to such a way of being? Surely *doing* ethnographic research forms the anthropologist in very significant ways, including theoretically. Changing theoretical problematic is not a problem about changing knowledge or changing theory, but a problem about changing ethnographic *practice*.

So what is involved in moving from a vernacular positivist problematic to a critical relational problematic? It is not, I would argue, a pedagogical project with either a smooth trajectory or a finish. I've always admired

Jeanne Favret-Saada's ethnography, *Deadly Words* (1980). It is a subtle and fascinating account of witchcraft in the Bocage in northwestern France in the 1960s, and of crossing uncrossable gaps, in practice, in the course of ethnographic work. Her book is an extended analysis of what the people of the Bocage do with the following dilemma: as dedicated followers of rationalist, indeed commonsense positivist, French national discourse, they do not believe in witchcraft—silly superstition. Yet some get deeply caught up in witchcraft episodes. Within these episodes, witchcraft looks like a war to the death and the rationalist stance appears not just silly, but dangerous. Favret-Saada's question is, how is it possible that folks in the Bocage (among other places) break from the first point of view into the second.

There is a similar question, it seems to me, about moving from a theoretical problematic embracing a conventional, descriptive, commonsense theoretical stance, one that does not admit the possibility of any other theoretical problematic (or even its own), to a theory of praxis that finds the conventional stance both naïve and imperialistic. There is no way from *within* either one to move in a theoretically principled way from one to the other. In part this helps to account for the improvisational character of ethnographic work. Fieldwork is a long disruptive process. The process of reworking the theoretical formation one brings to the task is also disruptive. The chapters that follow trace steps forward and backward, surprises and breaks, and shifts of direction in such a process.

"APPRENTICESHIP" IN DIFFERENT PROBLEMATICS

How is the process of research on Vai and Gola tailors' apprenticeship in the 1970s to figure in the ongoing discussion about critical ethnographic research practice? Answering this question requires some care. One way to rephrase the question is to ask, why should you care about research on apprenticeship or "informal education" or "learning transfer" in Liberia if your interests lie in the political economy of water use in Bangladesh or revolutionary struggles in Central America or the culture of Internet game playing in the United States? It will be tempting, I wager, to assume that there is a "general" theoretical argument here about critical ethnography, and then the particular example of research on Vai and Gola tailors to support the general argument. But this is precisely the kind of assumption about relations between the empirical and theoretical that furnishes commonsense theorizing, not social practice theory. There are questions on the table throughout the rest of this chapter (and the book as a whole) about how, from the perspective of social practice theory, the apprenticeship of critical ethnographers, the tailors' apprenticeship, and the changing process of ethnographic research in the 1970s are all three empirical-theoretical parts of a single empirical-theoretical project.

For one thing, ethnographers, whether they see themselves as pursuing knowledge about the world or trying to help bring about a more just world, or living the life of the mind, or taking part in "the knowledge economy," should be interested as part of their own research practice in how they and other people come to know and learn, and in the theories of knowing and learning on offer from their expert colleagues. These are not simple questions: Knowledge, knowing, and learning are understood differently in different problematics (Lave and Packer 2008). My late colleague Steinar Kvale argued that there is "an intrinsic coherence between conceptions of research and training, and of knowledge and learning" (1997, 4). His point was that there is fit, resonance, and iterative and generative relations between conceptions and practices of research and training and conceptions and practices of knowing and learning. They are closely interrelated parts of any problematic—and of all ethnographers' practice. He illustrated his argument by contrasting two clusters of relations, one he called "bureaucratic" and the other "pragmatic" (see table 1).

Kvale wrote about changing theoretical fashions in psychological theorizing as an unexceptional facet of changing sociocultural fashions more generally. He read the distinction he was drawing as a coherent set of modernist bureaucratic cultural relations on the one hand and as a set of postmodern cultural relations among concepts and practices of knowledge, research, and learning on the other. He argued that there is a close relation between theories of technical-rational learning based in schooling and a notion of research "method" as itself a technical-rational set of procedures for investigating the world. He treated his own work on qualitative research as craft, in a sustained exploration of relations up and down that "pragmatic" column. Starting with his 1997 paper, which explored graduate education as apprenticeship and drew on the biographies of Nobel laureates, he addressed relations of university training as apprenticeship, the qualitative interview, and training for qualitative interviewing as craft and art, necessary because of the situated character of knowing and doing in social practice (see also Kvale 2006; Kvale and Brinkmann 2008).

I disagreed with his view that the "pragmatic" column maps the "postmodern turn." Nor does each column represent a cluster of research interests that might fit the inclinations of some scholars and not others. Rather than looking at them separately, I see in his arrangement another possibility: a single coherent theoretical problematic, a conventional arrangement of binary distinctions (table 2).

TABLE 1. Bureaucratic and pragmatic approaches to knowledge and learning (after Kvale 1997)

"Theoretical problematic"	Bureaucratic	Pragmatic
Research training	Schools	Apprenticeship
Research activity	Methodology	Craft and art
Knowledge	Facts and rules	Situated knowing
Learning	Technical rational	Social practice

TABLE 2. Underlying binary relations

Formal education (schooling)	versus	Informal education (apprenticeship)
Experimental method	versus	Ethnographic/qualitative research
Decontextualized scientific knowledge	versus	Everyday knowing in context
General theory	versus	Specific applications, applied fields

The perspective laid out in table 2 ties Kvale's two sets of conceptual relations together into a single dualistic theory, a divide we can recognize as cemented in disciplinary boundaries, problematics, and politics. The contrasting columns are not equal in value or priority in theory or practice. The left-hand set features basic commitments of classical philosophy of mind and psychologies of learning. From a positivist, dualist perspective, the right-hand set comprises peripheral, subsidiary, even trivial facets of the mainstream issues.

"Apprenticeship" (whether in critical ethnographic practice or tailoring) is part of very different conceptual relations—it figures differently in different problematics—depending on whether you understand the contrasting columns of table 2 to reflect a historical sequence of theoretical fashions following one after the other or a single problematic. If the right-hand set of terms are taken together to be merely one pole in the scheme as a whole, the theory is always comparative; whether explicit or not, a discussion of either pole always relates to the other pole as well. Alternatively, the second set of terms may have other meanings made in other relations in a different theoretical problematic.[22]

I would not have written this book about apprenticeship in critical ethnographic practice if I had not first found the tailors' apprenticeship in Happy Corner a strategic way to engage in critical exploration of anthropological debates in the 1970s and later found it helpful in following through the different configurations of theoretical relations such as those outlined in tables 1 and 2. Future chapters show how this came about, in practice.

Taking the Measure of the Ethnographic Project

The official discourse on cross-cultural differences in education and learning in the 1970s comprised interlocking claims about the power of "formal" education to transform learners' knowledge and the corresponding lack of power of "informal" education.[23] This binary discourse was shared across several of the social sciences and beyond, and furnished a hierarchical politics justifying the polarized separation of means of producing lives, things, places, identities, and knowledges linked to psychological views of learning, literacy (Goody 1977), and "knowledge transmission." Sociologists and anthropologists of comparative education (e.g., Middleton 1970) divided the world into two "kinds" of societies (modern and traditional) with two forms of education (formal and informal).[24] Psychologists accepted and elaborated these distinctions to incorporate two modes of teaching, two sorts of mechanisms for learning, and superior or inferior "outcomes." A pervasive division between "formal" and "informal" education was one historical means of putting these abstract distinctions into circulation.

Early in my project, I made a synoptic diagram of the contrastive claims about formal and informal education in the arguments of anthropologists and cross-cultural psychologists. Figure 1 maps the relations that would require critical ethnographic exploration if I intended to mount a serious challenge to the binary comparative politics of education/learning. The Liberian research, its objects, questions, subprojects, and eventually its argument, were intended to challenge every node and relation in this web of assumptions and claims. A brief sketch of the different approaches of, first, anthropologists and then psychologists will give some sense of the issues involved.

FORMAL AND INFORMAL EDUCATION

During the period of my research, anthropologists interested in enculturation, culture and personality, or socialization in exotic places often took a broad view of (informal) education, asking how children grew up to become "members of society," as an effect of the transmission of "the culture" and "social norms" from one generation to the next.[25] In this genre, Meyer Fortes (1938) produced an exceptionally rich account of Tale education that was widely read in the '70s as a notable contribution to the anthropology of socialization.

Fortes began with the notion that education was a social process, a process of transmitting culture from one generation to the next. From the individual's point of view, it was the process by which he or she moved from

Traditional society
Informal education

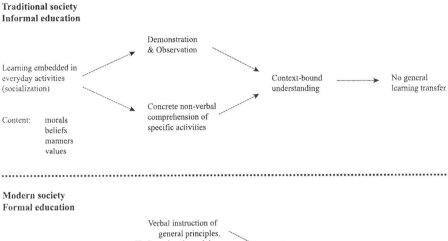

Figure 1. A comparative model of formal and informal education

a peripheral position to adult participation in the community. Fortes made the further point that children shared their parents' views about education, in fact identifying with their parents. Tallensi children were therefore eager to learn and parents were eager to teach and tolerant of the learning efforts of their children. Another Tallensi concept he labeled "the unity of the social sphere."

> As between adults and children, in Tale society, the social sphere is differentiated only in terms of relative capacity. All participate in the same culture, the same round of life, but in varying degrees, corresponding to the stage of physical and mental development. Nothing in the universe of adult behaviour is hidden from children or barred to them. They are actively and responsibly part of the social structure, of the economic system, the ritual and ideological system.

Children were also part of the educational "system" in that everyone taught—older children often acting as teachers for younger. This had educational implications, especially in relation to the motivation of the learner: "It means that the child is from the beginning oriented towards the same reality as its parents and has the same physical and social material upon which to direct its cognitive and instinctual endowment" (Fortes 1938, 9).

Within this social framework, learners categorized things to be learned differently, partly owing to the unity of the social sphere but more as a consequence of the embeddedness of education in the practical activities of daily life. A single, common, shared culture was both assumption and result of Fortes's claims for the unproblematic process of cultural transmission, the notion of *the* social sphere, the notion of *transmitting* culture with verisimilitude, and of education as transmitting *the* culture from one generation to another.

In insisting on the embedding of learning in ongoing activity for the Tallensi, Fortes took a stand concerning the situated character of learning—although at the same time, he limited this characterization to societies like the Tallensi. His work suggested a useful reversal of an analytic point of view: One reason that Fortes's description of Tallensi education seemed rich and promising was precisely because when he talked about Tallensi education, it appeared to be all there was. Instead of discussing how "primitive education" fell short of schooling, he created room to inquire how schooling was different from growing up Tale. This was not an easy task—as we shall see in chapter 2. What we learned when he divided those "primitive" societies with one sort of learning from the others, the not-primitive ones, was that he, like many other anthropologists, confined this kind of learning exclusively to the first set of societies, those less valued in politically polarized terms. What was learning like "on the other side?" The answer was unequivocal: The other side was implicitly "civilized" and literate, valuing change and creativity and learning distanced and removed from practical activities.

There are two important provisional lessons here: First, it is not enough to bracket off one pole, one "kind" of education from the other, to escape from the polarized enterprise as a whole. Given the ubiquitous, implicit (when not explicit), comparative claims with respect to formal education and informal education, no critical ethnographic approach can afford to neglect the mutually constitutive relations that give shape and meaning to both "sides." The second problem pertains more specifically to my project. Suppose I analyze ethnographic materials about Vai and Gola tailors' apprenticeship and then announce that they provide evidence for the situated character of learning and knowledge? The anthropologists or psychologists whose work in the 1970s is discussed here would find that completely ordinary—not in the least newsworthy. "That's how informal education is, of course," they might say. "That's what makes the products of informal education sticky, contextually limited, and unable to connect one scene with another"—unlike formal education. But I wish to argue that there are no exceptions to the situated character of social practice, most especially not schooling.

There are various ways to address this problem: Mine involved a turn to mathematics, at first because it simply looked like a common activity in tailor shops and schools and thus a useful medium for comparative experiments on the educational effects of schooling and apprenticeship. After a while, the underlying assumption of the unproblematic universality of mathematics came into question, as practices involving number began to look stickier and stickier. Eventually math took on strategic force in my work, for it provided a worst-case scenario. That is, if math, the pure "universal," is a relational, situated phenomenon, then so, goes the argument, is everything else.[26]

FORMAL AND INFORMAL LEARNING

Cross-cultural psychologists in the 1970s assumed that schooling was the most powerful site devoted to the acquisition of general rules and principles of knowledge that could be "transferred" from one situation to another, specifically, away from school to the varied situations of everyday life. This theory of the power of formal education correspondingly implied that informal education—designated as part of life experiences, the concrete learning embedded in everyday life—was bound to merely reproduce (if not simply to *be*) traditional knowledge, without the possibility of "general transfer" to new situations. The most serious social and political implications of this research followed from assuming that to say people were "educated" was interchangeable with saying that they had gone to school. Besides the appalling assumption that those who did not go to school were uneducated, it left unknown the heterogeneous, merely residual, contents of the not-schooled lives of the "others." The investigative method of cross-cultural psychology involved experiments carried out in far-flung corners of the world. But, as I will discuss in more detail in chapter 4, those experiments were designed by researchers whose lives were deeply tied up with Western educational institutions and practices. Experimental tasks were often drawn from or inspired by school activities. These experiments attempted to confirm—there was circularity in this procedure—that schooling was superior in its cognitive effects to the kind and quality of transferable knowledge to be acquired through other educational arrangements, including everyday life.

In "The Cognitive Consequences of Formal and Informal Education" (1973), a classic article on the subject in *Science*, Scribner and Cole gave a

carefully weighed account of this genre of research, arguing that the contribution of psychological analysis in their view, was to show *how* different educational contexts and different teaching/learning processes might
lead to different cognitive consequences, if schooling were doing something that other kinds of educational experiences could not. What was it
about schooling that was supposed to promote special cognitive skills? Formal educational processes were supposed to enhance the application of general, abstract, higher cognitive skills, resulting in flexible, general problem-
solving capabilities and hence learning transfer. Subjects educated in other
ways should acquire only particular, practical, and embedded knowledge
that would not transfer. Such arguments placed learning transfer in a privileged position as the major way in which schooling was supposed to affect
life outside of school.

In Figure 1, learning transfer and its absence are attributed to crucial differences between context-embedded and out-of-context learning. Scribner
and Cole pointed out that the tools taught in school related primarily to information processing, and that they were learned apart from the content
and the circumstances in which they were customarily used.

> At a simple level of technology, the use of a specific tool is ordinarily
> mastered in the course of exercising it for some particular purpose. . . .
> The intellectual tools of the school seem to differ from the tools used in
> practical activity in at least one other respect. [Note the equation of sim-
> ple technology and practical activity and the implicit categorization of
> schoolwork as not-practical activity.] . . . The intellectual tools used in
> school range over a wide variety of tasks and contents; how one oper-
> ates with a book or ruler is not much affected by the subject-matter or
> goal. . . . We believe that the existence of common operations that are ap-
> plied to a multitude of tasks underlies the tendency we reported of school
> populations to generalize rules and operations across a number of prob-
> lems. (1973, 557)[27]

What was to be generated by different educational forms (which end up
producing learning transfer or not on the part of schooled and not-schooled
learners) depended on different modes of instruction. The divide between
formal and informal education implied that the manner in which specific
skills were taught was crucial for whether learning transfer would follow.
Differences between informal and formal education included teaching by
demonstration versus explicit, abstract explanation of principles, and the
learning of bounded bodies of beliefs and values versus acquiring a general
understanding of knowledge and symbol systems.

DIFFERING CONVENTIONS OF COMPARATIVE RESEARCH

In the absence of critical examination of the implicit sociopolitical logic that generated a divide between schooling and every other educational endeavor, elisions typified much of the research. It often slipped without explicit comment between notions of socialization in other cultures and everyday life in the researcher's own, and from primitive or nonliterate cultures to ethnic minorities and women in the United States (cf. Lave 1996). Examples of informal or "everyday" learning were drawn almost entirely from "other" cultures. Anthropologists and psychologists cultivated thoroughly compatible theories, but nonetheless a good deal of work in their respective camps went into maintaining disciplinary boundaries (Lave 1988, chap. 1). There were disciplinary differences of value in interpreting the two sides of the theory—even given the civilization/primitive education templates in which all concurred. What Fortes, the anthropologist, called transmitting culture "with verisimilitude," psychologists tended to view as the mechanical reproduction of culture, without creativity. The unity of the social sphere and the synthesis of interests and skills that had a positive ring in Fortes's account became, in the hands of psychologists and sociologists, a lack of differentiation between cognition and emotion in "other" cultures (or in socialization, or in everyday life, or in primitives, or in women or children). What for Fortes was effective learning through engagement in everyday practices was viewed by others as the inability of informal educational processes to separate fact and value through lack of decontextualized, specialized, intentional pedagogy.

One argument that recommended a study of apprenticeship in 1973 focused on the comparative character of research contrasting formal and informal modes of education, learning, and thinking. Studying apprenticeship made sense as a way to break out of the standard comparative strategies of that time, most of which couldn't call into question the basic claims of the formal/informal model. Others were designed to seal and deliver those claims as fact. British anthropologists such as Fortes tended to take on socialization in one culture at a time. Their bracketing practices gained them some room to explore issues about everyday learning in positive terms, but those practices were rooted in a theoretical framework that had schooling and a theory of learning in the West as its implicit comparative basis. Those anthropologists who started with a broad view of education as socialization or enculturation tended to focus on early childhood, and on the inculcation of values and beliefs and induction into "society" or "culture." Those who started with schools as the prototypical form of education compared schooling and its consequences in different places. They lumped everything that wasn't schooling together as if all other educational practices were "socialization." Neither strategy offered obvious leverage for addressing the heterogeneous claims of the "formal versus informal" model of education, learning, teaching, and cognitive power. Cross-cultural psychologists, in yet another genre of research, tended to make asymmetrical comparisons between "schooled" and "uneducated" subjects, contrasting Western schooling with socialization processes in a single cultural formation. This *did* reflect directly the binary comparative theory, bringing the comparison center stage, but with a normative commitment to schooling and its effects that disparaged informal education and its practitioners in no uncertain terms.

A study of craft apprenticeship made sense to me at the time in simple empirical terms, for as Scribner and Cole pointed out, there was little information available then about "informal education" in "non literate cultures." But further, the apprenticeship study started with the decision to find a form of education that might appropriately be compared with Western schooling but that, unlike imported Western schooling, was homegrown, an unexceptional part of existing "social spheres," and further, that didn't stack the deck against "others" by comparing schooling in (or from) the West with some stand-in for "non-schooling" in the rest.

While contrasting the conventions of comparative research in the 1970s, I have pointed to the bracketing practices of anthropologists like Fortes. Their deep empiricism with respect to people, places, and practices that remained only abstractly comparative for the psychologists opened a space to appreciate and to be instructed by unanticipated facets of others' lives and thus to explore the limitations of their own (or more official) assumptions. This may help to explain how a *broadly* critical stance is "knitted into the very backbone of anthropology" (Cerwonka and Malkki 2007, 166), for even anthropologists with very different theoretical orientations find themselves delving (deviling?) into the details of everyday practice at the political/theoretical margins. It is still quite possible to ratify dualist comparative claims even without meaning to do so—ethnographic research doesn't determine ethical/political or theoretical conclusions, nor vice versa. But the everyday conduct of inquiry into everyday practice offers critical resources to the ethnographer so minded that are more difficult to arrange in other methodological genres.

The notion of opening a space to be instructed by the unanticipated is not inaccurate as a description of the research on the tailors' apprenticeship in Liberia. Chapter 2 begins where my naïve theoretical sensibilities took me—in pursuit of the institutional arrangements of apprenticeship, which I only gradually recognized in some unlikely places. Chapter 3 then asks how those arrangements shaped and were shaped by processes of learning. Both kinds of inquiry into apprenticeship were made possible by detailed field-work and created challenges to the assumptions underlying the standard comparative theory, especially to abstract claims about what informal education "ought," theoretically, to be.

European-American Ideologies of Craft, Art, and Science

The connotations of "apprenticeship" assumed in comparative theories of education and learning in the 1970s had a much longer history. Apprentice-ship was not just a random exemplar of "informal education" plucked out of thin air on a field trip to Monrovia; nor was the theory that framed schooling as the opposite pole to apprenticeship simply about "education." The binary politics opposing "formal" to "informal" education were part of more sweep-ing historical processes underlying cross-cultural research. Twentieth- and twenty-first-century theories of learning and education more often than not reproduce old—including really old—assumptions without recognizing or questioning their ideological origins and effects.

Raymond Williams's *Keywords*, originally published in 1976, is a fasci-nating resource for locating theoretical terms in their changing historical contexts and political relations. We can piece together rich connotations of craft production and the preparation of artisan labor across centuries of Euro-American history as they are implicated in theoretical distinctions between science, art, technology, knowledge, culture, learning, and prac-tice. The terms took shape in the changing capitalist division of labor, says Williams, in relation with each other. He points to the long negatively val-ued meanings of craft, its coupling with assumptions about how people think, and with other assumed characteristics of craft practitioners. (Wil-liams uses his own shorthand for denoting historical periods: C = century; e, m, and l = early, mid, and late. Thus lC20 would be read as "late twentieth century.")

Mechanical . . . was used from C15 to describe various mechanical arts and crafts; in fact the main range of non-agricultural productive work. For social reasons mechanical then acquired a *derogatory class sense*, to in-dicate *people* engaged in these kinds of work and *their supposed character-istics*. . . . From eC17 there was a persistent use of mechanical in the sense of *routine, unthinking activity*. This may now be seen as an analogy with the actions of a machine, and the analogy is clear from mC18. But in the earliest uses the *social prejudice* seems to be at least as strong. (1983, 201; italics mine)

We could scarcely look for a clearer example of the politics of categorical distinction-making, where kinds of labor in kinds of lives assigned to lower classes were branded negatively and neatly separated from those of their "betters." The shifting historical meanings of "craft" were not made in isolation. If craft was distinguished as low class, then it no doubt happened in relation to whatever constituted "the high"—upper-class (mental) labor, prized characteristics of people, and powerful ways of thinking.

Williams characterizes science as

> the general use of knowledge and learning . . . continued until eC19. . . . But from mC17 certain changes became evident. In particular there was the distinction from *art*. . . . [This] seems to express a distinction between a skill requiring theoretical knowledge and a skill requiring only practice. (1983, 277)

Then came a huge distinction between experience and methodical demonstration—experiment—supported in the eighteenth century by

> a distinction between practical and theoretical knowledge . . . , which was then expressed as a distinction between art and science. . . . The distinction between *experience* and *experiment*, however, was the sign of a larger change. *Experience* could be specialized in two directions: towards practical or customary knowledge, and towards inner [subjective] knowledge as distinct from external (*objective*) knowledge. . . . Theory and method applied to [metaphysics, religion, the social and political, and art] could then be marked off as not science but something else. The distinction hardened in eC19 and mC19. (278)

These lines drawn between experience and experiment, theory and method, and science and art frame one further distinction: "a now general distinction between artist and artisan—the latter being specialized to 'skilled manual worker' without 'intellectual' or 'imaginative' or 'creative' purposes" (41). Here also are shades of distinctions between formal and informal education and the devaluing of apprenticeship and manual labor both.

Williams's analysis emphasizes the emergence of meanings out of and in changing practice:

> This complex set of historical distinctions between various kinds of human skill and between varying basic purposes in the use of such skills is evidently related both to changes in the practical division of labour and to fundamental changes in practical definitions of the purposes of the exercise of skill. (1983, 42)[28]

Williams's analysis of this set of historical relations surely makes the point that the theoretical assumptions and webs of relations spun by social scientists in the late twentieth and early twenty-first centuries between political-economic structuring, everyday practices, and putative modes of thought (while often omitting to mention the first) have cultural/political effects.[29]

All this should encourage questions concerning the historical constitution of Vai and Gola craft practices and apprenticeship in West Africa: Where do they come from? What about the Vai and Gola themselves? There are two good reasons for these questions. One is to point to differences between West African historical craft practices and the Western historical practices that have generated comparative educational research. The second reason, *pace* the comparative theory of formal and informal education, is to insist that educational practices such as those of the Vai and Gola have a history and are part of larger historical forces and movements.

Historical Relations of Vai and Gola Crafts

Liberia today is in the aftermath of a long civil war, and it thus bears indeterminate relations to the country I came to know between 1973 and 1978 (cf. Moran 2006).[30]

In the mid-1970s, the capital, Monrovia, was a city of about 200,000 in a country with a population of about one and a half million, the only large urban center in Liberia (Ministry of Planning and Economic Affairs 1987). Today the population of Monrovia is about 550,000. It is still the center of the country in economic, political, commercial, and social senses, though not geographically.

The city lies on a small peninsula formed by the ocean on one side and the Mesurado River on the other. Broad Street, the main thoroughfare of the city, runs along the ridge dividing the river from the ocean. In the mid-1970s, the business district filled two streets on either side of Broad, with smaller, less prosperous businesses interspersed with apartments and shacks further away from the main street. Turning off Broad Street toward the river, a steep downhill walk down Mechlin or Randall Street led to the district of Monrovia known as Waterside. Along Water Street a mixture of commercial businesses owned and operated by Lebanese families and a multitude of street hawkers catered to the wholesale commercial demands of the construction and retail trades and the daily needs of the very poorest segment of the population. Cloth merchants were located here as well as hardware and lumber businesses.

Happy Corner came into existence in 1965, when a wealthy Americo-Liberian began to rent out small commercial spaces along a path by the river. By 1973, the area contained twenty tailor shops with 250 masters and

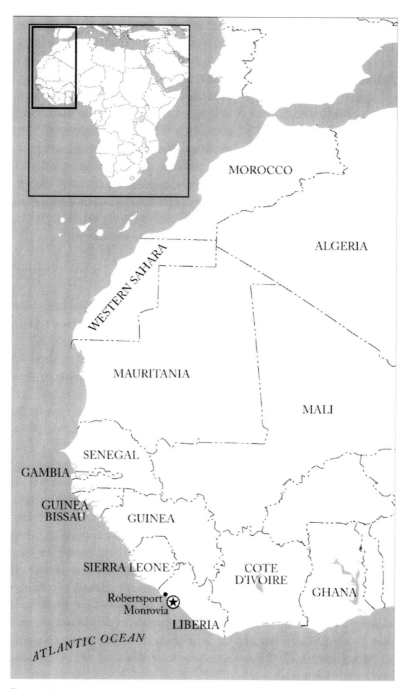

Figure 2. Liberia and its regional neighbors

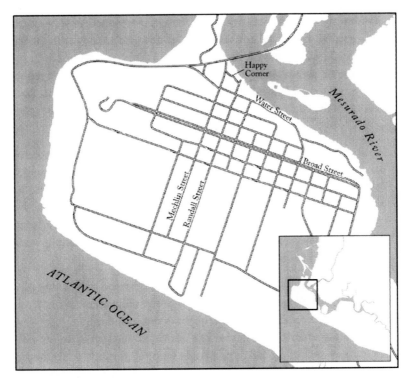

Figure 3. Downtown Monrovia

apprentices drawn from several ethnolinguistic groups and many different villages. The narrow, rock-strewn path lined with wood and tin-roofed
shacks was squeezed into a long narrow space between the backs of the
warehouses and the edge of the river. Happy Corner used to stretch between
Mechlin and Randall streets. It was destroyed, piecemeal, to make way for
an approach to a bridge over the river between 1979 and 1981. At the Mechlin Street end, the alley broadened, and there cloth sellers offered colorful
lengths of Fanti trade cloth displayed on long horizontal poles rising in tiers
eight or ten feet high. It was a beautiful and inviting sight, but the narrow
and crowded alley, which could not be explored without joining the throng,
had a rough reputation that discouraged the novice outsider. (Never in the
time I worked there did an unmistakable tourist wander through.) At the
other end of the alley, the entrance was practically invisible. It would be easy
to pass by the tiny tailor's shack that looked out on Randall Street, without
realizing that a whole world of work and learning lay behind it.

Craft production and apprenticeship are ubiquitous in West Africa, involving many crafts, widely distributed and frequently practiced.[31] This
stands in contrast with East Africa, where crafts were concentrated in East

Indian immigrant communities rather than in precolonial local practices (King 1977). Tailoring in Liberia is not handed down in families, as it is in Nigeria and Ethiopia. Nor is it a stepping-stone to other occupations or forms of investment, as it is among tailors in Kano and Dakar. Monrovian tailors serve a much longer apprenticeship than is typical of East Africa. Margaret Peil notes at the beginning of her survey of West African crafts in the 1960s that

> craftsmanship has a long history in West Africa. . . . Blacksmiths, weavers, potters, leather workers, silversmiths and goldsmiths were active long before the colonial period; carpentry and tailoring, which were introduced by early missionaries, soon spread widely. Printers were active in several towns in the nineteenth century. New trades are eagerly adopted, for they provide additional opportunities for wage employment or independent entrepreneurship. (1979, 3)

A study of craftspeople in Liberia should be understood as focusing on a large segment of the population, and a large sector of economic activity. Apprenticeship as an educational trajectory is common indeed.[32]

The history of craft practices in West Africa is bound up in the *nyamakwala* caste system of the far-flung Mande Empire, in which craft production and apprenticeship were practiced by endogamous groups of blacksmiths, bards, and leatherworkers (McNaughton 1988; Tamari 1991; Conrad and Frank 1995). There seem to have been three very old centers of artisan castes in West Africa predating Arabic/Islamic influences in this part of the world. These castes, sometimes more and sometimes less bounded and endogamous, were ubiquitous across the hierarchically organized societies of West Africa. Transformations in certain respects began in the nineteenth and twentieth centuries (Tamari 1991).

> The social organization of craft production in the Mande-speaking region (which would include some parts of Liberia, including the Vai—but not the Gola-speaking peoples) was . . . very embedded in the endogamous ranked specialized groups ("castes" or "nyamakalaw" in southern Mande) that seem to have emerged and been spread during the early years of the Malian empire (i.e. thirteenth century).[33]

The history of trade and empire in this area has been pursued much more widely by historians and area specialists than the history of craft and domestic relations. Indeed, relations of trade seem to have precipitated the intertwining of Vai and Gola people and their histories by the end of the sixteenth century (Hill 1972). This interaction began with the migration into Gola territory of Vai traders from the savannah-based Mande Empire. The

Vai, along with other Northern Mande–speaking groups (e.g., Kono, Mand-ing) arriving in western Liberia and eastern Sierra Leone, split resident groups of Mel speakers, including forebears of the Gola (Jones 1981). The Vai were seeking to establish an outpost on the West African coast for trade in salt and kola nuts.[34] The Mande Empire is known for its extraordinary trading relations, extending across the Sahara, bringing Islam with it, and across oceans, bringing Portuguese and other traders—slavers, notoriously, among them.[35] The trade routes ran all the way from the West African coast to savanna empires and from there to the North African coast, across the Sahara. Trade routes disseminated religious influences as well as commodi-ties.[36] The Vai became practitioners of Islam. Although clearly their accep-tance of Islam was deeply entwined with their participation in long-range trade with Muslim intermediaries, this seems to have had little effect on the *nyamakalaw* system.[37]

> Many of those people who became Muslims tended to be those who were most directly affected by the flow of commerce. Many of the Vai who be-came Muslims were important men such as rulers, traders, and people at the rulers' courts. Open conversion to Islam was especially notewor-thy among Vai leaders who gained economic wealth through trade with Europeans on the coast and the Manding coming from the interior. Al-though these men were often not of the lineages which normally sup-plied Vai rulers, these upstart *nouveau riche* Vai were sometimes able to replace the traditional backing of the "big men" in the Poro society with the sanctions of Islam to justify their attainment of political power. The new rulers invited Muslim clerics to live in their towns. These clerics would usually start Qur'anic schools and provide the usual types of ser-vices as diviners and scribes. . . . Perhaps by the latter years of the nine-teenth century a majority of Vai had become Muslim. Certainly this phe-nomenon had occurred by the first or second decades of the twentieth century. (Corby 1988, 48)

The Vai developed a highly stratified social system of chiefdoms, clans, and town chieftaincies that further included debtors, pawns, and slaves. Early Gola chiefdoms seem similar, divided into "the owners of the land" (members of the lineages ranked close to the founding line), "freeborn" (citi-zens of attached lineages), "followers" (noncitizen clients of kings and other important men), and "slaves" (d'Azevedo 1959, 73).

Over the course of the nineteenth century, despite a good deal of inter-mingling, the Vai and Gola swung between uneasy accommodation and out-right warfare. Their changing relations had much to do with long religious-political struggles around Poro and Sande secret societies and the practice of Islam. The Gola were deeply involved in these men's and women's secret societies, found in one form or another throughout much of forest West Africa (Holsoe 1976). They may be understood as major hierarchical organizations in polygynous, gerontocratic communities, Poro and Sande acting as different counterweights to a hierarchically organized lineage, ward, town, or clan political system (Holsoe 1977, 287). Poro elders exerted control over youth through initiation rituals of great duration, and over succession to ritual and political power. Poro and Sande were responsible for much of ritual life, and Poro also for fighting the frequent intergroup slave raids and broader political wars. The Vai are believed to have acquired variously land, lineages, and secret society practices through their long association and close proximity to the Gola (Holsoe 1967). Indeed, "Gola have retained the most conservative and exemplary traditions with regard to the structure and content of Poro and Sande," and "Gola Poro and Sande tended to discourage the emergence of rival associations, including Islam and Christianity" (d'Azevedo 1980, 14–15, 21).

The Vai and Gola faced not only one another, but increasingly in the twentieth century, various kinds of pressures from the Americo-Liberian government in Monrovia as it attempted to gain control over Liberian hinterlands. The two groups reacted differently, the Vai forming alliances with the Americo-Liberians, sending their children to be fostered by Americo-Liberian families, and establishing themselves as preeminent among the twenty-eight ethnolinguistic groups in Liberia (Holsoe 1967, 261–63, 265), while the Gola resisted as long as they could and fought with the Vai over their differences. The cessation of hostilities was government imposed and seems gradually to have become the status quo. By the 1950s, their proximity in western Liberia seemed to make close ties between Vai and Gola a matter of course (Fraenkel 1964).

There are glimpses of evidence that suggest how Vai and Gola may have come to have a special interest in the craft of tailoring in Monrovia in the 1970s. The abolition of internal servitude in Liberia in 1930 wreaked "absolute havoc" upon Vai society and "the economic base was destroyed" (Holsoe 1987, 142). Large numbers of former slaves moved to urban areas, Islamic practices became more prominent, and Poro bush school shorter.

> The Vai traditionally engaged in a variety of crafts including blacksmithing (working in gold, silver, copper, brass); carving in wood, bone and ivory; leather work; weaving and plaiting; pottery; and in professions as musicians, singers and dancers. After 1930 many freeborn Vai, disdaining the farm work and menial service work of their former slaves, moved

to a new community, Vaitown, in Monrovia and took up craft occupations. . . .

. . . The vast majority of men, who were traditionally weavers, turned to tailoring as an occupation. (Holsoe 1984–85, 13–15, 19; see also 22)

D'Azevedo says of the Gola:

In former times each large village had numbers of weavers attached to the households of well-to-do families. . . . The tailor . . . is a more recent type of specialist responding to the increasing use of European cloth and styles of clothing. Almost every village has at least one professional tailor who has learned his trade in some urban center. (1973, 328–29)

It thus appears that slave taking, pawning, and fostering (social, political-economic arrangements earlier, then forbidden under colonial regimes) gradually transformed in ways that have shaped contemporary practices of craft apprenticeship. (Goody 1989 and D'Azevedo 1959, 65, speculate along similar lines.)

Moving to Monrovia did not pose huge problems of coordination or incorporation into capitalist forms of production and commerce for the tailors, for the Americo-Liberian economy was concentrated almost exclusively in large foreign extractive enterprises. In the early twentieth century, the Firestone and Goodyear rubber companies established huge natural rubber plantations in Liberia, and European-based mining consortiums began operations in the 1950s. These enterprises and the Liberian government were in each other's pockets (and bank accounts) over many decades (Thomasson 1987, 6). Spoils were not reinvested in the country; indeed, the government in Monrovia didn't attempt to extend bureaucratic control, taxation, infrastructure, or governance over the interior territories and counties until after World War II. In the 1970s, a small number of elite, intermarried Americo-Liberian families dominated the government (Clower, Dalton, and Walters 1966; Liebenow 1987). By law, with the exception of the rubber and mineral concessions, only Americo-Liberians could own major businesses. There were not many of these in any case, but Americo-Liberians were prevented by government manipulation of educational and economic opportunity from gaining hands-on *management* of commercial or industrial enterprises that could provide a potential economic base independent of the ruling families. Americans and Europeans managed businesses but were enjoined from participating in politics on pain of expulsion from the country. Migrants from the countryside supplied the small amount of wage labor that the system could absorb. Many other upcountry Liberians like the Vai and Gola tailors moved to Monrovia to apprentice themselves in a plethora of trades, setting up craft shops from which they eked a living.[38]

In the Liberia of the 1970s, craft production and its practices of reproduction were surely being shaped by long- and short-term capitalist intrusions into the political economy of national and international commerce. As I will discuss in chapter 2, I did find direct economic threats to prospects for the ongoing reproduction of the tailors' craft by imported factories and the second-hand clothing trade. But whatever the future would bring, in the tailors' alley there was nothing about their means of production, the products of their craft, or relations among masters, apprentices, and customers that marked them off as anachronistic in everyday life in Monrovia.

Raymond Williams's inquiry into the changing meanings of art, science, craft—and modes of labor and thought—traced a history of conceptual objects crucial to the politics of European and Anglo-American theorists who divide formal from informal education, schooling from everyday life, and learning from the transfer of learning. West African historical traditions, as well as more recent capitalist economic changes, went into the making of the craft of tailoring and its particular apprenticeship processes as practiced by Vai and Gola tailors and their apprentices in Liberia in the 1970s. It should be clear that issues of comparison and translation seriously complicate ethnographic inquiry across such different cultural-historical practices. It should also be clear that critical ethnographic practice requires thoughtful concern about the techniques through which ethnographers and others *establish* comparative claims, for these reflect and are imbued with differences of power and political implications.

The Argument

So far our discussion has focused on the temporal end points of the book, on the exploration of critical ethnographic practice now and of ethnographic research in Liberia in the 1970s. But what about the book as a whole? What are the relations betweentimes and how are they produced in the chapters to follow?

At the heart of the ethnographic inquiry into changing apprenticeship in Liberia was a desire to pursue change in the theory and practice of research on learning and thinking, the bailiwick of experimental psychological research. It seemed useful to launch my project from a place, in a practice, nominated by historical, political, official Western commonsense theorizing to be marginal and inferior: "Only a challenge to the hierarchy of sites of discourse, which usually comes from groups and classes 'situated' by the dominant in low or marginal positions, carries the promise of politically transformative power" (Stallybrass and White 1986, 201).

I intended to translate what I learned from the fieldwork into new experiments, and to translate the results of the fieldwork and the experiments into terms "hearable" by those I wanted to challenge. But engaging in the practice of ethnographic work gradually led to the recognition that what I intended required deeper theoretical as well as empirical reformulation. This agenda was rife in all its parts with pitfalls as well as possibilities. Indeed, translating a determination to reject claims like those under challenge here in favor of a noncomplicit alternative stance is a very tricky business. Chapters to come grapple with how one might pursue alternative conclusions without reproducing the logic of inquiry to which they are opposed.

To address these issues, I lay out a (long, slow) process of breaking with a commonsense positivist problematic and moving toward relational social practice theory. Changing empirical and theoretical work over extended periods is another dimension of critical ethnographic practice: it is a long-term, uneven struggle, an ongoing, open-ended, and partial process to explore and develop a theoretical/empirical stance that addresses ethical/political issues in rigorous terms (and makes apprentice ethnographers of us all).[39] More often than not, this process is reflected in a series of projects, over an ethnographer's lifetime, but occasionally it takes over a book project, which becomes a boneyard of superseded understandings through many rewrites and rejected drafts. Not a lot of work that eventually emerges from such a process has the same form as the present book, but mine is by no means unique. Margery Wolf and Helen Verran are notable for following long-term, changing relations between their own earlier research and their present stance with respect to that work and their field. Their transformative accounts of changing analytical and theoretical practices were written, as this one was, to struggle critically and anew with their own earlier attempts to make sense of everyday practices in terms that challenged the received wisdom of the time (see, e.g., Verran 2001, vii, 19–20; Wolf 1992, 4).

In each case, we have written about ethnographic projects many years later. Wolf was engaged in field research in northern Taiwan in 1960 and published her book *A Thrice Told Tale* in 1992. The core chapters of her book each take a different focus on what happened in a village in northern Taiwan, one a short story, one excerpts from her field notes, one an article she published in the *American Ethnologist*. As she explains, "Each chapter is followed by a Commentary, in which I use the text to illustrate and argue with some of the problems and promises [of the period of ethnographic reflexivity in the 1980s]" (1992, 7). The commentaries lay out her critical views as a feminist anthropologist on postmodern debates about ethnography.[40]

Beginning in 1979, shortly after I stopped making field trips to Liberia, Helen Verran began years of work in Nigeria on Yoruba mathematics, "determined to take on the seemingly ridiculous task of showing 'natural number' as culturally situated" (2001, 18). In the same spirit, I had set out to take on the equally ridiculous-seeming task of showing "learning" as socially and culturally situated. Verran was incensed by the ethnocentric—what she identifies as "colonial"—assumptions about the "primitive" character of African thought, and especially the inferiority assumed to characterize African number systems: "I sought to demolish the claim that Yoruba quantification is primitive, to dissolve a claimed deficit in Yoruba psychology of either social or biological origin. I wanted to remake the problem as an issue in sociology of education and curriculum development" (143; see also, e.g., 82).

If I took on comparative educational theory and cognitive theorizing about learning as exemplars of colonialist politics, dualistic argumentation, and experimental method, Verran took on comparative claims about mathematical practices and Piagetian theorizing about the development of logical structures. She too tried her hand at conducting experiments and made a critical analysis thereof.[41] Math in both projects provided a worst-case scenario: As Verran asks,

> How can we expose the social foundations of mathematics? Natural number seems a good place to start, for it is among the most sacred of the Platonists' objects; it is one of the least problematic of the empiricist's reality; and for the psychologist, it is the most obvious of mental structures." (2001, 178)

Verran's critical reactions to her own earlier analyses, not unlike mine, led her eventually to a multilayered account of her changing understanding over the years:

> In a serious way, my analysis had failed. I was stymied. I abandoned the manuscript and began again. Eventually I came up with a method that had me overtly decomposing my previous . . . writings. That method determines the structure of this book. (2001, 20)

She grouped chapters in threes; the second is a commentary on the early work described in the first, and the third a commentary on the second. Verran was intent on moving from critiques of universalist claims about the inferiority of the mathematics of the "marginal other" to alternatives arguing that there are historically constituted multiple systems of number. Going on to a critique of this stance lead her to a relational account of mathematic practices. The present book has similar empirical/theoretical intentions.

The main parts of the next four chapters lay out just about everything I came to know about the tailors' apprenticeship practices. Each chapter concludes with a commentary written these many years later that takes on the specific issues of critical ethnographic practice it has raised. Together the commentaries address interrelated issues concerning the doing of apprenticeship in critical, changing, conceptually challenged ethnographic practice. Each chapter may look as if its two parts are divided between "then" and "now," or between a descriptive empirical account and theoretical conclusions, or for that matter, between a reflexive account of fieldwork and its interpretive construction. However, I see the commentary concluding each chapter as a critical attempt to wrestle with the empirical material inseparably from the theoretical practice of which it is part.

Structuring books as long-term critical accounts of ethnographic practice both comes from and contributes to assumptions that social life is a matter of historical process. Critical ethnographers' commitments to an ethics of social justice aim research at social change. For Wolf, Verran, and me, this approach no doubt reflects our location in intergenerational relations, but it also derives from our location in a particular historical cohort in a changing world. We have lived and worked through roughly the same changes in theoretical "central tendencies" in anthropology, the struggles in and out of the academy that have produced in each of us what I would call a democratic feminist sensibility whether with a capital F or not—a sensibility that has lent political weight to our focus on social process, open critique of our own work, and changing theoretical practice. This focus also follows from and creates conditions for addressing apprentice ethnographers, especially those with specific concerns about social inequality and changing practice.

To understand tailors or anthropologists or ethnographic projects, it gets in the way to treat them as finished products. For me the most productive question, central to a relational problematic, is, *What is the process by which something is produced?* My answer lies partly in conceptions of complex processes of apprenticeship, whether of tailors or ethnographers. In the chapters that follow, I present in detail apprenticeship and everyday practice among Vai and Gola tailors. How are trousers produced? How are relations of learning and teaching produced, or knowledgeable skillfulness or engagement in mature practice? I also provide an account of the process of production—the doing of—the research, from inquiring into life and work in Happy Corner and the trajectories of tailors' apprenticeship (chapters 2 and 3) to the experimental research (chapter 4) that followed and depended on the ethnographic work and finally to the postexperiment return to the tailor shops for further ethnographic work, given new questions that emerged during my analysis of experiments (chapter 5). Each chapter reflects the process of inquiry, beginning with conventional assumptions and questions. This leads to places where the ethnographic findings underwrite more critical questions that in turn begin to transform the direction of the work that follows. The fieldwork moves from uncritical descriptions to critical problems that sometimes provoke further, unexpected lines of inquiry.

I posed a dilemma earlier in this chapter of how to address empirical and theoretical relations as they constitute each other. Looking at the world in material-historical processual terms is essential to resolving that dilemma. We must therefore encounter empirical and theoretical work together, reading each through the other. It is difficult to do this sort of dialectical reading—unless you do so in practice and by asking how each is part of the production of the other. So, throughout this introductory chapter, I have been exploring different theoretical problematics through the lens of apprenticeship and apprenticeship through different theoretical lenses. Similarly, running through the next four empirically focused chapters is a growing argument for a more adequate theoretical basis for future research. Each of these chapters offers an ethnographic-practical account of changing theoretical concerns, and I conclude in chapter 6 with a theoretical account of the process of critical ethnographic practice. Taken together, read through each other, the chapters lead to a relational theoretical problematic—a theory of social practice.

2 Institutional Arrangements and the Uniform

Overview

I began the fieldwork in Happy Corner with a census and interviews to gather basic information about the tailors and apprenticeship. I watched the tailors working and learning and compared details of production processes in different shops, as well as observing and discussing relations between masters and apprentices. Eventually I began to explore what I came to call the "learning syllabus" of the apprentices.

The ethnographic project had several purposes. One was to establish that there was an educational form worthy of the designation "apprenticeship." I also intended to reconsider the comparative model of education in light of practices of apprenticeship in the tailor shops. I hoped to identify aspects of apprenticeship that might offer a basis for designing learning transfer experiments and explaining their results. The work described in this chapter moved toward critical challenges to the standard assumptions about differences between formal and informal education. It was not, however, a case of saying, "Now I'm going to leave off the mainstream stuff and start being critical." We will see that what happened instead offers a useful window on how understanding changes in ethnographic practice.

The Institutional Arrangements of the Tailors' Alley

The twenty shops along the noisy and crowded tailors' alley between Mechlin and Randall streets were exclusively men's businesses. Women also practiced tailoring in Monrovia, but not in Happy Corner. Most worked in their homes, a few in the public market not far from the alley. The tailor shops were crammed side by side so that there were only a few spaces between buildings wide enough to permit passage to the women's businesses, Vai cook shops, and brothels.

The typical tailor shop had wooden sides, a corrugated tin roof, large openings in the front wall, shutters to close at night, and a door opening onto the path. The shops were closed on the sides and back and had dark interiors, dimly lit here and there by patches of sunlight or a bare light bulb. Wherever a little extra space occurred between shops, a street seller sat on the ground or in the middle of a low display table, her goods arranged around her. One or two beggars and a couple of pickpockets had regular stations in Happy Corner as well. There were two tiny stores near the Mechlin Street end of the alley that catered to the tailors, selling thread, buttons, measuring tapes, and other notions. Walking down the alley could be an overwhelming experience, stumbling over rocks, trying to dodge through the crowds of hawkers and customers, and edging around the makeshift tables set out in the middle of the path covered with hats and children's underwear for sale—ears buffeted by the sounds of a hundred or more treadle sewing machines and loud voices competing with the blast of high-life music from portable radios, eyes trying to take in rows and rows of ready-to-wear trousers hung on the shop beams, shutters, window frames, and doors to attract customers.

PRODUCTION IN THE ALLEY

Inside, the Vai and Gola shops in Happy Corner felt almost as jammed as the street, typically accommodating four or five tailors and a similar number of apprentices. All the tailors in a shop shared a table for cutting out the garments. There was a small open space near the door where customers stood when they came to buy trousers or get measured for a safari suit, or just to visit. Each tailor had his own small area within the shop just large enough for his sewing machine, sewing bench (long enough for two to sit on), and wooden storage box for fabric, tools, and sundries. An apprentice spent most of his time sitting on his master's bench or the box or leaning on the stand for the sewing machine. The bench was the apprentice's observation post, and it was a good one since his orientation to the master's activities was very similar to the master's. Masters sometimes called the apprentice to watch and sometimes moved aside so that the apprentice could work on the sewing machine. (Masters returning from some errand not infrequently scolded their apprentices if they discovered that the boys had not taken advantage of the opportunity to practice.)

Tailors had frequent opportunities to interact with each other and with shop visitors. Customers, relatives and friends from upcountry, tailors from other shops in the alley, and food sellers were all part of this traffic. Tailors

Figure 4. Happy Corner, mid-1970s

were likely to have friends and relatives in the alley, and many of them were fixtures in each other's lives, having worked there together six days a week for several years. Two tailors among this predominantly Muslim group were treated with special respect because they had made the pilgrimage to Mecca. The multiplicity of relationships between tailors was as much a fact of life as the lack of privacy and as the close proximity and easy permeability of their space.

At the Mechlin Street end of the alley, a few shops housed tailors of other regional and linguistic affiliations. This partial segregation reflected greater cultural differences than those between Vai and Gola and necessitated use of Americo-Liberian English as a lingua franca in Happy Corner.

The tailors had characteristic ways of organizing their materials, producing garments, and selling them, putting most of their effort into ready-to-wear trousers (though they all knew how to make other kinds of clothes). They bought only enough fabric to make a few pairs of trousers. When a pair or two had been sold, there would be enough money to buy fabric to make another pair or two. Inventories and capital outlay were small, and stock was replenished as it was sold. The tailors went through the cycle of buying fabric, making trousers, and selling trousers often enough that it became virtually a single process. They sometimes stockpiled a number of pairs of trousers and went on peddling trips to the foreign-owned mining concession and rubber plantations. Sometimes customers commissioned custom-made clothing. But most customers simply came shopping, strolling down tailors' alley looking for ready-to-wear trousers.

When a tailor was ready to make a pair of trousers, he assembled cloth, thread, lining fabric, and waistband stiffening. He drew the pattern for the different pieces on the folded cloth using chalk and a yardstick and cut them out. He then set to work at the sewing machine. Interrupted only to press the stiffening onto the waistband at the shared shop table, he worked first on pockets, building them into each of the four main trouser leg pieces. Next he built up right and left sides of the fronts and backs of the trousers, finishing with the waistband, fly, and inner leg seam. Finally he gave the trousers to his apprentice to sew on buttons and hem the cuffs, or he did the job himself. If he planned to make several pairs, he might cut out two or more before starting to sew. He would sit down at the machine and sew one pair of trousers start to finish, beginning the second pair only after completing the first. Alternatively, he might give one pair to an advanced apprentice to sew while making the other pair himself. While the job could be done effectively by one person, it could also be broken down into steps, some of which required little skill and little coordination with the master's work.

The tailors bought cloth from the Lebanese cloth merchants whose concrete warehouses backed the alley. Their purchases were too small to command a wholesale discount, but the tailors did buy frequently. Merchants sometimes gave these steady customers credit or small discounts. The tailors knew how to utilize cloth more efficiently than amateur sewers. They could claim to customers that a certain amount of cloth was needed, while actually using less. A meager profit often rode on that difference. Apprentices made and sold children's underwear (known locally as "drawers") and hats. They bought the materials on which they sewed, though masters often gave them scraps of fabric, especially for their very first efforts, which might not be salable. Children's drawers therefore tended to be made of elaborate patchwork: scraps cost less, and labor was costless from the apprentices' point of view. They kept what they earned for themselves in order to buy more scraps of fabric or to use as pocket money.

Sales for the tailors fluctuated strongly during the year, with much brisker trade in the dry season (November to May) than during the wet season. Demand peaked just before Christmas, Ramadan, and Liberian Independence Day. At those times, having skilled apprentices benefited the tailors, for time was the main constraint on how much business they could transact. During other periods of the year, business sometimes almost stood still. At these times, apprentices represented mouths to feed and backs to clothe, not economic assets.

The tailors' expenses included $5 per month to rent a space to put the treadle sewing machine and gain access to the cutting table and an annual government "machine tax" of $25—in essence a police shakedown—avoided whenever possible. The 1976 mean income for a sample of eighty-one tailors was $75 per month, the median about $40. The chief capital outlay was for tools: sewing machine, scissors, tape measure, bench, and the wooden trunk for supplies. The sewing machine was clearly the major item, and the expense of purchasing one was a formidable obstacle to becoming a self-employed tailor (a new machine cost about $100 in 1975). Beginning master tailors often bought second-hand machines on credit or took loans from relatives who had money to invest.

The minimal technology, short production cycle, location at the margins of the urban economy in Monrovia, and their reliance on apprenticeship in reproducing themselves and their craft all confirm that the tailors were engaged in "informal education," in terms assumed in the polarized theory of formal versus informal education. The tailors were also actively engaged in what is often called the informal economy, that is, in the cash economy outside the surveillance of the bureaucratic, taxed, capitalist organization of commercial Monrovia.

How much had urban transformation in Liberia shaped their daily activities by the mid-1970s? The tailors with very few exceptions shared similar histories of growing up in small villages upcountry in polygynous households engaged in farming and occasionally in crafts or petty commerce. They came to Monrovia to be apprenticed as tailors and stayed on after becoming masters. Most of their brothers and half brothers worked as craft producers as well.

The distribution of sales of different kinds of garments reflected the relation of these Vai and Gola tailors to other tailors in Monrovia. The Vai and Gola had had a stranglehold on the tailoring craft in Monrovia until the recent arrival of Mandingo tailors from Guinea, whose incursion had created distinctions of language, nationality, and also differences of wealth and social position. No Mandingo tailors worked in Happy Corner—their shops were located closer to the main commercial thoroughfare of Monrovia.

The distribution of sales of different kinds of garments also placed the tailors in relation to the population that came to them for their services. Trousers might be thought of as cheap social universalizers for men; all the rest of the Happy Corner tailors' work took second priority to this. In more expensive Mandingo uptown shops, most products made and sold were elaborately tailored short-sleeved safari suits (known locally as "Higher

Heights" suits) and ladies' gowns and dresses. The Vai and Gola tailors in the alley sewed for poorer clients, often visitors to Monrovia who bought clothes before returning to their home villages.

There were two types of sewing the tailors didn't do—both of which involved embroidery. Such work fell at opposite ends of the rural/urban spectrum. The tailors didn't make machine-embroidered shirts and gowns that required more expensive, agile sewing machines than they could afford. These garments were sold uptown to tourists and other relatively wealthy folks by the Mandingo tailors. The other embroidered garment was the countryman's hat. It was made by hand by part-time craftsmen upcountry and worn by members of that same category: older, dignified men who mostly lived in small villages. In a sense, both the buyers of embroidered shirts (from uptown tailor shops near Broad Street) and the buyers of country hats (by upcountry elders) marked the periphery of the social world that the tailors in Happy Corner served. The tailors in the alley were mediators for those leading hybrid rural and urban lives. Part of their effectiveness came from the broad range of social personae they were able to dress. Their reach stopped just short of each end of their social spectrum.

The tailors' effectiveness in their role as mediators also stemmed from their own social position. They were in many respects very like their customers. They were mostly Muslims, and they were also involved in Poro. They wore the same kind of clothes they made for others. Even in Monrovia, the Vai and Gola tailors led lives quite similar to life in the villages from whence they came. All of the tailors were born upcountry. They came to Monrovia in order to learn tailoring or to work as tailors (on average they had ten years of tailoring experience and had been living in town ten years). The tailors ranged in age between nine and sixty years, on average twenty-five. Seventy percent were between the ages of fifteen and thirty-four. Other urban Vai, with a similar age distribution, averaged five years living in the city. The tailors therefore had spent a good deal more time in urban environments, on average, than other Vai in Monrovia.

But the tailors worked in Happy Corner, a community within which everyone came from a rural background and still made frequent trips home to visit, attend funeral feasts, and work on their farms. A little over half of the tailors maintained small farms near their home villages. Further, the tailors lived in large communities within Monrovia that were mostly homogeneous by geographic origin and language. It was quite possible to go back and forth from Happy Corner to Westpoint, Vaitown, Claratown, or other urban migrant enclaves day in and day out without ever going near downtown Monrovia or having contact with more Westernized Liberian social life or commerce.[1]

RELATIONS OF FORCE

Happy Corner was constructed piecemeal in 1965 and was bursting at its seams by 1973, when I first encountered it. It was physically destroyed to make way for an approach to a bridge over the Mesurado River between 1979 and 1981. But the tailors' livelihood was being economically shredded even before the bridge—destroyed by competition from imported second-hand clothing that undercut their prices and sent them out of business, or at least drove them away from Waterside. By 1978, warehouses on Water Street stored bales of used clothing plainly marked with their country of origin (Italy in this case) and with instructions from the charity Caritas that the clothing was to be given away, not sold. Clothes from those bales—for sale—lay in piles on the sidewalks outside the warehouses, attracting customers who would otherwise have gone to tailors in Happy Corner. I talked with a number of the tailors about shifting some of their efforts into refurbishing and altering second-hand clothes. They rejected this idea with disdain.[2]

Happy Corner was neither fully outside nor fully integrated into national bureaucratic institutions of economic and political control. They certainly took part in the cash economy, buying materials and selling trousers. "Taxation," such as it was, was a police matter. On several occasions while I was sitting in one of the shops, warnings of an imminent raid by police passed quietly from one shop to the next. The tailors and apprentices moved quickly away down the alley until within minutes the place was virtually deserted. Police searching the shops for tailors from whom they could extract the annual "sewing-machine tax" collared only an unfortunate few, who paid the police to avoid being carted off. The police also descended on the alley on December 1, Matilda Newport Day, to round up unwary tailors and apprentices to fill out the crowd along Broad Street for the annual parade (schoolchildren were also forced to attend). Matilda Newport Day was an Americo-Liberian celebration, invented in 1916, to commemorate an incident in 1832 in which a new colonist from the United States was supposed to have shot and killed a potentially threatening "native." I expected the tailors to explain their avoidance of the celebration in political terms, but they did not seem to identify themselves as the victims in this pageant, objecting more directly to police coercion than to the purpose of the occasion. (This rite was abolished after the 1980 coup.)

The Mandingo tailors' shops and production practices were quite similar to those of the Vai and Gola tailors in the alley in spite of differences in their products and clientele. But Monrovia also boasted a small capital-intense clothing factory, a mattress factory, and a shoe factory. These had wage-earning employees and used mass-production methods. Tailors from the alley had good prospects of getting jobs sewing in these factories. Young tailors without apprentices were most likely to try a stint in one of the factories, galvanized by economic hardship during slow times of year. One of the tailors' biggest complaints about working in Happy Corner was the erratic and unpredictable nature of their income. They told me they welcomed the predictable income of wage employment and the control that gave them over their financial lives from week to week. But they rarely stayed at a factory for more than a few months, returning to the alley in reaction to what they found to be confining, brutal discipline and excessive demands for high output, though they certainly had the skill to meet these demands. The clothing factory was the project of an Americo-Liberian who imported industrial sewing machines and other equipment from the States. It didn't last long. The tailors drove it out of business because they could produce ready-to-wear trousers more cheaply and quickly than the mass-produced products of the factory.

Tailors' Apprenticeship

There was no set pattern in West Africa by which would-be apprentices found masters and masters selected apprentices. Sometimes it was a casual arrangement, with relatively unmarked access for children to learn a craft; sometimes it was costly as well as difficult to get taken on. What apprentices and masters expected of each other varied as well. I spent a good deal of time early on trying to understand the specific character of these relations in the tailors' alley.[3]

Apprenticeship in Happy Corner took about five years, and almost every apprentice became a master tailor. A master tailor might foster a boy of thirteen or fourteen as an apprentice. He often had ties with the boy's senior relatives, and the decision that the child should become a tailor had been sorted out in discussions about how to create a diverse craft and trade "portfolio" within the extended family.

The new apprentice lived with other apprentices in the shop. He learned first to sew by hand, to take care of the sewing machine, and to run small errands for his master. Most new apprentices also did household chores for their masters, and some of them occasionally went to the masters' home villages to do farm work as well. Over the next several years, the apprentices learned to make all the different kinds of clothes that were made in Happy Corner, and to do so with an economy of effort and a speed that was amazing to behold. Midway through the process, when they were skilled enough, the apprentices' work began to augment and supplement their masters' output and income, and they continued to work for them until they themselves became masters, ready to begin their own small, independent tailoring businesses. Masters took in apprentices with little ceremony, no contract, and no fees. The apprentices became masters when their masters had given them their blessing.

Most, but by no means all, masters accepted the notion that having apprentices was a useful addition to their lives as craft masters. The variety of views on this point in part reflected the fluctuating economic effects of supporting and training an apprentice. Most masters had no more than one or two apprentices at a time. If there were two, they were taken on at intervals of several years so that each could contribute differently to the production process. None of the tailors was prosperous enough to take on two new apprentices at the same time. Across long careers, the masters trained at most ten apprentices, averaging about one trained apprentice for every five years of tailoring experience. The masters were in the business of training their own future competition, and indeed they worried that there were too many tailors "these days" and not enough customers to go around. Having interviewed each of the tailors in the initial months of fieldwork, I could count the number of masters who finished their apprenticeships at about the same time. The number of new masters increased from 1940 to about 1970 and declined after that.

In theory, both master and apprentice were on trial for a period of time after an apprentice came to live with a master. I asked a variety of masters whether they tested "applicants" in any way before accepting them. Tailors said that if a boy still could not sew buttons on trousers after three months, they would send him back to his parents—should it ever happen. But to be sent away for lack of aptitude would require an extraordinary exhibition of incompetence. Masters and apprentices were more specific when they discussed attitudes than when they were discussing aptitude. Masters agreed that if an apprentice were "frisky," that is, disobedient, or sullen and lazy, he could be sent back to his parents.[4] Apprentices spoke of being punished by their masters for swearing or other misbehavior. (The punishment consisted of being fined or given extra chores.) "Good" apprentices were expected through deference and service to encourage their masters to make the effort of passing on their knowledge and skill.

There were durable conflicts as well as common interests in apprentices' progress. Given the difference in power between apprentice and master, the most important concerned their long-term relations as patron and client and the temptation to exploit apprentices in the shorter run.[5] The master could employ an apprentice as errand runner, house servant, and farmhand, all of which would interfere with the boy's opportunities to learn. Masters had the formal responsibility to declare apprenticeship complete, return the

Figure 5. Apprentice at sewing machine

new master to his parents, and convey legitimacy on his mastery through his blessing (without which the tailors believed it would not be possible to prosper in business). Timing mattered: The master could hold on indefinitely to a skilled apprentice as a source of cheap labor and would be more likely to do so when demand for clothing was high. In bad times, the apprentice might not want to be pushed out on his own. Masters might be generous or tightfisted, and their apprentices thus either more or less able to set up in business for themselves. Apprentices thus had little leverage with which to negotiate the end of their apprenticeships.

But there were limits on the masters as well: If a master badly neglected his apprentice and didn't give him opportunities to learn tailoring, the boy's family could intervene, and the apprentice could leave his master and seek a new one. The tailors gossiped about certain masters who exploited their apprentices. And masters were, perhaps more compellingly, dependent on the skills and industry of their apprentices for their own livelihood. An advanced apprentice who left in protest could not soon be replaced.

All of this was common knowledge in Happy Corner. As one tailor explained:

> An apprentice goes to work for a master. He sees other boys working for another master. If they get ahead, learn to do more things faster than he does, then he knows that his master is not doing right by him. He tells his parents, and they speak to the master. If things don't improve they take him away from the master.
>
> But a schoolteacher, there is only one in town. Who can see if he teaches well or badly, much or little. Teachers, they get paid by the government; it doesn't matter if they teach three days or five days. They go get their money once a month even so.
>
> But a master: the boy watches and watches and pretty soon one day the master says, I have to go out, you sew this while I am gone. If it isn't sewn well the master doesn't get on well with his customer. And the parents take the boy away and the master loses his helper. A master knows he should teach the boy well and quickly so that the boy will be a master tailor.

One interesting point in these observations is that even in Happy Corner we find the comparative shadow of schooling.

The Syllabus of Tailoring

The broad question in my initial exploration of the social conditions and relations of Happy Corner was whether the tailors' system of apprenticeship could serve as an exemplar of informal education. But what of the *process* by which apprentices gradually turned into master tailors? Ethnographic work about the apprentices' changing knowledge and skill focused on questions of what and how apprentices learned. I started on these questions early on, but it took a long time before I got anywhere with this part of the project.

THE WRONG TROUSERS

Shortly after arriving in Monrovia for the first time, before I knew that Happy Corner existed, I spent my days in a Vai tailor shop not far from the alley. At the end of two weeks, I could see that the tailors were skillfully engaged in their work and that apprentices who had spent different amounts of time there were different from each other, some more and some less adept. There was abundant evidence that learning was going on. But I couldn't see it happening. There weren't any classes, no designated teachers among the masters, and no time set aside during the day for anything like tutorials. I thought maybe I did not understand how to be in the right place at the right time. So I began to ask masters with young apprentices to show me how they taught them. The masters were hospitable and kind. Obligingly they "gave lessons." In these sessions, a master stood over his small apprentice giving a monologue on the work to be learned and a running commentary on the apprentice's performance. The verbal detail was extraordinary. There was no doubt that the masters knew how to "teach." But it didn't feel right, even though it was what I thought I ought to see. I finally couldn't avoid facing up to the fact that I was pursuing the wrong issues when one master explained to his apprentice in a loud voice really intended for my ears that "the fly *always* goes on the *front* of the trousers." (I went home and wept.)

Even during the following year's fieldwork in Happy Corner, it was only after absorbing everyday goings on in tailor shops over a period of months that different sorts of questions began to arise. Meanwhile, I spent a good deal of time on questions generated by the assumptions of the comparative educational theory, trying to ascertain whether practices of tailoring and of training apprentices were uniform. It seemed essential to start with the most basic of questions—"Does apprenticeship as a discrete educational process exist?"—by which I meant, was apprenticeship anything more than everyday "hanging out" in tailor shops. The advantage of this rather severe skepticism was that I took my mission to be one of establishing whether, and if so, of what, a process of apprenticeship might consist. In the background was a rider, a conditional "if": Does apprenticeship exist as an educational form if the tailors do not intentionally separate learning from doing or teaching from master practice? From the perspective of the comparative theory of formal and informal education, it mattered where that pedagogical organization came from. There should be intentions to teach and methods of instruction. Occasions for instruction and learning should be removed from situations to which they were to be applied—decontextualized. Both conditions together were required to produce those "high payoff abstractions and generalizations" for later "transfer."

I began by trying to ascertain just how organized apprenticeship was as a form of education. Which aspects of apprenticeship could be better accounted for by craft production and sales activities? Which could not? At the time, I figured that if apprentices were learning what masters were doing, then they would only be learning the same things if the masters were doing things the same way, so I went looking for "a form"—a common, unifying, shared way of educating apprentices. This approach involved an uncritical commitment to investigating the world through a lens of homogeneity and uniformity.

Accordingly, I spent many hours watching the tailors work and asking questions about the sequence of steps they used in making trousers. I took hundreds of photographs of different tailors cutting out trousers and compared them, interested in what they did, but more so in whether the procedures they used were the same. I also had many conversations with tailors concerning the uniformity of practices in the alley: Do all the tailors know how to make the same things? What do they make? Is there anyone who doesn't know how to do x? Does anyone sew y differently from the rest? Some differences came to light: V.G. specialized in shirts instead of trousers. F.B. used a paper pattern for cutting out trousers instead of chalk and tapeline. And old A.K. had learned tailoring in Sierra Leone many years before. He made fly fronts differently from everybody else. (I sought out his apprentices and former apprentices in Happy Corner, discovering that they made fly fronts like the other tailors in the alley, however.)

The similarity of the activities of the tailors was impressive. The tools used and not used—there did not seem to be a single straight pin in the whole of Happy Corner—were identical. The process of drawing and cutting out trousers was strikingly consistent among the tailors, and for the same tailor on different occasions. The styles they made, as well as the process of putting the pieces together and cutting them out, seemed to be widely distributed and fairly standard for the tailors. One master commented,

> In big tailor shops, in small tailor shops, the way of teaching apprentices and the way masters learned and are doing their work is the same. You check any big or small tailor shop around here, you will see the same way

of teaching apprentices and the same kinds of clothes that we sew for our customers. . . . Only Vai and Golas sew here in all these shops, but the ways of teaching apprentices and working are the same.

There were also commonalties in the lives of the apprentices. To begin with, the boys spent a lot of time sitting on the bench beside their masters while they worked at their sewing machines. The apprentices hemmed cuffs, sewed on buttons, ran errands up and down the alley, and took newly made trousers out to be pressed. More advanced apprentices worked on trousers if the master was away and the machine was vacant. Less advanced apprentices might work at making a hat or a pair of children's drawers. Despite their regular tasks, the boys had plenty of time and attention for observing the passing scene. They did lots of things that took them out and about— far more often than their masters. Indeed, that was partly why apprentices were there to begin with. They carried out tasks that did not require close coordination with their master's work sequences. Furthermore, the masters' activities were routinely observable by the apprentices. The masters were models, just by being there, for what the apprentices were trying to become. Production techniques and sequences were easy for an apprentice to observe as he sat on the bench beside his master or looked at other masters and apprentices working a few feet away or when he wandered into other shops. The ongoing work of the shops, the short cycle of production from purchase of materials to the sale of a completed pair of trousers, provided vivid lessons about what "being a tailor" was all about.

Certainly the apprentices knew a lot about what they needed to be able to do to become master tailors. I asked many apprentices and masters what a master tailor must know how to make. There was a standard response, spoken rhythmically, a sort of litany: cloth hats, children's drawers, trousers short and long, sport shirts, Vai shirts, lapa suits, (Muslim) prayer gowns, and Higher Heights suits. That they agreed was clear. But I was bothered by the formulaic quality of the responses my question elicited, and I recorded their "garment inventory" without enthusiasm and certainly without insight. Clothes-in-a-sequence didn't reveal itself in the short run as an organizing principle for apprenticeship. What about skill levels? Grades? Seniority? None of those seemed relevant either.

THE CLOTHES LINE

After several months in Happy Corner, I began to recognize a number of resonating and similar sequences in the work of the apprentices and master tailors, in the garments they made, for whom they made them, and the social world they dressed. The patterns were ubiquitous in the everyday lives of apprentices. I began to consider relations between how the tailors divided their labor among the different kinds of clothes, and how they made divisions between ready-to-wear and custom tailoring work. Small variations were associated roughly with life stages in tailors' careers. At different times in their lives, they made somewhat different mixes of garments.

This, fairly suddenly, led me to reconsider the garment inventory and what it might mean to say that apprenticeship had meaning and organization even as it was part of ongoing practice: Young apprentices made only hats and drawers. Advanced apprentices still made hats from time to time, but a young master tailor would not do so.[6] Advanced apprentices and master tailors made trousers. Younger masters tended to sew for younger customers and made a greater preponderance of new-style trousers, while older master tailors sewed more often for a more conservative clientele and made a disproportionate share of Higher Heights suits.

I had an idea that it might be important to find out whether the shifts in patterns of garments produced by tailors of different ages and amounts of experience roughly reflected the order in the garment inventory recitations, as well as the order in which the apprentices learned to make the different kinds of clothes. I asked a number of tailors to describe their apprenticeship, explaining that I was interested in knowing about the order in which they learned different parts of their craft. One middle-aged master (who had not been to school) gave the following account in Vai; then another tailor, who was acting as my assistant that summer, translated it into Americo-Liberian English. Speaker and translator collaborated and spent a lot of time turning it into a kind of essay:

> *Research Assistant:* Mr. B., please tell us how did you learn your work and what was the first thing you learned, the second, the third, fourth, on to the time you became a master tailor.

> *Mr. B.:* I thank you very much. The first thing that I learned or was taught as an apprentice was how to peddle the machine. I sat behind the machine and my master taught me the parts to touch in order to peddle the machine. He taught me how to open the parts of the machine to clean it when it was dirty or in need of oil.

> The second thing he taught me was how to sew or fix buttonholes and also how to cut the buttonholes. He made me know that I should use needle and thread both to fix buttonholes and put buttons on trousers, shirts, and all ladies' dresses. He cut a piece of cloth and told me to cut the buttonholes myself and fix the buttonholes and I did it and he approved me satisfactorily.

Now, he was then sure that I could peddle the machine, loose[n] the parts and put them back. He was sure that I knew all about buttons and buttonholes.

The third thing he taught me was how to sew back pockets because back pockets are hard to sew to any other part of trousers. I learned it and knew it, so he tested me by cutting the trouser parts and called me to sew this trousers.

I sewed that trousers and he said that I did well, only the fly of the trousers was not sewn the right way. So the fly was my first mistake in sewing trousers as an apprentice in those days.

So he was sure that I could sew trousers (but couldn't sew flies too well). However, he didn't waste my time on trousers because of the fly. He kept giving me trousers to sew until he approved of me that I could now sew flies of trousers very well. He was sure of that about me.

The fourth thing he taught me was how to cut the cloth in order to sew trousers. Of course I could sew trousers already. He gave me a cloth to cut by myself to sew trousers. I cut the trousers even though it was not as neat as my master could cut it, but it was the right way as he approved me well. He taught the difference between numbers on the tapeline and also taught how to read the tapeline, knowing the difference between inches, feet and yard. He also taught me how to measure the pieces of trousers while cutting it. How long the trousers should be according to the length and size of the person, and how wide the pockets should be, how wide the strips and fly should be on trousers. I learned and could do all of them by myself. And he approved me well being sure that I could do everything about trousers.

The fifth thing he taught me was how to sew a shirt and put the collar on it and also put pockets on that shirt. He cut a shirt and told me to sew it. I sewed it and added the collar on it, but he told me that the shirt was good but the collar was not well sewed. He also taught me how to put pockets on shirts of all kinds. I was brilliant enough that I understood all of these in few time because I was always attentive and ambitious. But you know in tailor work it is different. Pockets are of many types. Shirt pockets are also of one or two types. But once you have learned how to sew one kind of pocket, you would learn the rest very easily because you already had an idea of how to sew one kind of pockets.

He told me that when you sew a shirt, measure the neck of the shirt first and if you know how long the neck of the shirt is, you use that same measurement on the collar and if you try it there, it will fit there exactly. He tested me, gave me another shirt to sew and I sewed it together with all the pockets and the collar and he approved of me very satisfactorily. He was then sure that I could sew a shirt completely without error.

He taught me how to cut the shirt because I could sew it already. He used his scissors, tapeline and marker to cut the shirts parts as he was teaching me.

He tested me on cutting of shirt and he discovered that I was very smart and fast to understand because I sewed that particular shirt that he cut and I cut my own shirt with the collar and the pockets exactly without error and he approved of me very satisfactorily. He was sure that I could do any sewing of shirts and trousers by myself.

So he told me that I had gone far in learning my work and that I had encountered the difficult parts already. I therefore could work now for myself and get money even though I was still an apprentice.

That was how I learned my work and how my master taught me. And these were the different things I was taught one after the other. So if you have any more questions, ask me.

Research Assistant: He never taught you anything else besides these?

Mr. B.: He taught me something, more and more, but these were the technical parts that I already covered. All what he taught me after these were an additional knowledge to my competence so far as tailoring is concerned.

Mr. B. didn't say anything about making drawers and hats before learning to make trousers. But in many respects his account corresponded with the differences in tailoring projects between younger and older masters, and with the order in the garment inventory litany.[7] Similar results from discussions with other masters and apprentices suggested a fairly consistent ordering to what they learned, beginning with rudimentary skills, then hats and drawers, then trousers, next shirts, dresses, and Muslim prayer gowns, and finally Higher Heights suits. The process of apprenticeship did indeed seem to foreshadow (through the apprentices' changing labors) the appropriate course of a typical career of a master tailor. Furthermore, the way different kinds of garments were learned incorporated, I gradually concluded, a pattern of relations of the tailors and their craft to the Liberian social world more broadly.[8]

GETTING DRESSED

Think of clothes as social skin, as socially prescribed markings of social locations and identities and relations among them. Indeed, clothing has quite special abilities "to mediate both individual and collective identities and desires" (Hansen 2000, 3). The garment inventory actually reflected many of these identities and desires. But it did more than act as a static classification system, for it defined the work of the tailors in relation to the world in which they labored. The garment inventory was also a major organizing device for the learning process apprentices went through in the course of becoming master tailors. A great deal more was thus conveyed about the nature of the social world beyond Happy Corner by this process than was at first apparent in the simple system of categories of garments.[9]

The tailors' apprenticeship as a learning process began with the most intimate, least formal clothes for socially not-completely-formed persons: children's drawers and hats for older children and young men. It ended with the most formal, public, and most prestigious social dress: the Higher Heights suit, worn by the relatively rich and powerful on formal occasions, above all, by President Tolbert at his inauguration in 1971. (At the inauguration, this outfit was christened with his campaign slogan, "Liberia for Higher Heights," and adopted as a symbol of unity of the country. Tolbert's gesture was meant to reduce distinctions—rhetorical, sartorial?—between Americo-Liberians and the vastly exploited, excluded, and impoverished majority.) During this process, the apprentices moved from a very peripheral position in the tailor shop to skillful participation roughly equivalent to that of their masters and finally to the formal status of master tailor.

Trousers, the trademark of Happy Corner and the pivotal garment in the garment inventory, were also the pivotal point in the movement of apprentices toward mastership. Trousers were worn by virtually all Liberian men. Trousers were constructed in such a way that they did not distinguish Americo-Liberian from other men, rich from poor, urban dwellers from upcountry folks, or old men from young. To be sure, there were trouser styles and color variants that did indicate age and attitude. A careful look at cloth and construction would reveal differences of wealth, but such details were not easily observable. In fact the genius of Happy Corner was to produce inexpensive trousers that on casual inspection were indistinguishable from expensive uptown trousers.

Next the apprentices learned to make shirts, dresses, and prayer gowns, and herein are traced major social divisions in Liberian society: gender, wealth, urbanization, Westernization, and religious differences. Only Muslims wore prayer gowns. Muslims constituted 15 to 20 percent of the population. For the Vai and Gola tailors, who were themselves Muslim, the distinction was one they supported and were concerned about.

Men's shirts, unlike trousers, did differentiate urban versus upcountry locations, and modern versus more traditional ways of life. The tailors

Figure 6. Higher Heights suit jacket displayed for sale

learned to make both Western-style tailored sport shirts and Vai shirts and other loose pullover styles that were worn by men from rural areas.

Women's clothes reflected social distinctions parallel to men's shirts. There were the long lapa skirts, more common in rural areas, consisting of lengths of cloth folded and secured by rolling and tucking at the waist. These could be worn with elaborately tailored blouses, the whole outfit called a lapa suit. There were also Western-style blouses, skirts, and even occasional pairs of pants, although the last were not made in the alley. For a man to wear sport shirts may not have meant a great deal more than that he had spent some time in Monrovia, although he may still have moved in the ambiance of village ties and engaged in modes of exchange and ways of living practiced by many who lived both literally and figuratively on the outskirts of urban life. Or he may have been a several-generation urban dweller with a job in a government office. It was hard to tell how "urban" a man was if he was wearing a sport shirt. Women wore more elaborately tailored blouses with their lapa suits as they moved into more urban ways. But only the most urban women wore Western garb. It was thus difficult to tell how countrified a woman in a lapa suit was. Except for these nuances of practice, men's shirts and women's dresses played similar differentiating roles in social marking.

In sum, the location of Happy Corner between the cultural and linguistically differentiated urban enclaves and the poorest commercial district of Monrovia, still part of the cash economy, gave the tailors a mediating role between country life and city life. They were purveyors of the garment that indicated male adult social membership, along with all the garments that helped people to express or create differences in identity as their lives changed. The customers who frequented Happy Corner were generally poor, little involved in the city, often newcomers, or just visitors. For them, garments from the tailors' alley served to mask rural, ethnolinguistically distinct cultural identities, replacing them with other categories of differentiation. All of these things were reflected in the organization of the learning process for apprentices through the garment inventory, whose categories sustained those social distinctions.

Further social differentiation was expressed through differences in garment styles. These generally reflected the spectrum of different social distinctions and impressed on apprentices in a tailor-ly way what they already knew about growing up Vai or Gola in Liberia. In Happy Corner, most style innovations were in trousers. There was clearly scope for a variety of trouser styles, providing differentiated possibilities for dressing social identities. Wealth distinctions were mainly made through the choice of a Happy Corner or an uptown tailor to provide the trousers and were only very narrowly expressed in the tailors' alley. Age and rural allegiances were reflected in dark colors and narrow trouser legs; youth and urban chic in flamboyant colors and bell-bottoms. Innovation was so well institutionalized that to wear trousers identified as faddish or fashionable was itself an indicator of youth and urban orientation. In general, in Monrovia, garments distinguished major social categories while styles subdivided them.

This analysis points to certain assumptions about what made for a popular trouser style in Happy Corner. The tailors clearly figured that a popular style should be general enough in its features so that existing techniques for style coding could be employed to produce old distinctions as well as a new one. Thus, the two-color bell-bottom trouser caught on in the late '70s. To some extent this trouser was identified as a young man's style—too radical for older men. But the tailors also produced two-color trousers in sedate, subdued tones, so that older men bought and wore them. And these trousers could be made with the straight cuffs that already differentiated older from younger men's styles. Another style, with pairs of straps and buckles on each hip, invented by a young tailor in the alley, did not catch on. Among other things, there was no way to create a dignified version. It did seem that there were routine assumptions among the tailors that generating and making new styles was part of their everyday work.

Figure 7. Bell-bottom trousers displayed for sale

MATURATIONAL CONSTRAINTS

Seventy per cent of the apprentices in Happy Corner had entered apprenticeship between the ages of eleven and twenty-one. Finishing ages clustered around eighteen years. The length of apprentices' training was influenced by the age at which an apprentice was sufficiently mature to assume the role of master tailor. Since most apprentices began between the ages of thirteen and fifteen, it appeared that the Vai and Gola tailors believed it took three to five years to master the trade. But one important requirement for becoming a master was socially acknowledged maturity. No matter how skillful, a young apprentice could not become an independent craft producer until he viewed himself and others viewed him as mature enough. Starting between the ages of thirteen and fifteen roughly coordinated the achievement of tailoring skills with sufficient maturity to become a master tailor. The expectation that the apprentice would be self-employed after becoming a master shaped these decisions. (If children went to work in a factory as wage laborers, attempts to coordinate maturity and skill acquisition might well disappear.)

The maturity of the apprentice dictated how long the basic skill learning went on (buttons, hemming, pressing, and learning to use the machine), and when he was ready to make trousers. Apprentices starting at fifteen were mature enough to make trousers although not mature enough to be master tailors. So they moved relatively rapidly through learning the rudimentary skills, hats and drawers, and into trousers. They made trousers and learned other garments for a relatively long period of time. Sewing a Higher Heights suit signaled the beginning of the end of apprenticeship and was timed accordingly. For the occasional apprentice who spent time in the shop from the age of three, the basics might take five years or more, and hats and drawers another year or two before he might start on trousers. On the other hand, an adult starting to learn tailoring at the age of twenty-six might spend a few weeks on initial skills, another few weeks on hats and drawers, a year or so on trousers, shirts, and prayer gowns. The added detailing of Higher Heights suits would be added to his repertoire in a matter of weeks.

Commentary

This account of the lineaments of apprenticeship among Vai and Gola tailors points to tensions between initially uncritical lines of ethnographic inquiry; discrepancies, differences, and doubts that emerged from that inquiry; and unexpected new research questions that led in unanticipated directions. All of these are surely involved in critical ethnographic practice. But since there is nothing inevitable about the process, we must ask how the change in understanding came about. The earliest Liberian ethnographic work was (uncritically) intended to establish that the tailors' apprenticeship met the criteria for "informal education" according to the comparative theory. Indeed, the Vai and Gola tailors were craftsmen, and apprenticeship was a marked, recognized arrangement that entailed lengthy opportunities to participate in the everyday life of the tailor shop. In the tailors' apprenticeship, learning was embedded in the context of the mature practice of tailoring, and masters and apprentices understood their relations in broad moral as well as technical terms. There was very little specialization or separation of educational circumstances and pedagogical intentions from everyday life in the shops. Everyone assumed apprentices were there to learn "with verisimilitude."

Critical exploration of the shortcomings of common assumptions about the comparative limitations of "informal education" was also part of the project. The hegemonic forces surrounding research on formal education, after all, a cultural pillar of social-political life in the United States, shaped the issues I first thought essential to pursue as I set out to learn about apprenticeship. This quickly became a major impediment to trying to understand the tailors' apprenticeship in something like its own terms. With schooling as the template, questions about apprenticeship were framed mostly in negative terms. True, the binary distinctions between "formal" and "informal" education posited some definite characteristics for informal education. Mainly, however, things present and important for carrying out schooling were presumed absent in apprenticeship—teaching as the central prerequisite for school learning, for example, and with its absence, a lack of effective organization to the learning aspects of apprenticeship. This tenacious perspective clearly directed the questions I asked in Happy Corner to begin with and defined my expectations about what should be happening if the apprentices were going to learn. It explains the difficulties I had in coming to see that other things that were happening were crucial matters of learning.[10]

I tried rephrasing questions about school versus apprenticeship (or "not school") symmetrically. How do organizational characteristics common to apprenticeship help to explain what's missing in school practice (or "not apprenticeship")? For one thing, the separation of schooling from arenas of mature practice leads to enormous weight on pedagogy to drive educational activity. It leads to contrived forms of evaluation, for example, testing. How, and how well, do these institutional arrangements of schooling compensate for the divide they draw between school practices and relevant practices of everyday life? "Learning transfer" is, of course, a common explanation, but it is itself in need of explanation. Reciprocally, this chapter addresses the question of what is absent or unimportant in schooling that is important in the arrangement of informal educational activities in the tailors' alley, for instance, the masters' stake in the increasing skill of apprentices.

Asking such questions, it became evident that there *was* organization to apprenticeship. But it was not first and foremost pedagogical, nor—as we shall see in chapter 3—was it merely coincident with the organization of daily labor in the tailor shops. "Learning tailoring" could not be reduced to the skills and knowledge necessary for making clothes. The masters' relations with apprentices could not be reduced to that of teacher, parent, boss, or even some combination thereof. Masters and apprentices were mutually dependent but also threats to each other's well-being. Their conflicting interests helped to make more than one characteristic path to masterhood likely. These critical ethnographic/analytic findings challenged the theoretical adequacy of distinctions between formal and informal education.

Other limitations of the formal/informal education dichotomy concerned its explanation of learning transfer. Claims that generative knowledge production cannot emerge from something like apprenticeship follow from assumptions that context-embedded learning is limited to the reproduction of existing practices both by the circumstances in which learning takes place and by a presumed cultural preference for tradition supposedly absent in schooling. It follows that the effects of informal education should be concrete, resulting in knowledge of a bounded content understood as specific skills, lore, and facts. Knowledge production and creativity are assumed not to infuse the lives and work of "ordinary" people, and are thereby reserved and set aside for the unusual and unusually privileged—more polarized dualistic politics. At the time, it was difficult to know how to address this issue except to argue that the tailors *were* creative—look at their trouser innovations. But this merely acceded to the narrow terms of the theory, not the best way to address its claims about the segregated character of creative production (or even what that might be).

I've been discussing ways that analysis of tailors' apprenticeship produced a critique of the comparative theory of education. But a more interesting take on the creativity question was not to be found in either the binary theory or its critique. The ethnographic research led places not anticipated by the formal/informal model. This unintended forward movement shows the critical, transformative potential of ethnographic research as I gradually came to take seriously the multifaceted learning syllabus of the tailors' apprenticeship, the complexity of what the apprentices came to know about social relations of production, social relations among the tailors, and Liberian cultural identities and social distinctions and how to clothe them. If all this was part of becoming a master tailor, then it was impossible to stipulate what the boundaries of tailoring knowledge might be. Even the tailors' understanding of garment construction could not be construed as only the literal learning of construction steps. Apprenticeship was rich in meaning *because* it played out in and through multiple contexts concretely related in the everyday practice of tailoring. A revision of assumptions underlying concepts of context-embedded learning would therefore be necessary if these concepts were not to depend on notions of bounded knowledge and circumstances.

Other problems (besides the literal and narrow definitions of the content of learning) took on salience in the ethnographic inquiry. Should things like the garment inventory be counted as the form or the content of the educational enterprise? I began to wonder whether my question—Is apprenticeship an educational *form*?—was the right one.[11] "The uniform" in the title of this chapter points to the interdependence of notions of unity and notions of form with which I started out to study apprenticeship. Based on an initial assumption about the shared nature of culture, I thought that the problem of establishing that apprenticeship was "real" could be solved by documenting a unified approach to apprenticeship across tailors and shops. This sociologic had a huge impact on my fieldwork. I regret that. It mostly kept me from considering how social life and its analysis are crucially constituted out of heterogeneous relations, conflict, and from commonalities and differences that come about in ways that require further analysis.

Both broad issues and specific language in this chapter should raise questions about the meaning of "formal" and "informal" as a contrastive pair. These terms have always seemed contentless to me. Perhaps what they mean is exactly what they say: that if there exists a form (e.g., of education), content of various appropriate kinds (e.g., knowledge and skill) can furnish it or flow through it. "Informal" implies that content exists without form, or exists perhaps in forms meant for other things. Or perhaps it implies that somehow form and content bond, melt down, are not distinguishable from one another. Assumptions of crucial polar differences between schooling and apprenticeship are recognizable in these themes. This may well become an untenable theoretical commitment as the argument develops. Further, it appears that evenhanded comparative analysis under the hierarchical politics of binary models is impossible. This problem looms, given that analysis under binary theory is always comparative.

In my experience, it is easy to agree with the thesis of the previous paragraph. It is much more difficult to recognize the myriad ways binary comparative theorizing constrains, blocks, and otherwise influences research questions and analysis—basic assumptions and their social and political implications are by their nature rarely met face to face. To move beyond such assumptions requires critical questioning of the way concepts such as "learning," "formal education," and "learning transfer" depend on the institutional practices of schooling, which they take for granted and in which they were developed. Where can we move theoretically instead so as not to compound the problem? Is it possible to shed a different light on things? The inquiry into apprenticeship among the Vai and Gola moved me from critical doubts about the formal/informal comparative theory to doubts about the *kind* of theory it is. My response has been to turn to a theory of social practice, as I will lay out in chapter 6.

I believe the practice of ethnographic research has a special kind of critical potential because it can focus on the mundane activities of marginal persons, practices, and institutional arrangements for long periods. Such a commitment assumes that daily lives are valuable sources of enlightenment about the complexities of social practice, contrary to the values associated in conventional theory with the marginal as merely that—a powerless foil or negative pole. This way of doing research contains possibilities for reversing the value of "high" and "low" in comparative analysis from a focus on the power of "high" discourse to a focus on the power of "low" practice to challenge the former.

I reported occasional stunning "aha!" moments when the ethnographic work forced a reappraisal of apprenticeship in ways that wouldn't have occurred if I had not been face to face with a recalcitrant world that didn't conform to my expectations. This happened early on, for instance, when the master announced that "the fly goes on the front of the trousers" and I had to start the observation and analysis of apprenticeship over again. Crystallizing moments like this matter. They are inflection points that lead to shifts in the direction of inquiry in pursuit of unanticipated questions and sometimes to a reversal in the value given to some facets of theory.[12] For instance, I came to admire the efficacy of learning how to tailor in the arena of mature practice. Educational circumstances were interwoven with other aspects of everyday life in the tailor shops. In the end, this seemed to be an advantage rather than a disadvantage, being rich in possibilities for the apprentices' complex appreciation and comprehension of what they were there to learn. Shifts in value as new perspectives emerge from the ethnographic research are an important part of processes of theoretical transformation.

Such processes are partial and piecemeal. Consider the work recounted in this chapter in terms of the power of Western assumptions to suppress inquiry at the margins. I made observations in passing that I found much more significant in later readings in other contexts, for example, the issue of "maturity," which emerged as an afterthought but could have led inquiry into the different trajectories of apprentices through apprenticeship. I acknowledged notions of conflict between masters and apprentices but did not pursue them in detail. Nor, in observations that apprentices were becoming master tailors, not merely sewers-of-garments, and that masters were concrete exemplars for their apprentices of "being a master tailor," did I address seriously enough issues of identity. I may have raised the notion of identity in considering what "being a tailor" meant, but all too often I retreated to the notion of tailoring as a matter of skill in producing trousers, displaying tunnel vision I now find heartbreaking. Last, but not least, early and occasional references to peripheral participation seemed unremarkable, and only some years later did this concept become central in my work (e.g., Lave and Wenger 1991). These early openings appeared in awkward sections or passing phrases, but in spite of my critique, they didn't fit the argument at the time. However, they would not be here at all if they had not grown out of ethnographic work.

Because processes of theoretical transformation are partial and gradual, they always need pursuing further. Thus critical ethnography is different from other, especially casual, notions of ethnography—of the variety "I did six whole weeks of participant observation" or "I interviewed major players." Critical ethnography must be linked to theory, and it raises questions about the adequacy of any given theory and kinds of theories. But what do you do, sitting with partial, changing ethnographic materials while theory is supposed to be comprehensive and general? This question appears in several guises in subsequent chapters, for working at relations between ethnographic and theoretical materials is the heart of the critical ethnographer's craft.

To anticipate the concluding chapter with one last point, this discussion of ethnography is intended to move toward a theoretical account of critical ethnographic practice. Such a practice subverts binary comparative research claims in specific ways. It is always partial, and locates school-centric, more generally ethnocentric, assumptions in relations between theory and practice and the institutional arrangements that shape those relations. A first step is to insist that fieldwork activity and analysis are an integral part of a theoretical stance, not some neutral technology for finding stuff out.

This chapter has focused on the social conditions of the tailors' apprenticeship. Yet in a sense, apprenticeship is still a black box. What happened during apprenticeship? How did it work? Chapter 3 turns to the processes by which apprentices became master tailors.

3 Becoming a Tailor

Overview

This chapter explores local conceptions of learning in long processes of apprenticeship. How did apprentices learn the tailoring craft? To begin to address this question, I turned to Burton, Brown, and Fischer's cognitive-science based research on skiing and computer-aided instruction (1984).[1] Their model was especially attractive both because it pointed to embodied activity outside the laboratory and because it seemed to offer a way out of the grip of cognitive theory and its embedding binary logic—a logic that concentrates ferociously on the mind and correspondingly excludes the body, creating a pristine divide between an adaptive subject and a determining "environment." Burton, Brown, and Fischer took a less school-dominated approach to learning than most. Rather than emphasizing teaching or knowledge transmission from experts to novices, they talked of novice skiers learning in specially contrived situations, simple "microworlds" that afforded novices entry points established with the help of coaches. Novices would move toward the acquisition and integration of conceptual and physical skills, and toward the possibility of self-correction of errors. This approach looked useful for questioning the conventional wisdom that informal teaching and learning must be concrete, literal, and limited.

Opposing one dualist variant of cognitive psychology by taking up another is not my research strategy of choice these days. I wish now that I had engaged in more broadly defined ethnographic research on the lives of all concerned in Happy Corner, to see how tailoring was a part of their lives, rather than reducing their lives to but one of its parts. I wish I had not followed the instrumental logic of learning narrowly defined, for it provided no means for understanding how changing knowledgeable skill was constituted as part of life more broadly. Changing the *scope* of inquiry did seem important at the time. I tried to broaden my analysis of learning from minutes of engagement in a cognitive task to years of participation in the process of becoming a master tailor. Whatever my notion of "the whole of apprenticeship," however, I still concentrated on knowledge in an instrumental mode until it nearly excluded consideration of other ways learners (and the practice of tailoring) changed. Ethnographic evidence presented in chapter 2 supports the proposition that there was more happening than changes in the task-knowledgeability of the apprentices' fingers, minds, backs, and feet. But the sociologic of such reductions was easy to succumb to: Apprenticeship was to "learn tailoring." What is tailoring? Making clothes. To study apprenticeship is to study how newcomers learn to make clothes.

During a summer of fieldwork, I followed several young apprentices who were making different garments for the first time. Little M. was nine or ten years old and had been an apprentice for several months. He was a shy, rather quiet but playful kid, whose master, referred to here as G., had no other apprentices at the time. There were several other apprentices and a number of masters in the shop where G. worked, some of whom helped shape what transpired during the summer. I talked with many apprentices about how they went about learning to make clothes. The apprentices told me that they watched in order to learn how to make something they'd never made before. In order to stop making mistakes, you had to practice, they added. As was not infrequently the case, they meant what they said (and more). But at first their comments seemed too obvious to offer any insight. I gradually came to think that they were telling me two things of importance for understanding apprenticeship, worth investigating further: that learning depended in good part on their initiative as learners, and that how they learned changed as they progressed.

It looked as if learning processes (writ small and writ large) were divided into phases. The first phase, which I called a "way in," involved initiation into the mysteries of some particular activity, to the point of being able to produce a first approximation. Then the apprentices practiced—engaging in a variety of activities designed to take them from a first approximation to a high level of mastery. "Way in" and "practice" looked promising as ways to describe the apprentices' activities. I decided to take apprenticeship as a whole as the object of analysis, whose parts were learning processes organized by the garment inventory and much else. The first half of this chapter maps my understanding of kinds of ways in, including initial construction attempts, practice sewing and practice cutting out, and self-correction techniques. The second half of the chapter steps back to consider the process as a whole: relations among the garment-learning processes, the question of teaching, and things all apprentices needed to learn for which there was no customary place in the apprenticeship process.

Figure 8. Little M. at work

Learning Processes in Apprenticeship

I first tried to analyze the tailors' apprenticeship as a linear whole, as if it had one grand, initiatory way in followed by a long trajectory of practice. After all, apprentices learned many new things during the first years of apprenticeship, and fewer new things later on, as practice took up more and more of their working time. Further the trajectory of the apprentices looked roughly unidirectional. But this rationale wouldn't do: ways in were required for a wide variety of production processes at many different points within the trajectory of apprenticeship as a whole.

The problem, then, was to map sequences of learning that had several different scopes within which way in and practice organized learning processes. Their overlapping and intertwining produced a learning career. A map of apprenticeship as I conceived it at the time comprised three levels of learning processes. Each (I thought) subsumed the next more detailed division of production activities. At the most inclusive level, there was the garment inventory. Then there were multiple ways in and kinds of practice while learning each garment. Each phase of learning to make each garment, principally sewing and cutting out, required a separate sequence of way-in and practice activities.

Throughout the apprenticeship, apprentices were peripheral participants with legitimate access to the arena of mature practice. They could observe both the processes of garment construction and the products that resulted. Master tailors and apprentices in the shops embodied all levels of skill in ways that made it possible for learners to infer directions in which they were going to move and the changing steps that would be involved over months and years. Tangible products were abundant, made with varying degrees of conceptual and physical skill by apprentices with different amounts of experience. All of these factors enriched the learners' possibilities for understanding what made up the process of apprenticeship—as well as for understanding tailoring. That is, knowledge could be obtained directly by the learner and did not depend on the initiative of a teacher.

Much of what the tailors needed to learn included a large component of physical skill. Cutting, sewing, and even measuring are physical skills as well as mental ones. The tailors also needed to learn to conceptualize processes of garment construction for different kinds of garments, including style variations. And they needed to learn to put skills and conceptions together in the process of constructing a garment.

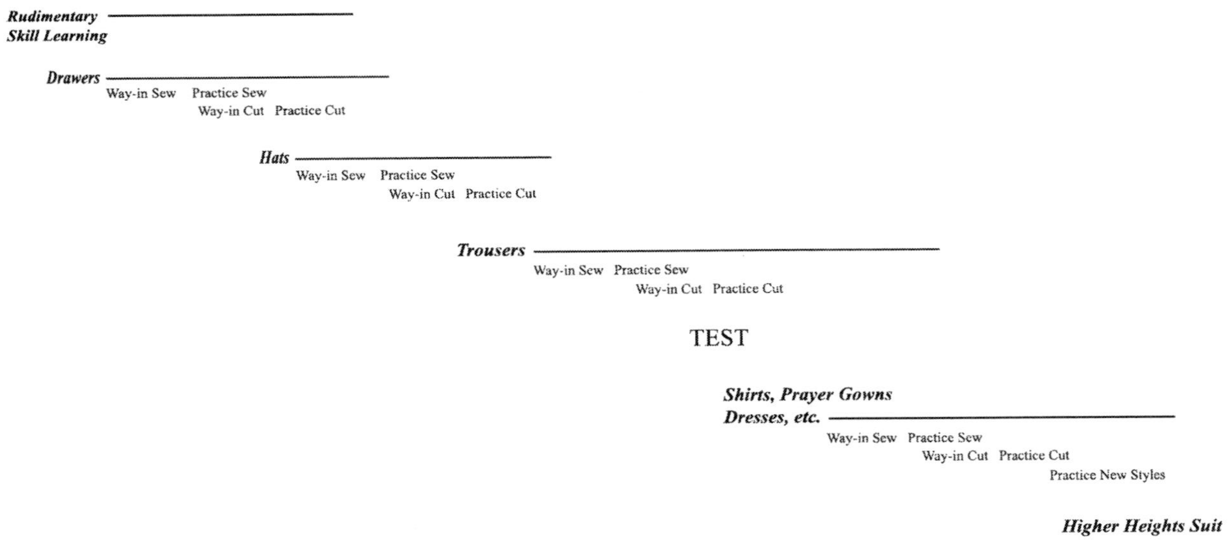

**Rudimentary
Skill Learning**

Drawers ———————
Way-in Sew   Practice Sew
    Way-in Cut   Practice Cut

Hats ———————
Way-in Sew   Practice Sew
    Way-in Cut   Practice Cut

Trousers ———————
Way-in Sew   Practice Sew
    Way-in Cut   Practice Cut

TEST

**Shirts, Prayer Gowns
Dresses, etc.** ———————
Way-in Sew   Practice Sew
    Way-in Cut   Practice Cut
        Practice New Styles

Higher Heights Suit

Figure 9. Apprenticeship as a process

Entry Points

There were ways in for the apprenticeship process as a whole and into the learning of each item in the garment inventory.

The very first things a tailor's apprentice learned were rudimentary; that is, he was given opportunities to learn and practice skills separately from the construction of garments. Apprentices learned how to wield a needle and thread, to hold cloth, make even stitches, and sew in straight lines during the time in which they also learned to sew on buttons, to sew buttonholes, and to hem. (Mister B.'s description in chapter 2 is typical in this respect.) They practiced on scraps of cloth before attempting to make actual garments.

Likewise apprentices became familiar with the sewing machine, the major piece of equipment they needed to learn to use, cleaning and oiling it, and learning how to treadle. One master commented, "First you learn to make buttonholes, then how to peddle the machine, *not on cloth*, then to sew *straight*" (emphasis his). The apprentices practiced sewing on scraps of cloth, tried to follow lines in the fabric or parallel to the edge, to sew even stitches, and to sew the cloth without puckering it. Occasionally they sat around with large pairs of scissors, which for the little boys were practically too heavy to lift, and snipped scraps of cloth or thread, practicing cutting. They learned to press with the iron, usually simply ironing stiffening fabric onto small strips of cloth for trouser waistbands. Over the course of two days, I watched Little M.:

> Little M. is trying to cut bits off a piece of elastic. Later I ask his master, G., whether Little M. was playing or learning. G. says, "He does it to learn, he is not playing."
>
> Little M. is pressing some yellow trousers that G. made Saturday night. He obviously knows how to press. But he isn't strong enough to iron well. B.S. (another master in the shop) takes over and irons with a good deal more power and authority. B.S. has finished some belt loops while Little M. presses. Then after B.S. finished that job he presses, and Little M. watches him.
>
> Little M. is sewing on a scrap of cloth at M.P.'s (another master's) machine. Fifteen minutes later he is still sewing tiny strips of cloth. Little M. then sits sprawled, with his head on his arm on the machine, still sewing. A few minutes later G. sends Little M. to get trousers from the cleaners (errands take precedence over this level of practice activity). In the afternoon Little M. makes more strips at the sewing machine.

Burton, Brown, and Fischer (1984) assumed that there were "entry points" for learners, provided by "coaches." In the tailors' apprenticeship, other aspects of the environment besides coaching and other long-term goals besides teaching organized the learning process. To the extent that the master did guide entry for the apprentice, he mainly intended to provide himself with help on a variety of small sewing tasks and errands. These intentions had implications for learning activity. They allowed apprentices to learn hand sewing and in the process to handle the garments the tailors made. As G. said to me one day,

> When an apprentice is newly arrived, you force him to learn things so he'll get on quickly: buttonholes (to help you with the work), cuff trousers by hand, tie [sew] buttons on trousers, how to hem, and press. These are the first things the master needs for him to know. Later he can learn by watching.

Besides entry into rudimentary skills, most of the rest of the craft learning (narrowly defined) was a matter of learning to produce most or all of the kinds of clothes in the garment inventory. Entry into the first garment the apprentice learned to produce represented a shift to a new, different step in the apprenticeship process.

Repeated Learning Processes: Learning to Make Garments

The process of learning to make a garment happened in a way that reversed the order of production work by the tailors. A great deal could be learned about sewing a garment from turning it in one's hands while hemming trouser cuffs and making buttonholes. Sewing a pair of trousers was a great way to come to understand, before trying it, why trousers were cut out in a certain way. And cutting out provided occasions for coming to know about the contours of bodies, and about the kinds, amounts, and prices of cloth and how to handle it. In this way, the process of apprenticeship was different from the process of production: Learning segments of work processes was reversed from the masters' construction procedures. (Though we shall see that apprentices did practice making each item from start to finish. Indeed, this was a two-way and complicated set of practices.)[2]

Another pervasive set of arrangements also shaped learning, garment by garment. For each garment, the apprentice first went through a way-in process up to the point where he could produce a first approximation of sewing or cutting it out, followed by practice until he could produce masterful products and do so rapidly.

Figuring out the details of a sewing process was the first activity the apprentices encountered that they would repeat for each new garment across a series of way-in procedures. A tailor's apprentice did not try to sew a hat at the same time he first observed hat sewing. Later he would try only to sew a hat, not to construct it from start to finish. Both the skills an apprentice needed and the products he wanted to make were highly visible. Other apprentices frequently made hats, so many versions of the relevant events could easily be seen.

Apprentices told me that the way to learn was to watch until you knew how to make all of a garment. I wondered whether this observation effort over time would lead to the development of a conceptual model of the process of putting the garment together (the goal of learning activities, according to Burton, Brown, and Fischer). Certainly observing was dependent on the ongoing work in the shop rather than on pedagogical demonstration. The focus of observation could not be reserved to the work of masters, since master tailors never make hats or drawers. During the summer, Little M. made not only his first hats, but also a money bag with (atypically) a zipper. With a multitude of examples around him, he went off by himself and sewed the hats, without interaction with his master. His first hats showed a grasp of the construction process. On the other hand, the money bag, his own invention, bogged down in conceptual difficulties. Let us start with a hat:

> There is very little work these days and masters as well as apprentices are sitting around with little to do.
>
> I look at Little M.'s third hat. (He sold the second to J.K., a master tailor in the shop, for ten cents.) Little M. made double rows of stitching on each seam as an expert would. He made several rows of stitching on the brim to give it shape; he faced the bottom edge of the hat. (Even master B.S. sometimes omits to do that, when he is in a hurry.) That is, all the details of a "masterful" hat are present. It is, however, extremely messy, the rows of stitching waver, the thread is tangled, there are places where the fabric is wrinkled and puckered, and on one row of stitching around the brim he sewed the brim to the hat and didn't bother to take the stitches out and re-sew it. As G. and I are looking at the hat, however, G. rips out this row of stitching, a kindness that improves the hat.

Little M. clearly knew the sequence of steps and orientation of pieces of cloth and the inside and outside positioning of seams necessary to make a hat. He actually tried making a simple shirt six weeks later. It exhibited a similar set of characteristics: All of the steps were there, all the pieces right side out and in proper relation to each other. His problems in both cases were in execution, not in conceptualization.

In contrast, for the next project, Little M. had no consistent model to follow. The tailors rarely made money bags or used zippers. Little M. could not have observed more than a very few widely scattered instances of putting in a zipper. He had a very difficult time with it.

> Little M. is making a money bag. G. glances at him from time to time, but lets him go on without comment. When Little M. is finished, G. takes the bag, holds it up for him and says, "M., is this the way to sew a zipper?" (It is in backwards, so the slide is on the inside of the bag.) Little M. looks at what he has done, and then looks embarrassed. He says, "I forgot." G. rips out the stitching and hands it back. Little M. puts the zipper to the cloth, then shows it to G., saying, "Is this the way?" G.: "Yes." G. then comments to me that he saw the mistake earlier, but since sometimes Little M. forgets to look before he sews, he let it go, in order to teach him a lesson. "Sometimes M. does it right, and I don't need to tell him . . .sometimes he forgets."
>
> G. talks to J. while Little M. tries again on the zipper and sews the cloth all the way over the zipper. Little M. looks at it (it obviously won't open) and rips out the stitches himself. He tries again. He succeeds this time. The seams are crooked. The threads are not trimmed off. He has used white thread on dark red fabric. But it is a money-tight money bag.

Putting in a zipper is a pretty complex problem; the two sides are not sewn symmetrically; the fastener goes between the cloth and the zipper cloth, and it is easy to get confused and put the fastener on the side that is accessible while sewing but wrong when finished. However, the conceptual difficulties of making a hat, which has eight wedge-shaped pieces, a brim with two pieces, stiffening, and a facing, is also complicated. The contrast between Little M.'s hat construction on the one hand and the money bag project on the other suggested that a good deal of conceptual modeling had gone on during his observations of hat making in the shop before he made one himself, and that this had an impact on his initial productions.

Such observation was not the result of some vague demand for the apprentice to "be observant." By virtue of the apprentice's circumstances, it was an active, focused process. How so? Since the apprentice could already use the machine by the time he was handed the pieces of a pre-cut garment, he only needed to figure out the spatial orientation of the pieces and a sequence for putting them together in order to sew them. That is, raw edges had to end up inside, right and left sides of the fly had to be on the right and left sides of the trousers, and so on. Only a few specific kinds of observations needed to be made. The apprentice's knowledge that he had to sew his first garment from beginning to end and that all of the pieces would be cut out for him focused observation on sequence and orientation. Such relations seem especially apt targets for observational learning.

INITIAL CONSTRUCTION ATTEMPTS

After acquiring sufficient rudimentary skills, an apprentice who thought he grasped the process of constructing a garment retreated to make an attempt to sew it, usually at night when the business of the day was concluded and masters were not around (but other apprentices were). If successful, he would bring the finished product to his master for inspection the next day. If unsuccessful, he would watch other apprentices and masters make the garment until his grasp of the steps in the process and the orientation of pieces improved sufficiently to try again. Presumably the number of tries it took to make a garment straight through varied among the apprentices. But tailors consistently told me that it took five or six attempts to produce a garment sufficiently well made to sell at the going price in the alley. This fifth or sixth approximation to a well-made garment marked the end of a way-in period, represented the achievement of some degree of skill, and indicated the beginning of a practice phase, the goal of which was to improve both quality of production and speed.

The apprentice practiced sewing the kind of garment he'd just learned to produce for a while before he undertook the way-in process for cutting it out. The way in for cutting, just like the way in for sewing, required careful observation by the apprentice of many instances of the real thing. But the cost of making an error was usually higher for cutting out a garment than for sewing it together. In their attempts to cut out, therefore, the apprentices were likely to ask for help from more advanced apprentices and sometimes even to pay for their help. Each way in was staggered so that it overlapped with practice sequences, but not with other way-in periods. The learner's life was different from a master's, then, since the master had to be able to sew and cut out every garment at any given time but wasn't learning to make them, while apprentices were working to learn to make garments, a small number at a time. The timing of requests for help mattered more with cutting, since the possibility of irreversible errors was ever-present. Apprentices' interactions with masters over early sewing attempts typically occurred in relation to a second, third, or fourth effort. The exact timing of these interactions was unlikely to have significant effect on eventual skill.

The money bag example shows how Little M. began to detect and correct his own mistakes. He looked at how he sewed the zipper the second time, recognized his error (albeit a different error than the first one), ripped it out, and fixed it himself. Apprentices had to deal with most of their mistakes themselves or they would have been unable to produce a complete garment before subjecting it to the master's inspection. In fact, the masters were presented with only those errors their apprentices could not correct. This maximized the apprentice's practice at coping with mistakes and focused the master's attention on the apprentice's more persistent difficulties. The rapid shift to self-correction helped to account for the intermittent and circumscribed nature of the masters' coaching. The cost of apprentice errors at this stage was low, except in time, since repair involved the tedious taking out and resewing of machine-made stitches.

PRACTICE: SEWING AND CUTTING OUT

After an apprentice knew how to make a garment, he made more and more of them until he could make them well. Mr. B.'s description of his apprenticeship illustrates this approach to practice:

> So [the master] was sure I could sew trousers (but couldn't sew fly too well). However, he didn't waste my time on trousers because of the fly. He kept giving me trousers to sew until he approved of me that I could now sew flies of trousers very well.

He made similar comments about learning to sew shirts. This practice strategy might be called "successive approximation," in which the whole process of sewing a garment (or cutting it out) was repeated from start to finish until all parts were equally well made.

I talked to many apprentices and masters about which parts of making trousers they found most difficult to learn. There was near unanimity: set-in back pockets and fly fronts on trousers. I did see isolated subassembly practice in the shop from time to time. Mr. B. described working on back pockets separately from making trousers. Little M. spent a great deal of time working on miniature shirt collars. G. told me, "If you practice at night on a piece of cloth, hip pockets and side pockets, then when you sew your first trousers you do it quickly." But when I approached a number of tailors, armed with information about the steps they considered especially difficult, to probe for special practice techniques for learning them, the tailors actively resisted the idea that their strategy was to practice difficult subsequences separately: they insisted that practice was a matter of successive approximation. As G. commented: "When you start trying to sew trousers you do the *whole* trousers. What spoils, spoils. The next time maybe it will not spoil" (emphasis his).

Practicing subassemblies might have been a way to reduce mistakes. But practice by successive approximation was a better way to integrate rudimentary skills and a conceptual model into a smooth process of garment production. It could be learned by observing masters and advanced apprentices at work, and it would serve the apprentices well as they became mature practitioners. Successive approximation was an efficient form of practice so long as the costs of making mistakes were not much higher than they would be if difficult aspects of construction processes were practiced in isolation first. After all, the exceptional skill of these tailors did not lie in their ability to make trousers, but in their ability to make a dozen pairs of trousers from start to finish in one day.

How did the apprentices divide their practice efforts among different garments? When apprentices could both cut and sew children's drawers but didn't yet know how to make other garments, they simply practiced the two procedures (now in correct order) by making drawers from start to finish. When they could make both hats and drawers, the choice of which to make depended on materials available and personal inclination. By the time the apprentice was seriously engaged in making trousers for his master to sell and was learning shirts, gowns, and dresses, the allocation of practice effort had become almost entirely a function of the master's preferences about what he wanted to sell, and what customers demanded.

SELF-CORRECTION TECHNIQUES

How easy was it for apprentices to recognize and correct their own mistakes? Here is an example in which Little M. made a series of miniature shirt collars. This took place before he had made his first shirt.

> G. has gone to buy cloth for B.S. to sew. Little M. cuts something out of a cloth scrap, with scissors. He folds it in half, cutting what looks like a miniature dress front. He works on another scrap, squaring it off. Little M. now sews the "dress-like" scrap on top of the rectangular one. Then he cuts the rectangular piece to be the same size as the "dress" piece. He starts to turn it right side out, but shakes his head, smiles, and stops, as the stitching starts to come out. He restitches the end of the row of stitches. The bobbin runs out. He refills the bobbin, spool held between his teeth like a pro. Little M. finishes stitching. Then he turns his creation right side out. He uses the point of the scissors to turn it with. He stitches across the fourth side.
>
> G. comes back, talks to several people, carries out his business with

B.S. Then he asks Little M. what he is sewing. Little M. says shyly, "Sewin' collar."

G. has no work at the moment. And he likes to play too. He cuts out a much larger paper collar. Little M. watches. G. then takes Little M.'s second attempt and recuts it, and lays Little M.'s out on top of the new paper pattern. Then he tells Little M. to make a paper one. G. lays his own paper one and the little cloth one where Little M. can see both. Little M. doesn't look up, however, he just does his cutting. This time he gets the angle better. He trims the top long edge, as G. did. Then he opens it and looks at it. G. takes it from him and reshapes the top long edge, hands it to Little M., who smiles and looks at it, then folds the collar down in half the long way, as G. had done earlier, to produce the finished collar shape. Little M. trims it up a bit. Opens it. Folds it again, and trims some more. G. looks at Little M.'s current trim job, which now has curved collar bottom corners so it does not look like G.'s. G. asks Little M., "Who cut that?" Little M. gestures to himself.

G. gets ready to cut trousers, and Little M. wanders off. G. says, "Little M. doesn't like to stay in here." "Why?" I ask. "I don't know." He goes out and gets Little M. Then he picks up a whole bunch of collars off of M.P.'s machine. They are cut with round collar bottom corners like Little M.'s.

G. measures trousers, Little M. fiddles with the sewing machine, not paying attention to G. M.P. is cutting out more collars.

B.S. sends Little M. out to buy two machine needles. Half an hour later he is back, sitting close to G. at the machine, neither Little M. or G. doing anything in particular. After a few minutes Little M. starts making miniature shirt collars again. He cuts two pieces together (previously he cut one, sewed it to a piece of cloth, then cut the second using the first as a guide.) He remembers to shape the top edge, which he forgot the last time.

He turns the two pieces inside out, puts the edges carefully together. He's got the tabs on this one too long.

G. cuts out some miniature thing, but Little M. doesn't watch. He is, instead, getting ready to sew his collar on the machine. He sews it at the very edge of the cloth. When he turns the first point, much of the cloth pulls out of the seam. He doesn't bother to turn the second point; he just tosses it on the floor and goes out. Ten minutes later he is back, with a handful of purple scraps that he must have found discarded on the floor in some other shop. G., meanwhile, has pressed a piece of cloth, cut a large collar shape out of it. He sends Little M. off again, on an errand. G. turns under the edge of his one collar and stitches it. Then he stitches it onto a bigger piece of cloth, starting at the side, then across the tip, then down the other side. He trims the big piece of cloth to shape. (This is the technique Little M. used the first time I saw him making collars.) G. turns it and hems the raw bottom edge, stitches across the narrow part and around.

Little M. has been wandering around and now he watches this stitching and careful folding then turns away and goes out. G.'s nifty creation, now fastened and pressed is about 6 inches around. I comment that Little M. doesn't seem to watch much. G. says, "Well. We don't sew many shirts around here." Then nods for emphasis (so there is no reason for Little M. to learn). Then G. says, "Well, if you want to learn, you make trousers. Shirts are just for money."

There were several moments in this collar exercise when Little M. showed that he was able to correct himself. Shortly after he began, he realized that his stitching wouldn't hold and went back to restitch it (successfully). When he cut out a collar, G. took it from him and trimmed the top edge. Little M. then folded, trimmed, unfolded, and looked at it, then refolded and trimmed again, correcting his own work. As testimony to the rich learning resources of the shop, notice that Little M. cut the tabs on the collar differently then G., copying another master, M.P., who in fact had a stack of shirt collars already cut out, sitting on his machine. It seems likely that it was M.P. making shirts that sparked Little M.'s efforts in the first place, since G. and B.S. were not making shirts at the time. The next day, Little M. still had trouble stitching the seam securely, but he remembered to trim the top edge as he had learned from G. the previous day. The products the tailors often produced bore diagnostically powerful traces of the construction process. And the immediate problems caused by mistakes, for example, stitching too close to the edge of the cloth, presented themselves immediately and transparently.

Burton, Brown, and Fischer (1984) talked about this sort of thing in the vernacular of computer programming as "debugging" and treated error correction as its major form. But perhaps another aspect of such corrections in craft production is the communication of masterful standards. Information about the quality of what the tailors produced was readily available: When Little M. sold his second hat to a tailor for ten cents, both he and the tailor were aware that the customary selling price for hats was a dollar fifty. There was a clear message to the apprentice in this transaction concerning the quality of what he produced. Sales provided a general evaluation; mistakes in construction were more specific. So feedback to apprentices was available in different relations of detail and hence was rich and informative: apprentices received information not only on what constituted an error but also on what errors were serious and how much they would impede a sale.

The Apprenticeship Process

I have described the entry into apprenticeship via rudimentary skills, along with the recurring pattern of learning how to make each new kind of garment through building a conceptual model of the construction process, practicing sewing it, watching how to cut it out, then practicing cutting it out. And I've said a little about the development of self-correction techniques. Further analysis requires considering the apprenticeship process as a whole.

There were relations between the learning of different garments. When apprentices began to learn how to make clothes, way-in activities were widely spaced. Until the apprentice knew how to sew a garment he did not learn how to cut it out; and until he had produced a good approximation he did not begin the way-in process for learning another garment. These principles applied through the time it took to learn to make trousers but contrasted sharply with the tempo and pattern of learning thereafter.

Learning to make trousers defined several changes in the learning process. The distinction between "before trousers" and "after trousers" was made by the tailors and marked ritually. Every tailor who described his apprenticeship to me included an account of the day his master left the shop in the middle of sewing a pair of trousers for a customer and told him to finish it. The "test" indicated the master's willingness to have the apprentice's work treated as though it were produced by the master, for sale by the master in the shop. Following the point at which the master "tested" his apprentice's ability to make trousers, the pattern of learning changed to haphazardly overlapping, often simultaneous ways in for different garments, although the order of learning to sew before learning to cut out was maintained throughout. The apprentice now ranged widely into learning processes for a variety of garments, rarely in response to personal interest or playful impulse, more often in response to customer demand.

This broadening of ways in occurred after the apprentice had attained a high level of rudimentary physical skill. By the time the apprentice could make passable trousers, he was no longer preoccupied with basic skills. Conceptual models of the new construction processes might address only the new steps to be fitted into existing sequences. Execution became a matter of specialized new requirements but did not present the brand-new problems of early garments. At this point, the rate of learning to make different kinds of garments could increase because much of what went into making unfamiliar garments had already been well learned.

This shift occurred in relation to making trousers. Trousers were the product that distinguished these tailors from Mandingo and other tailors in Monrovia. These garments were ubiquitously displayed in Happy Corner and accounted for the bulk of sales. Because making trousers was the tailors' major income-producing activity, the economic contribution of an apprentice increased sharply when he had become skilled enough to make trousers for sale. At that point, he stopped making hats and drawers and went to work in earnest for his master, making trousers for which his master both bought the material and reaped the profits. Before this time, the apprentice sold his own drawers and hats and kept the money for himself, purchasing fabric to construct other hats and drawers. Masters sometimes grumbled that apprentices were too happy making hats and drawers, making their own money, and that they didn't want to learn to make trousers. In the short run, the apprentices undoubtedly did lose financially as they became dependent on their master for pocket money. The ritual marking of the move to "serious" tailoring—beginning to sew trousers *for* the master meant beginning to sew trousers as a master made them—supported a change that had disadvantages from the immediate view of the apprentice. But it is difficult to imagine that an apprentice would have acted out the tailors' worst fears and never bothered to learn to make the full inventory of garments. After all, apprentices wanted to become master tailors. (And the garments the master tailors *didn't* make guaranteed that the apprentices would leave off making them as well.)

I have contrasted the carefully ordered learning processes up to the shift to trouser making, and the subsequent opening up of simultaneous learning processes. I am concerned that this characterization of the earlier course of apprenticeship gives an impression of systematic and narrowly defined activity on the part of beginning apprentices. In fact, during these early steps, the apprentices did many things that they would probably have labeled play, for example, making miniature shirt collars, or a money bag, or even a shirt, long before such things were "appropriate." They ran lots of errands and spent hours waiting patiently to be sent off again. Broad initiative was lodged with the apprentice to practice on whatever he wished (within the limits imposed by his meager economic resources). In trying to assess the educational efficacy of the apprenticeship process, we can ask what effects this idiosyncratic activity was likely to have on the apprentice.

In apprenticeship narrowly defined as "learning to tailor," the tailor shop furnished a benign educational environment. Almost any garment, or piece of a garment, an apprentice played with could be a vehicle for improving his execution skills, no matter how inappropriate the object in the general scheme of learning activities. Snipping bits off a scrap of elastic, making a money bag, watching someone make shirts when the apprentice was just learning to make hats, or making miniature shirt collars could not hurt and did contribute to the total amount of practice the apprentice got at sewing, cutting, and measuring. (Little M. became absorbed in those miniature shirt collars over a period of two days. Neither his master nor Little M. took the activity seriously. Yet it was an occasion for a good deal of learning.) Furthermore, self-correction techniques learned early in the apprenticeship process applied across a variety of garments so that playful practice was unlikely to produce bad habits even if it went unmonitored by the master or more experienced apprentices.

The last achievement of apprenticeship involved just one garment, the Higher Heights suit. The apprentice had acquired the skills and knowledge to make various kinds of clothes at different times, over a period of years. But making a Higher Heights suit acted as a kind of summary of the apprenticeship process, calling on just about everything the apprentice needed to know how to do. The only new conceptual and execution skills to be learned at this stage were details for the carefully finished pockets, cuffs, vents, and so forth, for by this time the apprentice could sew, cut out, and finish all the items in the garment inventory. In a sense, this already included the Higher Heights suit, for the suit was composed of trousers and a tailored shirt or jacket that between them accounted for the basic construction principles for everything in the tailors' repertory with the exception of hats. This suit took lots of expensive cloth and much work. An apprentice could not make a series of only partially successful attempts before he made a salable suit. The Higher Heights suit was an appropriate summary, a masterwork displaying the apprentice's skill. Constructing a well-made Higher Heights suit was a fitting (so to speak) signal for the master to take the apprentice back to his family and confer on him his blessing as a master tailor.

The Question of Teaching

COACHING

A master had responsibilities to and for his apprentices, and imparting tailoring skills directly may have been the least of these. Only a master could offer someone who wanted to become a tailor legitimate access to the workplace and opportunities for gradually changing participation in tailoring work. The master also was the only one who could draw the apprentice into making garments for sale after the "test," as part of the apprentice's obligation to serve him. A master needed to agree to, more often decide on, the timing of the move from apprentice to master status. He needed to have intimate enough knowledge of his apprentice's progress to exercise reasonable judgment about when to make these moves. To be sure, master tailors and their apprentices worked and lived in such close quarters that it is hard to imagine a master lacking sufficient information.

A new apprentice arrived at a shop where the different trajectories of older apprentices, stories told by masters about their own apprenticeships, and the arrangement by which new apprentices had to furnish cloth for their own projects—any and all of these effectively kept him from starting at what non-tailors might assume to be the "beginning." A naïve newcomer walking into the shop would probably identify cutting out trousers as the first step in these tailors' work. Identifying appropriate ways in, most of them uninterestingly modest, was not something a starting apprentice was likely to be able to do for himself. But arrangements of life in the shop directed the attention and efforts of apprentices into sequential arrangements of their projects and efforts, without masters acting as teachers.

What about the need for masters to furnish "expert knowledge"? There were many sources of tailoring knowledge in the shops, including not only the master tailors, but given their capacity for self-correction and improvement, the apprentices themselves. This rendered the role of the master qua teacher optional. The apprentice was in a good position to interrogate his own activities and the garments he made. Most masters were not as approachable as Little M.'s, nor would G. himself have been as indulgent had there been more work available at the time. Approaching a formidable master with a novice question would be an ill-advised breach of the respect owed by apprentices to their masters. That meant that the more skilled the apprentice, the more he would be watched, questioned, and emulated by newer apprentices. Such relations could be instructive for more experienced apprentices as well as the less skilled boys. Customers provided another source of useful information when they bought and bargained for clothes. Though they were not construction experts, they made critical choices on the basis of a wearer's knowledge. Other boys' masters and the more advanced apprentices in the tailor shops were also resources, working, being themselves, occasionally responding to requests for help from less knowledgeable apprentices. There were more "humans as resources" than "learners" in tailor shops, as masters and near-peers served as models and occasional tutors.[3] But the apprenticeship process in Happy Corner assigned *responsibility* for the transformation of an apprentice into a master tailor to that apprentice's master.

Some of the mistakes made by apprentices, and the means to correct them, would not have been known by customers in selecting and bargaining for a garment. I once asked a group of tailors how to decide which tailors were good ones, when you walked into a shop where you didn't know anyone. They had a number of ideas, sufficiently technical to suggest that only a tailor would catch them all: "Look at how they sew on trousers. Look at pockets and waistband—if the waistband wouldn't be laid straight; if the lining is coming down [showing] then the trousers are no good."

To show me, one tailor brought out two pairs of trousers, one made by an apprentice who was not very skilled. The waistband was wider in some places than others, including where the two ends met. This seemed transparent as poor construction, but it would be difficult for a non-tailor to tell an apprentice how to make it better. The tailor went on to point out other failings:

> Also, it is cut so that the two fly pieces are different lengths. (To show me this, the tailor folded the band under so that it was clear that the trouser pieces themselves weren't cut the same, that it was not due to the uneven waistband.) Then we compared linings of the waistbands. On the good pair the lining was smooth and flat. In the poor one it was bunched up and sewn in folds in places.

Another way to tell a tailor's skill, I was told by another master, is to look at how the pockets have been sewn:

> Hip pockets: [The facing] should fit right to the top edge of the pocket, there should be no space between the bottom and top edge of the pocket. ... Another way to tell is leg seams. [The two seams of one leg] should have the front crease right between them. If they aren't opposite each other, then when one puts on the trousers the front crease will twist around and won't hang straight. This is caused by how you sew it. Sometimes it could be from cutting, if you don't cut it good.

Knowing more than one procedural error that would produce the same apparent problem seemed to be a level of knowledge that only skilled tailors (including advanced apprentices) were likely to have. While the apprentice might have been able to identify the existence of the problem (pant legs hanging crookedly), he would probably have had trouble diagnosing the cause (cutting? sewing?). In short, an argument can be made that diagnosis by a knowledgeable tailor of those mistakes an apprentice couldn't figure out himself was useful when learning to tailor.

I do not know how well someone faced with only a completed garment as a template, or alternatively, with the pieces but no example of a finished garment, could figure out an order that would work for constructing the whole thing. Neither the unassembled pieces nor the finished garment would reveal how to fit the waistband and seat seam in the way this was done in Happy Corner, let alone how to interleave the operations of sewing the waistband, fly, and inner leg seam. By watching other tailors work, that is, by observing the process rather than by simply looking at the finished product, such difficulties could be avoided—no need for a master as guide so long as someone skillful carried out the construction process sufficiently often. This is exactly what master tailors and advanced apprentices did all day, as they engaged in craft production.

OTHER THINGS TO BE LEARNED

Tailors needed to learn how to sell what they made and how to measure, but these activities had no fixed place or arrangement in the apprenticeship process. Counting, reading numbers, arithmetic, bargaining, and making change were skills that Vai and Gola people acquired whether they became tailors or not. (Using a measuring tape was a specialized skill, but to measure required numerical skills that were broadly distributed.) Tailors were not willing to share with each other or with their apprentices what it took to make a profitable sale. Economic control was one's own business, so in a sense not part of apprenticeship, but rather part of being a master. Under these circumstances, shop talk and gossip were important but only indirect and unreliable sources of advice.

While tailors may have reasonably assumed that all apprentices would begin with complete ignorance of clothing construction and have no knowledge of how to work a treadle sewing machine, they could also assume that newcomers would have some (varied) numeric literacy and knowledge of arithmetic and commercial transactions. It seems likely that measuring and selling had no specific locations in the apprenticeship process because useful ways in would have been different for different apprentices. Further, measuring, buying, and selling were ubiquitous in every phase of their work.

Moreover, in certain respects there was an uneasy accommodation between masterhood and apprenticeship. Since carrying out business and determining the sizes of garments to be made were "things masters do," practice by apprentices within that arena would be inappropriate. The tailors also preferred money transactions to be private. Financial arrangements were an aspect of mature practice that was purposefully hidden from apprentices.

When I interviewed the tailors, I asked which of their peers in Happy Corner were successful, and how they had achieved success. There was strong agreement on who the successful tailors were, but not one of my informants suggested that good bookkeeping skills, or exceptional accuracy in tailoring, or anything else remotely associated with arithmetic, played a role in that success. Instead, to a man the tailors said that having a rich father who provided capital for setting up business in the first place was the major factor determining success. They argued that the more money one had, the bigger the inventory it was possible to keep; the bigger the inventory, the more you could sell. This was not just a tautology—they also argued that customers were more likely to buy the wares of a tailor with a large selection to choose from.

Among the tailors there were strong pressures for keeping transactions of a monetary nature private. The tailors worked and earned their living in close proximity to one another; it was discourteous to refuse to make a loan to a fellow tailor; they were all impoverished. Under the circumstances, sharing access to knowledge about their financial affairs did not make good sense. Writing down financial transactions would not be safe unless one could be sure of an absolutely private place to keep the record. The tailors preferred as a solution not to keep track of cash flow and to grumble about how this lack of knowledge hampered them in living their lives.

Commentary

In my description of apprentice learning, we have seen how ethnographic practice, though still circumscribed by conventional theoretical assumptions, could generate complexities that challenged those assumptions. Here as before, the results and effects of critical ethnographic inquiry were partial. My ethnography was focused on learning processes within long trajectories and followed the least powerful participants in the tailor shops, the apprentices. The central question concerned just how much of apprenticeship unfolded in situ without teaching as a precondition or propellant.

Indeed, in some ways I shared this project with Burton, Brown, and Fischer (1984), who considered how the world could be made into the teaching entity and teachers into coach/inventors of special pedagogical worlds. They began with the school-saturated view that to be a good teacher, the world needed to be reconfigured specifically for learners. I set out to show that the tailors' world was virtually always available for the apprentices in instructive ways and that it was (almost) all they needed. Our differences hinged on different conceptions of "teachers" and "teaching," which in turn depended on assumptions about institutional arrangements for teaching and on our concepts of learning. I'll begin with the assumptions underlying Burton, Brown, and Fischer's theory of learning, in order to then consider its complement—their approach to teaching built around concepts of coaching and microworlds.[4]

Burton, Brown, and Fischer's novel, but not critical, cognitive approach to learning divided conception from skill and with it the mind from the body. They defined a relevant learning process as the internalization and accumulation of knowledge in an "individual." Rather than taking "conception" and "execution" to be inseparable in principle (as would be the case in social practice theory), they saw as a key educational problem the issue of how to bring about their integration in "execution skills." (So did I—think of the example of the hat and the money bag). While Burton, Brown, and Fischer's approach to learning constituted an advance at the time, it rested firmly on binary assumptions.

Their conception of teaching centered on coaching and the notion of microworlds. Their "coaches" were authoritative parties (ski instructors, educators) arranging microworlds for novices so that they would be able to do what teachers wanted them to learn. A given microworld was conceived as a simplified problem-solving context for learners. The goal was for learners to internalize concepts and skills (with verisimilitude) via manipulation of the carefully contrived environment. This "environment" was a teacher-initiated curriculum (or computer program) prefabricated for novices' education, its microworld status deriving from its *separation* from the contexts of everyday practice.[5] In short, Burton, Brown, and Fischer's model was still a version of learning-through-teaching, one that cleanly divided subjects from world, and educators who know and teach from learners who don't know and must be taught. The instructionist bias of this concept leads to assumptions that teaching is the first and only preoccupation of the teacher. Even "coaching," à la Burton, Brown, and Fischer takes instruction to be a thing in and of itself that organizes what is going on around it; it is lifted out and bracketed off from everything else.

The closest thing to a contrived, simplified microworld in my own analysis was my map of the tailors' apprenticeship process in figure 9. Certainly the map, like the pedagogy of microworld construction, represented the apprenticeship process as a series of simplifications (compared with the work of master tailors) by the spacing and other ordering arrangements of their early efforts. But problems arise when one asks how those simplifications came about, along with resistance to simplification—for example, the tailors' insistence on practice by successive approximation. How did the work of learning actually go on and get done? My (not the tailors') synthesizing diagram imposed on the apprentices' everyday practice a hierarchical form of more- and less-inclusive "levels" delimiting a specifically educational form.[6] But relations among garments and construction processes lay not in some abstract hierarchy of levels of learning organization, but in the fact that they were all interrelated facets of tailoring practice, the sorts of things that apprentices were impelled to connect in the course of production, or to intersperse or coordinate for many different reasons. The interesting question is what organized what. Did the relations highlighted in the apprenticeship process map organize learning sequences, or were learning processes organized by ongoing everyday practice? Surely both. This stands in contradiction to a view of "teaching" as a matter of isolated microworlds and their prefabrication.[7]

I certainly played with the idea of master as coach, probing for how much coaching Little M. needed, how that coaching took place, and how timing mattered for laying down good skills. There were a number of ways in which a guide of some sort for the tailors' apprentices was helpful in rectifying complex errors (e.g., the poorly hanging trousers), or in assembling the various parts of trousers, or in finding out where to start into learning tailoring. But it doesn't seem appropriate to reduce the master to coach here any more than to reduce him to teacher in chapter 2. There was ample evidence, for example, that other tailors, most especially other apprentices, along with customer input, sales, occasional projects, and much else, helped shape the apprentices' changing activities. In exploring apprenticeship processes, the notion of "coaching" did seem more interestingly to stretch across various aspects of the apprentices' everyday encounters with their craft rather than being embodied in a particular individual. We might call it a notion of "the world-as-teacher."

Any concept of "the world-as-teacher" depends on how that world is conceived, its institutional arrangements, and more. But it also depends on assumptions about what counts as a "teacher." We've seen one set of assumptions: That teaching is a prerequisite for learning and instruction involves prefabrication of learning occasions by teacher/knowers. Teachers are knowledge/skill transmitters. The work of teaching requires control over learners' learning, but it is about transmitting knowledge/skill to individuals. Call this a "cognitive pedagogical view." Further, in that conventional theoretical stance, there is complete silence about the relations of power that inform the enterprise, leaving teaching as benign, power-free, and about nothing more than the transmission of knowledge.

The ethnographic focus on learning in apprenticeship offered a second set of assumptions about teaching, for following the apprentices' trajectories through apprenticeship raised a number of doubts and questions about the tight links assumed in conventional theory to bind learning to teaching.[8] These doubts focused on the apprenticeship process as a whole, taking seriously the apprentices' views that learning was their bailiwick, not their masters'. It felt like good sense to assume that learning—not teaching—was the phenomenon to follow in order to open up questions about learning. In apprenticeship, the master knowers/doers did not adopt identities as teachers, though they certainly knew how to produce a sharp teacher caricature. I argued that "teaching" (as defined in conventional cognitivist terms) was not required to produce learning. This led to two problems: First, uncoupling learning from teaching loaded the relations of power and authority of teachers over students onto teachers, in negative terms. Correspondingly, this left "learning" (instead of teaching) as a benign, power-free, organic endeavor: a romantic, uncritical view with the same problem as the cognitivist view of teaching—a taboo on political analysis. Second, having said that it was not acceptable to reduce masters to teachers (still using a cognitivist definition of teaching), or to reduce apprenticeship to a dependent outcome of teacher control and direction, the ethnographic account still included much activity that looked as if it belonged in the instructional ballpark, although more often as a response to learning (and other) activity than as its cause. Call this "situated instruction." Throughout this chapter, I described a number of occasions on which apprentices, their masters, and other masters were thus engaged. In the course of ongoing practice, exchanges about how to do something, or other events inspiring ways in, occurred in the midst of many other things.[9] Situated instruction rarely took precedence over the meanings and priorities of doings underway, and no one person (or facet of practice) was the designated instructor. Indeed, this chapter, focused on conceptions of learning in whole trajectories of apprenticeship, could be read twice, once as a description of how apprentices did the learning of tailoring and again as a description of this process as a matter of "situated instruction." Both terms, "situated learning" and "situated instruction," are apt characterizations of the apprenticeship.

There is more to be said about the erasure of issues of power from conventional theories of teaching and from romantic views of learning (especially clear, but among many others, might be Csikszentmihalyi's concept of "flow" in Nakamura and Csikszentmihalyi 2002). Both views bracket off and deny the centrality of relations of power. It is possible to be more specific about how this suppression worked. A move to reduce education to a cognitive analysis of mental learning processes erases the relations of power that act through and shape apprenticeship (and everything else). There is no place for concepts and analysis of authority wielded, transformations legitimized, vulnerability exploited, conflicts, threats, conformity cajoled or otherwise enforced in the production of clothes, or in the production of tailors, or for that matter in the production of the binary logic of comparative theory. If you block issues of force, power, and conflict, it is all too easy to see learning and teaching as completely benign processes, making unaskable questions about the conflicts and tensions, the relations of mutual need and potential threat, that masters and apprentices represented for each other. These relations were also constitutive of the processes of apprenticeship and craft production in Happy Corner (and are part of learning relations everywhere). Further, while it is no doubt true that the apprentices' varied efforts to learn to make garments contributed to their growing prowess as tailors, conflicting stakes over which masters and apprentices struggled were integral to this process as they engaged differently in the production of future tailors. Where then, in either Burton, Brown, and Fischer's account of ski coaching or in my account of learning in apprenticeship was there critical consideration of issues of inculcation?[10] Where was the iron(ing) fist of daily disciplines (however smooth and wrinkle free)? In my case, they were lost in the project of exploring first, how master-apprentice relations were complex and different from conventional teacher-learner relations, and second, how learning from the apprentices' perspective was not the dependent product of (conventional) teaching. On this issue I stopped short of political analysis that needed to be done.

Despite—or perhaps because of—its political shortcomings, the ethnographic work described in this chapter focused on practical daily arrangements of the *doings* of learners learning. Such a focus is precluded by conventional learning theories, for focusing on questions of the mental, the individual, and on teaching in the conventional sense obscures or suppresses questions about what learners do, how in practice they come to change. It was surprisingly useful, then, to follow learners instead, for that made possible an account of how they did the learning/changing, in practice. And if learning gets done in part through varied moments of situated instruction, the way to see situated instruction is through/in processes of the doing of learning. In this fashion, it was possible to see how apprentices came to be able to cut out and sew trouser flies so that they reliably appeared on the front of the trousers.

I see this chapter and the previous one as piling up invitations to consider a distinctively different assemblage of conceptual tools for inquiring into the changing apprentices in the changing social life in Happy Corner. But the ethnographic inquiry at the time was intended as preparation for investigating through experiments the comparative effects of schooling and apprenticeship on learning transfer. Chapter 4 provides an account of two rounds of learning transfer experiments, moving from questions of the tailors' comparative success and failure at problem solving to descriptions of the processes by which they solved problems, and eventually to exploring relations between multiple Vai and Gola number systems and their different effects on problem solving. The best moments in the ethnographic efforts described above and in chapter 2 captured the multiplicity and complexity of relations comprised by apprenticeship. Observational efforts in the shops did contribute subject matter for the experiments—but as we shall see, not in ways that incorporated those complexities. For experiments rely on the presumption that there are shared common bodies of discrete information that can be taken up for comparisons of people, forms of education, and indeed continents and cultures. Given the simplification imposed by comparative experiments, I abandoned new and hard-won insights from earlier critical ethnographic efforts, looked around for some sort of activity that was comparable across schooling and tailoring in Liberia, and lighted upon what was surely the most universal of subjects—arithmetic.[11]

As in chapter 2, I managed to take "two steps forward and then a step back." In that chapter, I made some progress as I began to recognize the rich multiple relations that furnished everyday lives in Vai and Gola tailor shops. But when I decided in the present chapter to look at learning processes in apprenticeship, I ignored the lessons of chapter 2 and went back to conventional terms and questions about learning and teaching, thereby narrowing once again what constituted the stuff to be learned (garment-making skills). The critical ethnographic work in this chapter again pressed on these boundaries to implicate the everyday doing of learning in tailor shops and situated instruction in ongoing practice. Even so, my psychologist colleagues insisted that ethnographic evidence concerning the apprenticeship process did not constitute a *test* of the claim that "informal" learning in the context of use (and all that this implied) would lead to the acquisition of less generally applicable knowledge than learning occurring in school contexts segregated from the settings of its intended use. I was determined to respond in terms they could take seriously. The ensuing learning transfer experiments, described in chapter 4, once again pushed me back to subject matter that reflected the assumptions of conventional theory about the nature of (a) formal and informal education, (b) learning, (c) knowledge, and (d) teaching. The terms "partial" and "struggle" surely apply to the process of critical ethnographic practice.

4 Testing Learning Transfer

Overview

In preparing to return to Happy Corner, I invented a dozen learning transfer experiments. During that next summer in Monrovia, most of the tailors and apprentices in the tailors' alley participated in them. This was crunch time— the moment in the project to find out whether previous cross-cultural experiments were or were not fair instruments for comparing forms of education and their effects. I suspected that the cross-cultural experimental evidence for "learning transfer" (patchy at best) was an artifact of the design of those experiments and assumptions underlying the design, both because they embodied ignorance about "other" sorts of education, and because they were fine-tuned to schooling through the employment of school-derived experimental tasks and assumptions about the superior institutional arrangements of schooling. Given that many cross-cultural experiments at the time took school-based tasks and instruction as the gold standard against which to measure everything else, the experimenters had no reason to specify relations of experimental tasks to anything but schooling. Furthermore, if they assumed the "cognitive abilities" captured in experimental tasks were natural and universal, they had no reason to acknowledge the institutional arrangements of schooling as the source of the tasks they borrowed for their experiments. I was determined to design experimental tasks whose relations to the everyday activities of apprenticeship were specified in detail.[1]

According to the theoretical assumptions that divided formal from informal education, transfer of training should follow after learning in formal educational circumstances that separated contexts for learning from contexts for the application of what was to be learned. Transfer of training should occur much less powerfully where learning was embedded in arenas of ongoing practice. In practical terms, it might seem sensible and obvious that if situations of "learning" and "use" were identical, no "transfer" would be required. But this was not the point for the learning transfer theorists: For them it was abstraction from specifics that was supposed to enable transfer. School was supposed to provide this abstract learning, while other kinds of education would not. The question of transfer was important, as Michael Cole explained in an editorial comment at the end of the first short paper I published on the experiments described in this chapter:

> A long-standing problem in educational psychology, currently recognized as a central problem in cross-cultural psychology, is to determine the extent to which knowledge gained in one setting can be applied to other settings. In educational psychology, this centers around the concept of transfer of training: do certain training techniques result in more, or broader, transfer than others? . . . There has been a good deal of interest in how education affects cognitive development. This has been addressed by comparing schooled and nonschooled populations with respect to their performance on selected cognitive tasks. (In Lave 1977, 3)

The binary comparative theory of formal versus informal education made clear predictions about where we should find more and less learning transfer. But it did not furnish a specific theory of *how* transfer should take place. There were competing theories in play, both dating from the early twentieth century. E. L. Thorndike championed a raw empirical, bottom-up approach, and Charles Judd a hierarchical, abstract, top-down theory—polar opposites in commonsense dualist (duelist?) theorizing. Thorndike suggested that transfer occurs when a sufficient number of elements are shared across learning situations; Judd suggested that the more general and abstract the principled understanding of some area of knowledge, the more likely a new problem is to be perceived as one of a class of existing problems for which problem-solving procedures are at hand (and it follows that they will then be applied). Both of these psychologists reviewed much more striking evidence for lack of transfer than in favor of it. Both focused on knowledge, tasks, and problems narrowly defined. Thorndike's view did not preclude introduction of elements of context as basic to making associations. But since he did not attempt to specify what elements of context might need to be similar in order for people to approach tasks in similar ways, his was not a theory of transfer, but only a suggestion about how one might go about devising such a theory. Judd so narrowed his theory to the organization of specific task knowledge that it did not invite attempts to relate processes of problem solving to the contexts in which they arise.[2]

Not surprisingly—Judd was the influential founder of the first U.S. graduate school of education (Lageman 1989)—cross-cultural comparative education theory took his position. Perhaps that helped to direct the focus of my experimental investigation to quantitative, mostly arithmetic skills.

Arithmetic seemed the epitome of universal, formal rules; it was taught in schools; and I knew it was used during apprenticeship in measurement, money transactions, and production processes. Further, arithmetic was one of the few genres of knowledge at hand for which there was a conventional notation system useful in describing fine-grained variation in arithmetic procedures.

But convenience from the perspective of the researcher shouldn't be the only consideration in experimental research. It was crucial to ask what role math learning played in tailors' apprenticeship and schooling. In chapter 3, I made the point that math knowledge was not assumed by the tailors to bear a determinant relation to the different periods in the process of apprenticeship. This stood in contrast to their assumption that new apprentices would be completely ignorant of defining characteristics of tailoring, for example, how to peddle a sewing machine or make trousers. Nor—as is the case in Western schooling arrangements—did it appear that for Vai and Gola tailors supposed aptitude or skill at math defined significant symbolic differences between social categories of identity, in the way, for example, that class, ethnicity, and gender distinctions are coded in the United States. Knowing more or less arithmetic did not differentiate the tailors among themselves or from other Liberians. Apprentices came into the tailor shops with differing amounts of practice in math, acquired elsewhere in the course of their daily lives.

Within the process of apprenticeship, math made a practical difference without having symbolic significance as a marker of elite knowledge or personal distinction. Analysis of the experiments showed that the major difference between young apprentices and older masters was the size of the quantities with which they felt at ease—not the kinds of arithmetic operations they did and didn't know. There were different kinds of garments to be learned, and math was used in making all of them, for no garment could be learned without learning to measure at the same time. Both learning to sew a garment and learning to cut it out required counting and measuring skills. Way-in and practice phases for learning each segment of the production process employed arithmetic skills. To use math learning as a major segmenting/organizing device in the apprenticeship process, then, would have required a reorganization of the rest of it. It is very difficult to imagine how math could have been elevated into such a principle.

Institutional arrangements of schooling designated arithmetic skill as an end in itself. Like peddling the sewing machine and making trousers in the tailor shops in Liberia, children in school were presumed not to know arithmetic before arriving at school—a fiction that in both cases helped to legitimize the organized character of inclusion and exclusion of peripheral participants. In schools, teaching arithmetic was a major goal. In the tailors' apprenticeship, math was instead a means for realizing other goals. These differing institutional arrangements surely affected how different tailors approached the experiments, but not, as we shall see, for the reasons presupposed in learning transfer theory.

Transfer of Training Experiments

In the cultural logic of psychological experimentation, if you wanted to know how successfully people could transfer—transport and apply—their "knowledge," you devised a series of problems increasingly unfamiliar in their particular features to create a kind of yardstick with which to calibrate just how far a subject's knowledge "traveled" as the problems to be solved looked less and less like the familiar problems through which knowledge was "acquired" in the first place. Some of the experiments I invented first turned out not to fit this logic. One involved talking through the process of sewing the waistband on a pair of trousers. I recorded descriptions by many apprentices and masters and transcribed each one. But I couldn't figure out how to analyze them in a way recognizable in conventional cognitive experiments. What if one tailor gave a lengthier explanation than another? What if one mentioned more steps than another? What might one infer about tailoring knowledge from differences between tailors (or vice versa)? I couldn't think of a sensible theoretically informed answer to these questions. In another attempt at inventing experimental tasks, I bought a tattered commercial Vogue Pattern catalog from a store in downtown Monrovia, selected a number of different patterns, copied each variation of each pattern (some variations were pretty obscure, all depending on the cut of the garment), and asked the tailors which went together and which were different and why. I was impressed by their facility in recognizing common construction features, but ran into another difficulty: Transfer of training experiments were occasions for comparing people with different educational antecedents. I couldn't imagine an analogous task in school settings. Among my experimental efforts, then, the only subject matter that survived in subsequent experiments was arithmetic.

The experimental tasks included arithmetic problems and exercises in estimating circumferences and lengths, extrapolating simple functions over a wider range of numbers than was customary in constructing trousers, and matching the proportions of two-dimensional figures. After describing these tasks in more detail, I turn to the predictions I made about the relative contribution of tailoring skills and school skills to problem-solving performance. Detailed analysis of the data follows after that.

ARITHMETIC TASKS

Arithmetic concepts. I concentrated first on areas of arithmetic skills characteristic of tailoring work, especially those involved in measuring and fitting
clothes for customers: the ability to recognize and name numbers on a number line (e.g., a tape measure), an understanding of the ordered relationships between numbers, and skills in using arithmetic operations. I selected
problems on the basis of observations of tailors using arithmetic in their
work, supplemented by intensive questioning of individual informants.

Number recognition. A few of the boys who were beginning apprenticeship
could not yet name Arabic numbers on the measuring tape. To establish
their familiarity with the number line, I asked questions about particular
number locations: "Show me the number 20 (11, 27, 38, 3, 45, 58) on the tape
measure." The first four numbers occurred often in sewing trousers; the
last three were rarely, if ever, used in actual tailor work, but were present on
the tapeline. The tailors saw them several times a day in the course of using the tape. In order to explore skill at recognizing and naming numbers
not used in daily practice, I next asked for numbers (65, 72, 80, 103, 139, 148)
that were not on the measuring tape as it was customarily used (the side
measured in inches), but that did appear on the reverse side (measured in
centimeters).

Ordered relationships. In the recent past, Vai and Gola tailors had measured
people and cloth by knotting pieces of string to mark the correct lengths.
The measurements could be directly transferred from customer to cloth
without numbers. Were the tailors using the tape measure as a number
line or as a sort of preknotted string on which unique symbols happened to
stand for unique possible string lengths? Did they understand the ordered
relations between numbers, measuring from a zero point, and the concept
of equal intervals between numbers?

Several questions depended on a grasp of these concepts. The problems
included giving the number that falls halfway between the two ends of the
tape and the number that divides the upper half of the tape into two equal
segments. I asked the tailors to display lengths of a yard, a half yard, and
a quarter yard on the tape, as well as lengths of one inch, two inches, and
twelve inches, and then these same distances anchored elsewhere on the
tape than at zero.

Computation. It seemed likely that if tailors used the measuring tape as a
number line, they would also make use of the number line's properties

for addition, subtraction, multiplication, and division, since all of these operations were required in the course of cutting out and sewing clothes. The task included multiplication and division problems. For example, "If trousers are lying on the table, and you measure the cuff at eight inches, what would it be if you picked it up and measured all the way around?" The converse was asked in this way: "If you measured the waist all the way around and found that it was thirty inches, what would it be if you laid it on the table and measured it flat?"

I used two strategies for making the problems unfamiliar from the tailors' point of view. For some problems, I inserted unusual numbers in a familiar problem frame, for example, doubling a flat cuff measurement of fifteen inches. If this measurement were actually used in making trousers, it would produce an absurdly large cuff, and none of the tailors had ever made such a garment. For other problems, I embedded numbers from the tailoring problems in a context that was not common to tailoring. In an example that used the same numbers and operation as one of the waist-size problems, I asked, "If you had sixteen spools of thread and divided them with your friend, how many would each of you get?" The total score possible was 74. The tailors' scores ranged from 3 to 74, with a mean of 55 and a standard deviation of 14.[3]

ESTIMATION OF LINEAR MEASUREMENTS

Like the arithmetic task, the estimation task was constructed so as to have some familiar and some unfamiliar items. In this case, the problems were designed to form a continuum from very familiar to unfamiliar, and were presented to the tailors in order from most to least familiar to encourage the possibility of transfer, or at least not to inhibit it. The most familiar items were pairs of trousers. I asked the tailors to estimate the size of waistband circumferences for different pairs of trousers. The trousers were identical in appearance except for their waist measurements, 26, 29, and 31 inches respectively. These were all typical waistband measurements for ready-to-wear trousers. There were also three loops of string that could be sized up in the same way as tailors inspected trouser waistbands for purposes of estimating length. These measured 17, 29, and 34 inches. The last two were common waistband sizes, one identical to one of the trouser waistband measurements. Seventeen inches was typical of a trouser cuff, with which the tailors dealt every day. Three lengths of string, not tied into loops, provided the next set of problems, and these were of lengths 8, 18¾, and 30 inches. The first was a reasonable measure for a trouser cuff lying flat, and such measurements were routinely made. Eighteen and three quarters might be encountered if making a 37½-inch waist, measured flat, but this was not as common as the other measurements. I included the 30-inch length because it was a typical waist measurement, although it would never be encountered when measuring the trouser waist flat. It should be said that while the tailors occasionally measured to the nearest half inch, they did not use finer-grained units of measurement and the 18¾-length was poorly chosen on those grounds. String lengths might evoke old linear measurement techniques; conceivably they could be formed into loops for estimation purposes. But taken as given, they were (intended to be) less similar to the waistband problem than the string loops. The last set of problems consisted of judging the length of sticks of wood 10 inches, 12 inches, and 24 inches long. Rigid, dense, and linear, there was nothing cloth- or clothing-like about these objects. The 24-inch piece was a relatively familiar waistband size, 10 inches was a common cuff size (measured flat), but the 12-inch piece would not be a common measurement. The best that could be said for it was that it was in the ballpark of common cuff-waist measurements.

I presented the four groups of estimations in the order given above (trouser waists, string loops, lengths of string, lengths of wood), moving from familiar to unfamiliar measurements. For the trouser waistband estimations, each tailor looked at only two of the three pairs of trousers. I tried to make it obvious that the two pairs were chosen haphazardly to discourage tailors from discussing their estimates with other prospective subjects. One pair of trousers was handed to the tailor. He could take as long as he wished and do what he liked in making his estimation so long as he did not use a measuring tape. When he had made a guess, the trousers were folded before handing the tailor the next pair, so that there was no visual basis for comparing one to the other.

I followed the same procedure for the loops and lengths of string and the pieces of wood. But within each of these sets of objects, there was no variation in the order of presentation for different subjects. The loops were presented in the order biggest, smallest, medium-sized; the lengths were ordered so that the medium-sized came first, then the smallest, followed by the largest; and the wood pieces small, medium, large.

EXTRAPOLATING A FUNCTION

For each waistband, the tailors were asked what the appropriate hip size would be, then what the appropriate fly length would be. The tailors gave repeated evidence, mainly in the form of requests for a repetition of waist size (but never hip size) to suggest that they were relating both hip and fly estimates to the waist size, not to each other.

The fourth task was designed to utilize presumed skills of the tailors at judging the similarity in proportions of two things that were not the same size, but still basically the same shape (e.g., two pairs of trousers). I made a set of twenty cards, each with four figures on it. The first figure, colored brown and separated by a vertical line from the other three, colored blue, consisted of a drawing of a pair of trousers, or a rectangle, a triangle, a square, or an irregularly shaped figure with several right angles. I asked the tailors to point to the blue figure that was "most like the shape of the brown one." I presented two example problems first and told the tailor immediately whether his choice was the correct one; then we went over the examples until the tailor appeared to have a clear idea of the task. I gave frequent reminders of the instructions for the task throughout the session. Each problem was presented three times with the correct answer in a different position on the card. The cards were interleaved so that the same problem was not presented on adjacent cards.

Participants in the Experiments

The tailors who took part in the experiments ranged in approximately equal numbers from apprentices (beginning to advanced), to masters who had never trained apprentices, to masters with apprentices, and from no schooling to seventh grade. I worked out the group of participants so that it included tailors with various combinations of tailoring and schooling, from little of the first and a lot of the second (and vice versa) to similar amounts of both.

I was able to create this sampling scheme because I had interviewed most of the tailors at the beginning of the fieldwork in Happy Corner and had a certain amount of background information about each of them.[4] This made it possible to check for likely sources of selection bias in the sample. The object of this exercise was to distinguish the impact of education on cognitive skills from the possibility that experimental subjects as a group either came to Happy Corner equipped (for whatever reasons) with unusual skills because of the way they were "selected" into apprenticeship or were dismissed selectively because they didn't have them. The 138 interviews included questions about the tailors' apprenticeship history and school history, their family background, their "modernity" (based on a borrowed attitudes scale), any practices that might have directed their choice of tailoring, and their beliefs about teaching and learning. From the tailors' responses, I sought commonalities and patterns of relations—in, for example, their educational histories—in the form of statistical in- and interdependencies via multiple regression analysis.

Learning transfer experiments would typically assess the effects of schooling and apprenticeship separately by having two unrelated experimental groups. I decided to draw on a single group of tailors with different mixes of tailoring and schooling experience. But that made it important to establish that tailoring and schooling were independent in several senses. For example, to understand the roles of apprenticeship and schooling in the lives of the tailors, I compared the mix of educational experiences taken up and forgone when a Vai or Gola child became an apprentice tailor or went to school. If either set of experiences had an impact on participation in the other, conclusions about their *different* impact on cognitive skills would be ambiguous. I explored the frequency of various combinations of educational experiences; the effect of the timing and length of apprenticeship and schooling on each other; the impact of relatives' educational experiences and occupations on the educational experiences of the tailors; and the nature and comparative stringency of recruitment criteria both into and out of apprenticeship and school. With rare exceptions, all of the tailors had been initiated into the Poro society, involving months (more recently, weeks) of seclusion in a bush "school." They had also joined other boys in their village for a year or so each morning to learn verses of the Qur'an.[5] The Vai tailors could have learned the Vai script in a short period of tutoring from someone who already knew it—but none of the tailors had done so. Western-style schools were another, increasing possibility for the tailors, and especially for younger apprentices.

The interviews included information on what grade level the tailors had completed in school; whether they learned the Vai script or not; how much of the Qur'an they had memorized, whether they could read and write it, read it only, or neither. I gave everyone an English literacy test and found that whether a tailor was likely to go to school or not was simply not predictable from knowledge of his participation (or not) in other kinds of literacy. In the '70s and '80s, development theorists drew heavy distinctions between "modern" and "traditional" people, institutions, attitudes, and values. By this logic, those who learned "traditional" literate practices would oppose going to school, and "modern" folks would go to school and refuse the "old stuff." It was news of a sort, then, to find that in my sample, Vai script, Qur'anic, and occasional Arabic learning neither precluded nor was precluded by going to school.

Nor were any of the forms of literacy related to the number of years the tailors had been engaged in tailoring. Suppose that those who learned Arabic or went to school only moved into apprenticeship afterward. Then if two tailors were the same age and only one knew Arabic, the other should have more tailoring experience. In fact there was no statistical relationship (positive or negative) between any kind of literacy learning and years of tailoring experience. This was true whether the tailors' age was held constant or not and was a crucial point for the analysis of experimental outcomes. The fact that literacy and tailoring experience were independently distributed was reassuring with respect to the plan for the experiments to draw on a single population of tailors with different mixes of schooling and tailoring experience.

Schooling or other forms of literacy learning might have had more specific effects, perhaps on the length of apprenticeship or its timing in the life of the tailor. A positive relationship would imply that it took longer to move through apprenticeship while attending school. A negative relationship would imply that the more time the tailor spent in school, the quicker he learned tailoring. Multiple regression analysis provided statistical evidence that schooling had no impact on starting age for apprenticeship, nor did schooling affect the length of apprenticeship—or vice versa.

What about the impact of the tailors' close relatives' educations and occupations on their schooling and apprenticeship? Elder brothers' schooling did have some predictive value for the tailors' schooling. However, neither tailors' fathers' nor brothers' education or occupation helped to account for differences in tailors' years of tailoring experience (as we might have expected).

In general, the interview-based multiple regression analysis of interrelations among available educational options suggested that the tailors faced a smorgasbord of educational possibilities, no one of which had a strong constraining effect on access to the others. This appeared to be true whether considering the choices available to an individual or considering relations between the tailors' education and occupations and those already existing for other family members. Multiple educational experiences within quite different kinds of educational arrangements were common. In fact, the tailors' exposure to different educational arrangements was probably more varied than that of most American adults.

By choosing this sampling strategy, I biased experimental results (but probably not a lot) in the direction of increasing the probability that learning transfer from school might look stronger than it would have had the sample of school students not also been tailors. For the school student / apprentice would have had the opportunity, however brief, to bring school-learned skills into the apprenticeship process before the experiments took place. School students without any experience in the tailors' alley would not have had this advantage. Given this method of sampling, however, little transfer from school to tailoring tasks would be a stronger *disconfirmation* of school-based transfer than if "school" and "tailor" samples were constructed separately.

The interviews explored how decisions were made to enter and leave apprenticeship. I asked questions about who the decision makers were, about what issues had to be decided, and about processes of decision making. The more homogeneous these practices, the more likely they were to contribute to selection pressure or bias; the more varied the pathways to apprenticeship, the less likely they were to shape the tailoring population in systematic ways. The tailors differed in the following ways: starting age (and therefore whether his family or the apprentice himself chose a craft, indeed *this* craft), ethnolinguistic affiliation, family size, brothers' occupations, and whether parents thought they were choosing a livelihood that reflected the child's predilections or to help establish a portfolio of services within the family. The tailors were alike in their reported desire to become tailors at the time they were apprenticed, the fact that they said they would opt for another craft occupation were they not tailors, and that so many of their fathers were farmers. There were slightly more tailor fathers than would be expected by chance. Here was a whiff of bias, but it was pretty ephemeral I thought. That most fathers were upcountry farmers and many brothers in one or another craft provided evidence of occupational change across generations. I concluded that the decision makers, decisions, and decision processes were varied enough so as to be unlikely to produce a powerfully homogeneous group of tailors.

Another possibility for bias lay in the manner, frequency, and timing with which apprentices dropped out of apprenticeship before becoming masters. What if only an atypical minority survived? I tried several ways of finding out who had quit and concluded that about 85 percent of those who started apprenticeship completed it. Those who quit did so for a variety of reasons, most having nothing to do with the performance of the apprentice in learning tailoring. The reasons given were rather evenly divided between an apprentice's dislike for tailoring or bad treatment by a master, family decisions to remove the apprentice for reasons unrelated to apprenticeship, and a few masters' decisions to leave town, abandoning their apprentices.

In sum, it appears that decisions concerning entrance into apprenticeship were fairly casual. There were no prerequisites and no long-term preparation required to become a tailor's apprentice. No one had to decide about becoming a tailor at a critical early age. Individuals, out of work and desperate, were still apprenticing themselves as late as the age of thirty. Apprenticeship cost time and service to the master, but not money (except in the form of forgone income). A person entering apprenticeship had a high probability of completing it. Tailor's apprenticeship offered an attractive mix of high status and high accessibility. It did not automatically cause big changes in other educational possibilities. Nor did it narrow beyond repair the apprentices' range of occupational alternatives. I concluded that selection pressures on apprentices were not likely to produce experimental results that would confound the effects of learning transfer.

In contrast, the pressures to leave school were much stronger. Lack of financial support was the only reason given by the tailors for leaving school without completing the primary grades. Clearly access to schooling involved heavy financial pressure for those who participated in peripheral ways in the cash economy. Schooling was less accessible than craft training in geographic, social, and economic terms. There was also far heavier selection out of school than out of apprenticeship. So the strategy of choosing a sample of tailors and then letting that also select the sample of those who attended school was more likely to produce a reasonable representative sample of Vai and Gola urban dwellers than would choosing school students and then trying to find among them tailors' apprentices.

Two Perspectives on Task Familiarity

Table 3 lays out a continuum of experimental task familiarity from the perspectives of the tailor shop and school. The initial problems in the first two tasks (waistband estimation, extrapolating hip/fly measurements) were very familiar in the tailor shop. For example, on several occasions I had heard one tailor say to another the equivalent of, "Come on, if you're so good, tell me how big the hip ought to be if the waist is twenty-eight?" Estimating the size of a waistband was another thing that the tailors did frequently in their work; it too was "played" as an interactive game among the tailors. I thus copied from daily life not only the problems themselves, but also the forms in which they were posed in the experimental setting.

There was less similarity to ordinary practice in how the tailors' arithmetic problems were presented experimentally, although the content was certainly as familiar as in the estimation and extrapolation exercises. Thus, masters did figure out the circumference of a pair of trousers from its doubled size, flat on the table, but I did not observe tailors playing with this problem. A few times I observed masters asking apprentices to take the circumference and figure out the doubled measurement or vice versa, and the task "show me numbers on the tape" was taken directly from such master/apprentice interactions. In sum, the tailors' arithmetic problems were real problems encountered occasionally when the apprentices and masters were

TABLE 3. Predictions of task familiarity in tailor shop and school

TAILOR SHOP	
Familiar task	*Unfamiliar task*
Estimating waistbands and string loops	Estimating string and wood lengths
Extrapolating waistband sizes to hip/fly measurements; common waist sizes	Uncommon waist sizes
Tailors' arithmetic problems	Non-tailors' arithmetic problems
	Two-dimensional proportions (matching geometric figures)

SCHOOL	
Familiar task	*Unfamiliar task*
	Estimating waistbands, loops, string and wood lengths
	Extrapolating waistband sizes to hip/fly measurements
Non-tailors' arithmetic problems	Tailors' arithmetic problems
	Two-dimensional proportions (matching geometric figures)

taking time out from work. However, the experiments did not present them in a manner similar to daily encounters with these same problems.

Moving along in the direction of problems unfamiliar to tailors, estimations of loops of string, lengths of string, and lengths of wood were meant to form a progression of problems with which the tailors would have had less and less practice. These problems were posed to the tailors in the same way as the waistband estimation. Hence the form of the tasks was familiar, but the content most definitely was not. Likewise, in the extrapolation of unfamiliar waistband, hip, and fly measurements, the presentation was the familiar one of the game, but the sizes were quite out of the ordinary.

School arithmetic problems were placed in the context of homely objects—trousers, buttons, and spools of thread. But the tailors did not encounter these problems in practice on a daily basis. I doubt that any of the tailors ever had a large number of spools or divided them with someone else, for example. So these tasks were not familiar in either daily form or content.

The proportions-matching task was the least familiar from the tailors' point of view. The best that can be said for the drawings of pairs of trousers is that they were simplified, stylized, and used the perspective convention of one of the tailors, whose unsolicited drawings in my notebook provided the pattern for the picture cards. While the tailors could make judgments about the relative proportions of trouser waists to lengths, the task they were presented with was to match proportions in highly conventionalized two-dimensional drawings. The tailors customarily encountered varying proportions serially as they cut out one pair of trousers differently from the next. This task was unfamiliar except in content, very narrowly defined. Of course, the rest of the pictures in this task were of geometric shapes that none of the tailors encountered in any circumstances.

We can make the same sort of review of the tasks from a school-centered point of view. Most did not have familiar school content, since tailoring was not part of the math curriculum in the Monrovia schools. I doubt that geometric proportionality was a topic in the grades the tailors attended, and I doubt that estimation and extrapolation were taught either. Trouser waistbands, loops of string, lengths of string, and pieces of wood were unfamiliar to school students in a school context. The various waist (and hence hip and fly) measures were equally unfamiliar. The form of the waistband and waist/hip/fly activities was foreign to school settings; and even though the two-dimensional proportions task was a bit closer to interrogation styles in the classroom, the task as a whole was quite unfamiliar to school pupils.

The arithmetic problems were in a format familiar in school, although "show me numbers" and similar tasks recognizable in tailoring were not as common in a school context as the word problems that might be devised by an arithmetic textbook writer ("If I had sixteen spools . . ."). Thus, the school math problems were the most familiar and the tailoring problems least familiar.

The predictions on learning transfer that followed from this review of task characteristics were straightforward. Tailoring experience should have an effect on tailoring arithmetic problems, but not on school arithmetic problems. It should have an effect on waistband estimation and a decreasing effect on the estimation of loops, lengths of string, and lengths of wood. Tailoring experience should have a big effect on extrapolations from familiar waistband sizes to hip and fly sizes, and a smaller effect on the unfamiliar ones. Finally, we would expect that experience with tailoring would have very little effect on the two-dimensional proportions matching. School experience should have little effect on the proportions-matching problems, estimation problems, or extrapolation problems; some effect on the tailoring arithmetic problems; and a major effect on the school arithmetic problems. If the major impact of schooling was through its enhanced effect on general problem-solving skills, schooled tailors should do somewhat better on *all* of the tasks than the tailors who had not gone to school.

Doing in Experiments

Sixty-three tailors (thirty-three masters, thirty apprentices) took part in the arithmetic task. The arithmetic problems were presented orally in English to each tailor individually. In fact, all of the experimental work was carried out under similar circumstances. During this phase of the research, I rented a tiny space in the tailors' alley, partitioned off from the end of a larger shop. Two research assistants helped, one a Gola tailor, the other Vai. When a tailor came to work with us, one of the assistants asked the questions in English and wrote down the responses, but was ready to clarify answers in the tailor's first language. A measuring tape was available, and the tailors were free to use it in any way they wished during the arithmetic tasks (but not during the other experiments). I was present at all sessions, trying to get an intuitive sense about what was going on. Others were not allowed to be present while experimental activities were in progress.

I used regression analysis to explore the impact of tailoring and school-like problems of various kinds of educational experience. General experience variables included age (the most general measure of experience), years of tailoring, age at which the tailor started apprenticeship, stage of apprenticeship, and number of trousers the tailor could make in a single day. More specific measures of skill included whether or not the tailor could sew and cut out trousers and the amount of his experience measuring customers. Path analysis, an elaboration of multiple regression that compared series of equations to infer relations among the explanatory variables, supported the characterization of the variables either as specific measuring skills or as general experience. The general experience variables dropped out of the equations when the specific experience variables were introduced, and overall, general experience accounted for less variance than the specific experience variables. Schooling was measured by both last grade completed in school and by the English-language literacy test. On some tasks, I tried to explore the impact of Qur'anic training and Arabic literacy on math skills, and not surprisingly, I found no significant relationships.

Results

In order to draw conclusions about learning transfer as an effect of apprenticeship and schooling, I analyzed the performance of the tailors on each of the experiments: the arithmetic problem-solving task, the estimation task, the extrapolation task, and the geometric figure comparison task. Multiple regression analysis was central here, too, combined with simpler methods of comparison and ways of checking on the validity of my initial predictions of familiarity/unfamiliarity of problems within each task. In each case, I was looking for confirmation or disconfirmation of the predictions in table 3.

For different groups of tailors on different tasks, the learning-transfer experiments showed statistically significant patterned success, greater on familiar, less (or none) on unfamiliar problems. Patterns of relations among performances on the problems in each task confirmed pre-experiment estimations of the familiarity and dissimilarity of the problems from both tailoring and schooling perspectives. Regression analysis made it possible to go beyond simple questions of who performed better to explore patterns of relations in the tailors' lives and work, asking which educational experiences accounted best for differences in their performances on the various tasks and on the set of tasks as a whole. This meant shifting the emphasis of the regression analysis away from tweaking equations in order to maximize the amount of variance accounted for in performance measures (though I did that too). More attention was directed at exploring relations among the independent variables (the best, if impoverished, picture of the tailors' experiences available through statistical analysis).

The regression analysis produced several interesting results. First, there was quite a range of scores on the arithmetic task, including some perfect scores. The regression equations showed that the more schooling the tailors had, the better their scores on the familiar and unfamiliar school-like problems. Second, various measures of tailoring experience were good predictors of the tailors' performances on tailoring problems, familiar and unfamiliar, in the arithmetic task; the regression equations showed that the more tailoring experience the tailors had, the better their tailoring-problem scores. Thus, there seemed to be evidence of learning transfer for tailors who had been to school, just as the comparative theory of education and its corollary, cognitive learning transfer theory à la Judd, would predict. But also and equally present was evidence of learning transfer for apprenticed tailors who had not been to school. This finding ran counter to the predictions of the theory. Further, not only did tailoring experience have a statistical impact on tailoring-problem scores, but on the school math problem scores as well. So the "learning transfer" of tailors who had not been to school extended beyond "tailors' math" to "school math" problem solving. This was a stronger argument for the transfer capacity of apprenticed tailors than their ability to solve unfamiliar tailoring-derived problems. One additional finding gave added confidence in these results. Regression analysis is able to detect interaction effects, or conversely, to confirm that two variables act independently of one another. Had either schooling or tailoring experience influenced and intensified the effect of the other, we could not appeal to the result as evidence for either "school" or "apprenticeship" as a basis for learning transfer. In order to claim that both greater schooling and greater tailoring experience contributed to better performances on the arithmetic task, the statistical analysis needed to show that those effects were separate and independent of one another—and it did. It was possible to conclude, then, that the more tailoring experience the tailors had, no matter what their experience of schooling, the better they did on the math task.

My skepticism about comparative claims with respect to schooling as the engine of learning transfer was only deepened by findings with respect to the other experimental tasks: The uniform lack of impact of school experience on solving the mathematical problems built into the estimation, extrapolation, and proportions-matching tasks did not confirm the claim that schooling enhances general problem-solving skills across the board.[6]

A more serious challenge to the comparative theory was buried in these results: Considering the narrow scope of problems included in the arithmetic and other experimental tasks, the impact of *both* school and tailoring experiences looked quite small. Indeed, there are more significant meanings to the term "significance" than its statistical sense. Consider that other kind of significance—just how much difference could the "learning transfer" demonstrated in the experiments make in the tailors' lives? How many more problems could they solve? How important in their lives were these kinds of problems to start with? Would one or two or five or ten more years of schooling or tailoring experience be worth the resulting increase in calculational prowess (assuming we'd captured adequate measures of it in the first place)? Good grief, no. In fact a sensible weighing up of the experimental work concluded that there was *equivalently trivial* transfer from schooling and tailoring to unfamiliar problems in the experimental context.

Two conclusions seem clearly warranted now, although they felt much more tentative then. According to my experiments, schooling did not seem to provide psychological tools for learning transfer superior to those furnished by "non-" or "other" educational practices. And further, the negative findings of these experiments, when combined with earlier ethnographic inquiry, raised questions quite insistently as to whether a mentalist, individualist approach to doing learning, doing experiments, moving knowledge across contexts, or anything else, was a promising tool for capturing serious aspects of social existence.

Another Round of Experiments

After the experimental work, it might have made sense to claim a successful conclusion to the Liberian project and call it quits. Instead, worrying that I had done only a single set of experiments whose results were at odds with (some) common wisdom, I retreated into a technical assessment of possible problems with my "method" of designing and carrying out experiments, exactly as I complained that other cross-cultural experimenters were doing. I thought maybe I needed a better experiment. I wondered if the problem-solving activity I had observed represented "learning transfer," or another or several other phenomena. I got involved in a new round of discussion with psychologists who were sympathetically and similarly engaged, including Scribner, Cole, Ginsburg, and Serpell—we were all reading Gregory Bateson (1972)—and Ginsburg's students Andrea Petitto (1979) and Jill Posner (1978). Cole and his colleagues were working on issues of "ecological validity" (Cole, Hood, and McDermott 1978).[7]

There seemed to be several arguments for undertaking another round of experiments: The first round of arithmetic tasks had not explored the upper limits of the tailors' math prowess. Also, I wondered if a one-dimensional yardstick of problem "familiarity" was adequate for analyzing learning transfer. Perhaps "problem familiarity" should be decomposed into several "dimensions." Further, Ginsburg had made a critique of my experiments in a paper on the meaning of learning transfer:

> A comparison of success rates in the initial and new situations may be informative, but it is not directly relevant or conclusive so far as transfer is concerned. Knowing that a person succeeds at old and new tasks does not necessarily mean that he transferred anything from one to the other. To demonstrate transfer, one must show that he approached both tasks with the same strategy, principle, or response. Failure to demonstrate this is the chief weakness of most transfer research in the areas of cross-cultural studies and experimental psychology. . . . It is imperative to collect information concerning the processes of solution as directly as possible. This may require the use of naturalistic observation, the clinical interview procedure, and other relatively unorthodox . . . procedures. (1977, 8)

I thought Ginsburg's point was well taken.

In preparation for the next summer's experiments, I made a short list of ways to improve:

- Make the math more difficult by including several sets of problems varied systematically from a *mathematical* point of view.

- Differentiate the concept of familiar/unfamiliar problems into three dimensions of familiarity, exploring increasing numerical difficulty, a range of subject matter from the mundane to the exotic, and varying problems from concrete button arrays to pure numbers.
- Collect more careful data on problem-solving processes.

So, in a really giant step backward, I generated a systematic composition of problems from math and money "domains" combined with a systematic exploration of (school-organized) mathematical operations. The problems were designed to sample addition, subtraction, multiplication, and division at five levels of numerical difficulty: (1) one-digit numbers, (2) two-digit round numbers, (3) other two-digit numbers, (4) three-digit round numbers, (5) other three-digit numbers. Numbers and an operation were combined to produce the "skeletons" of the problems at each level.

Other criteria were used to assign additional context to the problems, for example, creating word problems with roughly the same degree of familiarity to the tailors in their daily arithmetic activities. The problems were divided into three series, scaled on the basis of my intuitions to reflect three dimensions of task familiarity that might conceivably affect transfer of old problem-solving methods. For the numerical difficulty scale, it seemed likely that big numbers would be less familiar than small numbers, so a series of problems ranged from below ten to several hundred. Some content presented in problems should be less familiar than other kinds. A mundane (familiar) problem would be, "You need to cut out seven pieces to make one hat. How many pieces for three hats?" A moderately exotic problem was, "You have sixty-four spools of thread and give eight of them to another tailor. How many do you have left?" And a very exotic problem was, "If Fanta bottles had four legs, and six bottles walked over to you, how many legs would you see?"

The third dimension was "abstractness" of problems. Cognitive theory assumed the concreteness of everyday experience, along with the more rarified character of abstract generalization. According to this theory, the more abstract the problem, the less familiar it should be in the tailoring milieu. So three types of tasks in this sequence were intended to provide a dimension of abstraction to the test: First, arrays of buttons were laid out on the table, and the tailors were asked to perform some arithmetic operation on the buttons. At the next level of abstraction were word problems using the content from the tailors' everyday work. And finally, some problems were asked as abstract number problems: "What is seven times five?"

The first fifteen problems ranged over five levels of numerical difficulty; nine problems ranged over four levels on the dimension of mundane to exotic content. Two concrete object problems, several word problems, and two pure number problems created a three-level abstractness dimension. I initially imagined giving problems representing all combinations of the levels on all three dimensions for each of the four arithmetic operations. But this would have severely overloaded the time and attention of the tailors. Instead, I made up a series of problems that varied along a single dimension while holding the other two dimensions constant at middle levels of their ranges. The middle level of abstractness being word problems, all of the exotic-mundane problems and the problems on the numerical difficulty scale were presented in word-problem format.

The outcome was an elaborate task in which essentially none of the problems were familiar *problems* in the tailor shops. Most were word problems. They came in sets clearly generated on the basis of contrasting operations, and it could be presumed that the task, viewed as a series of problems, was quite familiar from the schooled tailors' point of view. It resembled nothing more than a set of exercises in an arithmetic textbook—a very different approach to generating an experimental task than the ethnographic approach of the first round of experiments.

With this doubtful instrument in hand, I went back to Liberia. Seventy-five tailors took part in the new math task. They varied in tailoring experience from a few months to about twenty years (and from no schooling to about seventh grade). I watched and took notes, observing attempts early in the sequence to establish a sense of the pace and rhythm at which each tailor solved problems. I wrote down what I could see and hear: pauses, groupings and movements of groups of buttons, grunts, twitching fingers and eyebrows. After watching a tailor solve a problem, I asked how he had solved it. Responses very often made sensible the pause or the grunt. In general, the tailors were articulate in describing the procedures they used.

When I returned home with this second summer's experimental data, I struggled for months with their analysis. I began by sorting the tailors' performances on the concrete-abstract dimension by how much tailoring experience and schooling they had. The results did not support the comparative theory of learning transfer. Tailors who had and had not been to school did equally well on button arrays (no problem) but also on supposedly abstract numerical problems, where the tailors who had been to school should have done better than the tailors who had not attended school. Further, everyone's performance on number problems was as successful as on objects in arrays, when in theory the more abstract the problems, the worse everyone should have done. Meanwhile, the tailors who had been to school did better on word problems than they did on either problems involving objects *or* on symbolic number names. The tailors who had not been to school did notably worse on word problems than the tailors who had been to school, but they performed better on number problems, which theoretically they should not have done. What on earth was going on?

Word problems are a signature facet of arithmetic pedagogy in schools and were really unfamiliar to tailors who had not been to school. If we made a table of predictions for this math task like that for the first round of experiments (table 3), all those arithmetic operations and numbers combined into problems along numerical difficulty and mundane-exotic scales but presented at the "middle level" of abstraction (i.e., couched as word problems) would be shown as more unfamiliar to tailors who had not been to school than either number or button-array problems. Since these tailors could solve problems with buttons or numbers that were identical to ones they could not solve as word problems, it appears that the format—not the arithmetic relations—was giving them grief (cf. Lave 1988, 60–61; 1992). It thus seemed impossible to discover reliable (and valid) measures of the tailors' comparative arithmetic performances by exploring performances on the other two dimensions of problem familiarity.

All that work. Not much to show for it—about the tailors—though the exercise did lead to some critical findings with respect to the comparative theory of learning transfer. I confess to a certain amount of despair. The best that could be said for the summer's field experiment was that I now had on hand a good example of the distorting effects of an experiment designed on the basis of cognitive theory, notions of a decontextualized universal math "knowledge domain," and unexamined school-centric assumptions about arithmetic. There was still the third item on my short list of (now doubtful) ways to improve the second round of experimentation: "Collect more careful data on problem-solving processes." But with such a dog of an experiment, why bother?

Regrouping

A few months after giving up on analyzing group performance differences in the experiment, I described the problem-solving data to a mathematician, H. J. Reed. I told her about the notes I'd taken during the experiment. They afforded the possibility of looking at processes of problem solving by a single problem solver, or to contrast the practices of different groups of problem solvers. One feature of the second arithmetic exercise had been a number of parallel problems, couched in numbers and quantities of things on the one hand and as problems about money on the other. There were contrasting arrangements of numbers and operations in sets of problems as well, for which comparing problem-solving processes might help answer questions about the tailors' math practices. It was also possible to analyze the errors made by each tailor.

Reed's response to this inventory breathed life back into the project. In her view, arithmetics have not sprung forth like Athena, fully developed and ready to attack daily problems. In fact, they have slowly evolved as people have found better and more efficient ways to solve certain kinds of recurrent problems. She insisted we must establish the structure of Vai and Gola number systems before trying to analyze problem-solving processes and errors. To speculate about the particular problem-solving processes used in arriving at the solution to a problem required basic information about what Reed called an "arithmetic system"—a complex cultural-historical artifact being used by multitudes of problem solvers. An arithmetic system is composed of a set of number names (a numeration system) and a set of strategies for performing addition, subtraction, multiplication, and division. Most people make use of several numeration systems on a daily basis; most people use several strategies for performing arithmetic operations; the numeration system may or may not affect the strategies (Reed and Lave 1979).

For instance, in the United States, native speakers of English use at least three:

> spoken English, written English, and written Arabic. Any given number name in one of these three systems has a corresponding name in the others and stands for the same discrete quantity. Thus, it is irrelevant whether we enunciate "fourteen" or write 14; our audience will know the precise quantity we have in mind. (Reed and Lave 1979, 572)

There are also written numerals with their own independent rules of grammar, as well as permissible verbalizations within a given language. For example, we can say "two and a half dollars" for $2.50, but "a dollar and a half" is preferred to "one and a half dollars" for $1.50; and certainly it is not commonly accepted to say "two and forty-seven hundredths dollars" for $2.47. This can be contrasted with readings for 2.50 that would include, among others, "two point five oh," "two and fifty one-hundredths," and perhaps even "two and a half." One of the effects we considered was the interaction of written Arabic numerals, which were familiar to all the tailors, with their native language and with spoken English.

This multiplicity of ways of representing numbers occurs in widely different cultural-historical locations; it certainly occurs anywhere people are multilingual or know how to write. One of the major features of multiple numeration systems is that, though they represent the same concepts, they involve both distinct symbols and distinct rules of grammar for relating those symbols to produce number names. As a consequence, a given individual may use numeration systems that are either similar and perhaps reinforcing or dissimilar and mutually interfering.[8]

Reed argued that there are two classes of strategies for performing arithmetic operations, those that deal with quantities as such and those that deal with number names. Strategies that work with quantities are very widely used and manifest themselves as counting on fingers, manipulating pebbles and the like, or using an abacus. The tailors made use of counters—either movable ones, such as buttons, or marks on paper. Strategies using number names are typified by the Western algorithmic manipulations learned in school, for example, the litany for addition: "put down the four and carry the one." In such treatment, it is the manipulation of symbols that carries the burden of computation. Beside the common algorithms in U.S. school math practices, there are many others throughout the world, each tied to a particular numeration system but usable in related systems.

These observations made possible a fuller explanation of the tailors' performances on the misnamed "abstractness dimension"; those button-array problems and straight numerical problems required, respectively, quantity and number name manipulation strategies—basic to the use of any arithmetic system in Reed's terms, and in constant play in the tailors' lives.

We considered four arithmetic systems—the Vai/Gola, the Western school-taught, and the monetary version of each of these—in terms of their similarities and differences and the ways in which these affected the tailors' processes of problem solving. Reed's analysis allowed us to see that Vai and Gola five-, ten-, and twenty-based number systems worked differently than imported base-ten school arithmetic (the basis of the experimental task, of course). Monetary arithmetic, different spoken than written, supported yet two more ways of counting, combining, and decomposing quantities. For most problems on the arithmetic task, it took more, and more difficult, steps in the Vai and Gola arithmetic system to solve a problem than in base-ten school arithmetic. It was possible to determine for many of the tailors what arithmetic systems they were employing by drawing on the descriptions of their problem–solving processes, including analysis of the process through which errors were produced. We concluded:

> The "high-resolution" picture of individual differences . . . has made it possible to demonstrate consistent differences in the methods employed by tailors who have learned arithmetic in shop and school and among tailors with different amounts of shop experience. . . . We have good evidence that all but the youngest and least experienced apprentices have a clear understanding of general principles of arithmetic problem solving.

Errors, for all the tailors, are sensible: they stem from the arithmetic system in use.

The data do not support speculations by some psychologists and anthropologists that a skill learned incidentally in the course of daily activities necessarily leads to less general understanding than one learned "from the top down" in school. Rather, our data suggest that the practice opportunities available in the learning environment, and the social costs associated with various types of errors, account much better for the problem-solving difficulties encountered by tailors with different educational experiences. The tailors who learn arithmetic in the shop setting double and halve with alacrity; rarely do they encounter three-digit numbers, or even large two-digit numbers in the shop, however. They do have difficulty on the math test with large-number problems. Tailors who have been to school and have switched to school-taught arithmetic apply algorithms to problems of all sizes with greater ease but are more often the authors of wild errors that are left unnoticed. In the tailor shop, a very large error in trouser measurements or a customer's change would have more serious social consequences for the tailor than a very small error; but there is no different penalty for large errors than for small ones in school. The tailors' performances reflect these differences in their daily uses of arithmetic. . . . The organization of practice, rather than early instructional circumstances, may account for much of the variance in solution strategies. (Reed and Lave 1979, 580)[9]

The analysis of problem-solving processes, focused on how tailors used different arithmetic systems to solve problems, added to the conclusions of the earlier round of experiments concerning the artifactual nature of previous cross-cultural comparative experimental work. The second math task had posed exactly the question I had worked to prevent in the first round: "How do apprenticed and schooled tailors do arithmetic when faced with a specifically school-derived genre of math problems?" The legitimacy of a comparative analysis in search of an answer would depend on an assumption that the problems presented equal difficulties to tailors who approached the task with different arithmetic systems, or alternatively, on an assumption that all of the tailors used the same arithmetic system. Neither of these assumptions held up under closer analysis.

As Reed and I concentrated on a varied array of local arithmetic systems, I made an assumption in passing that we did not subject to critical review: a distinction between "school-learned" and "shop-learned" math. This was surely problematic, as we tentatively speculated at the end of our paper (and at the end of the quotation above). But since we didn't pursue it further, our uncritical silence left open the question of learning transfer. From where, in the little space and time blocked off at the end of the tailor's shop in which the experiments took place, did we think the tailors' problem-solving techniques had come? It was all too easy to slip back into assumptions of mental, individual transfer when that issue was not the main one on the table. But also, as argued at the end of chapter 3, pursuing conventional questions and methods for investigating learning transfer kept us from following the tailors through and across the different situations of their lives, which would undoubtedly have led to a more complex picture of the located character of the doing of learning math.

Obviously a next project, which arguably should have been a previous project, was a careful study of math teaching and learning in Liberian schools, especially schools that the tailors might have attended. In the early 1980s, Elizabeth Brenner did go to Liberia to make an ethnographic study of pre-first, first, and fourth grades in two rural primary schools and two in a larger town, attended by Vai children, with close attention to the teaching and learning of math (1985a, 1985b). Had it come earlier, her analysis of Vai schooling and math learning might have expanded and enriched our understanding of "school-based math" in the experiments, and conceivably it could have provoked more serious critical attention to the notion of "learning transfer."

Similarly, although I had recognized that math learning was a flexibly situated, incidental facet of apprenticeship, and although math had gained importance to the research project, moving front and center as the topic of two summers' (and two winters') of comparative experiments and analysis, math learning and situationally varied math practices were not a focus of inquiry during my initial ethnographic work in the tailor shops. I'd only been looking in the shops for common quantitative knowledge and the tailors' shared versions of riddles. Another round of fieldwork in tailor shops, if not yet plans for looking more carefully at Liberian school math, might now entertain more complex and interesting questions about math practice.

Commentary

"Learning transfer" is an impoverished idea for analyzing moving persons' knowledgeability in practice. First, the dualist theory strips life, active participation, and meaning away from all aspects of human existence except the individual mind. It then sets the mind in motion as a receptacle for transporting and applying unchanging knowledge-in-general to different situations in which knowledge is expected to change things in particular— to solve problems—without being changed in the process. The institutional arrangements of schooling as they appear thinly disguised in learning-transfer theory make knowledge a fixed product of instruction whose value lies in reproducing it with verisimilitude.[10] This view of the world is not only implausible; it embodies an authoritarian politics of "knowledge transmission" and "acquisition" that is questionable in every sense of the term. Second, a binary division between subject and world precludes questions about how they mutually constitute each other. If we think of the world as composed of a variety of places, locations, and institutional arrangements for life's activities, we must ask what holds them together and interconnects what goes on in one with another. To reduce these interconnections of history, culture, economy, politics, and activity to merely "transferable knowledge" is to impoverish and distort our understanding of social life.

So why, besides the binary comparative politics that insists on an unchanging, disembodied knowledge, does the concept of learning transfer continue to cast such a spell? The hegemonic domination of schooling and mathematics, separately and together, holds cross-cultural research in thrall, hangs over the hinterlands of schoolgoers' everyday lives, and makes "learning transfer" a ubiquitous political and symbolic concept (cf. Lave 1988). The concept of transfer is vital in justifying the institutional arrangements of schooling: sequestering learners and places of learning from other activities and locations while attempting to manage, for example, the uses of math in those other times and places makes "learning transfer" essential to the logic of schooling. If official knowledge (intended to displace or transform the knowledgeabilities of everyday life) is claimed to be vitally available only in school, this leads to the notion that "knowledge" must be pitched at a general level so as to be "applicable" in varied non-school situations. The notion of general forms with changing specific content is a fundamental assumption here.[11]

If not transfer, what? Where lie the continuities, connections, relations, and movements of time, objects, people, and ideas that a concept like "learning transfer," whatever its shortcomings, is trying to address? The experimental work with the tailors generated one of those unforeseen responses to an unanticipated invitation to change the direction of inquiry. At various points in the experimental work, questions had arisen about the lack of "transfer." As these questions persisted, they drew attention to the social-historical complexities of the tailors' lives/work/math. For instance, the frustrations of the second round of experiments stirred up unanticipated work on Vai and Gola number systems and their practical shaping of calculational practices. Analysis suggested that even for so-called universal, context-free knowledge—arithmetic—differences in the local social-historical constitution of number systems made a difference among the tailors in calculation practices.[12] My concern about what the tailors were doing, and indeed, doing differently from each other—for reasons that weren't heavily shadowed by the heavy hand of schooling—took over, leaving behind the question about the comparative impact of schooling on tailors' performances.

Two other candidate explanations for the triviality of the transfer effects in the experiments emerged in the course of analyzing the second round of experimental results. One was speculation that the experimental task did not match the grain size at which the tailors created sense and meaning. This was essentially the Thorndike problem. Did familiarity operate for the tailors at the level of problem components? Did they perceive problems as wholes? Were there dimensions of familiarity? There didn't seem to be an a priori answer. Any answer depended on the tailors themselves in the midst of their engagements in ongoing activity. This seemed to be an invitation to further ethnographic work. The other explanation of why there appeared to be so little transfer focused on the possibility that problem-solving processes depended on the circumstances the tailors found themselves in, physically, socially, and emotionally, when they were solving problems. This led to further questions: What if appropriate strategies under some circumstances did not work in other circumstances? What if the understanding of problems changed (or did not change) under differing circumstances?

These critical questions expanded to focus on popular claims that both math and psychological experiments had sui generis status in an otherwise historically, political-economically entangled world. It certainly looked as if the character of that "most universal" of subjects, arithmetic, was more complicated than assumptions about its universality were accustomed to encompassing. And I was coming to realize that comparative cognitive experimentation constituted an elaborate cultural practice as exotic as any other unexamined practice, and equally in need of careful analysis because of its built-in theoretical, social, and political implications.

This change in the place of experiments in the project should not be a surprise—the previous two chapters similarly trace a turn from the use of everyday concepts for analytic purposes to wondering about how those concepts facilitated conventional meanings in the world, and to realizing that those concepts needed to be turned into objects to be analyzed. This progression is a crucial, typical part of what is meant by the "critical" in "critical theory" and "critical ethnographic practice."

One of the most crucial "aha!" moments of the project was the result of working for months on detailed descriptions of the tailors' processes of problem solving. Reed and I had found that tailors who had gone past fourth grade in school used base-ten place-holding algorithms, worked on paper with a pencil, and underlined their answers. Their errors were often large and in powers of ten. Tailors whose arithmetic practice had developed in the shop used Vai and Gola number systems, made mostly small errors, and employed a maximum-effort version of what I thought of then as shop arithmetic. Many of their effortful performances appeared to be invented on the spot. Tailors who had been to school but only for a short time sometimes used school methods and sometimes used shop methods. But in spite of these careful descriptions and distinctions, I found myself increasingly uncomfortable with this work. It finally dawned on me that I had never seen any tailor, whether he had been to school or not, use the methods he employed in the experiments to deal with math in daily life in the tailor shops.

I went back to Liberia for another summer to pursue questions about the doing of everyday arithmetic in Happy Corner.

5 Multiplying Situations

Overview

Much of my analysis of experiments in chapter 4 focused critically on the practice of taking school math as the "gold standard" for interpretation and evaluation of experimental performances under the assumption that math cognition is the same anywhere and everywhere. In this chapter, I focus on problem-solving processes in the tailor shops. During my last round of fieldwork in 1978, I looked carefully at tailors' daily activities, trying to translate their interests in relations of quantity into well-formed—read, "school-like"—arithmetic problems. Even though I'd gone to great lengths to confirm the skewed ethnopolitics of learning transfer experiments, I began fieldwork again with the same old conventional assumptions about what constituted math problem solving. I did expect that the tailors' problem-solving processes in the shops would be different from those in the school-saturated experiments, but only gradually did I come to see how profound the differences were. This realization led to a question I found increasingly welcome over the life of the Liberian project, "What instead?"—an invitation to further ethnographic inquiry in order to travel off in new directions away from conventional theory or even its critique. In this case, that invitation raised unforeseen problems. It meant trying to find a different analytic stance, different questions and units of analysis less dominated by the formal/informal model of education and its assumptions and institutional arrangements. I invented my own comparative "mundane math" model for this purpose. After a while, I began to see that quantities were being produced in the tailor shops not just in mathematical relations with each other, but also in relations with other concerns of everyday life. Relations of quantity were part of the tailors' social fabric in inextricable ways that helped shape its meaning. Conversely, relations of quantity only had meaning as part of ongoing practice.

It was possible to employ the mundane math model to compare problem solving in the tailor shops to problem solving in the experiments described in chapter 4. Further, the ethnographic work on mathematical practices in the tailor shops made it possible to shift focus from individual problems and individual tailors to compare instead the shops and experiments as *settings* for problem-solving processes, enlarging the scale of comparison beyond two problems or two tailors. The mundane math scheme offered different, modestly less typical criteria for carrying out the comparison of tailor shops and experiments.

The Fat Man's Higher Heights Suit

During a two-week period, I kept track of all arithmetic problem-solving situations that I could recognize as such and many encounters with quantities that I could not. I made detailed notes concerning the activities of eight tailors and of incidents involving roughly as many more. Some of these tailors had been to school for a few years and others had not. Most of them had taken part in the experimental tasks of previous summers. By this time, I had known the tailors for five years and had spent many hours with them in the shops where most of these incidents took place. The tailors in the many examples that follow include G., age about twenty-eight, the Gola tailor who was Little M.'s master. An acute informant and good friend, G. had been a master tailor for almost ten years. He was currently enrolled in seventh grade in school. B.S., a Gola tailor in his early twenties, had been a master for two years and had never been to school. Little M.—the apprentice whose initial efforts at making a money bag, hat, and shirt collars were described in chapter 3—was also Gola. Only nine or ten years old, he was making rapid progress according to all the masters in the shop. J. was a Gissi-speaking tailor, unusual in several ways. He was in eleventh grade in school, and he was acknowledged by all to be the worst tailor in the shop, although he had been a master for three or four years. J.K., a middle-aged Vai man, had been a master for fifteen years and had never been to school. M.P., a Gola man who had not been to school, was in his early twenties. Very serious and very shy, he worked hard and said little. M. was one of the most respected tailors in Happy Corner, certainly one of the wealthiest. He was a devout Muslim who could read and write a little Arabic. (All of the tailors were Muslim except J.) A Gola man, M. had not been to school. While prestigious because of his relatively large business, he was unassuming, friendly, and well liked. V.G., a Vai in his early twenties, had been a master for about six years. He was outgoing and intense, with a flamboyant style of dressing. He had not been to school. A.K. was the oldest tailor in the alley and the judge in local disputes. He was Mende, from Sierra Leone, a devout Muslim, spoke Vai, and had not been to school.

Examples of problems in the tailors' daily activities that I could identify early on included arriving at an agreement with a customer about the price for a Higher Heights suit, figuring out how much cloth to buy to make a given number of a particular style of trousers, how to deal with a master who couldn't pay his share of the rent until a week from Friday, or how to cut out trousers to fit a big man. Here is an example of a negotiation over the sale of a Higher Heights suit:

> J. bargains with a customer over a Higher Heights suit the customer wants J. to make. At the same time, J. who is the least skilled tailor in the shop draws M.P. into the transaction (so that M.P. will do the hard parts of the suit). Other tailors take part in peripheral ways.

The tailors' desired outcome was quite simple: they wanted to get the highest possible price for making a Higher Heights suit. But the problem was still complex. The encounter involved negotiating a price, figuring out how much cloth was available, measuring the customer, arguing about how much time the job would take, deciding on buttons, making future transactions dependent on how this one went, figuring out how to cut out the suit for such a broad and tall customer, establishing that J. was who he claimed to be, waiting while M.P. went out to buy lining fabric and stiffening, dividing up the work, sharing the change, arguing over who would pay for pressing, and dividing the final payment. The customer was present for an hour in the middle of one afternoon and returned to complete the transaction and pick up his suit at 1 p.m. the next day.

> The customer comes in with a suitcase, which has cloth in it for a suit. He already knows J. He asks J. how much it would cost to make him a suit, conveying what he wants without committing himself to having J. do it. J. says, "It will cost about $18."

J. kept the amount inexact so as to secure maneuvering room for more money without scaring the man off. The customer countered that $14 or $15 would be a good price.

The man had brought with him a bit more than three yards of cloth. Cloth for a suit cost $3 a yard, so the man probably paid $10 for the cloth. There was a Higher Heights suit hanging for sale across the way for $25 for which the tailor supplied the cloth. So the customer was about right in his guess of $15 for labor and incidental expenses.

Meanwhile, M.P. takes the cloth and measures it to find out how much there is. He takes the tape and cloth in hand, while standing up, puts the 0 point at one edge of the cloth and measures to 36 inches. Holding the cloth at that point, he puts the tape down, folds the cloth back from the 36-inch mark to the 0 point, and then back to the 36 mark again and has a bit left over. G., who is simply observing the proceedings, says to M.P., "Three yards."

This was unsolicited help, two persons engaged in confirming a quantitative claim.

J. wants to take the man's measurements. It is to his advantage to get the man committed to having him make the suit before arriving at a price; instrumental moves towards making the suit have that effect. J. measures the man's waist and says, "35." He starts measuring and doesn't anticipate that he will need to record the measurements until he has a number and no place to put it. He looks for one of his school notebooks as he calls out the numbers. Meanwhile, he gets G.'s help, asking G. to write down the measurements each time J. calls a number. J. says to G.: "Waist 25." G.: "What?" J.: "35." G. writes it down while J. measures hips. J.: "Hip 42." G. writes, J. measures length. J. shows G. the point (39) on the tape that he pinched to mark the bottom of the trousers the customer is wearing. J. says, "39." J. asks the customer how wide he wants the bottom of the leg. I miss the customer's reaction, but infer that he wants it like his current trousers. J. measures the cuff of the trousers the man is wearing by doubling the cuff first. He measures 9 inches on the tape, then says "18" (by multiplying or adding two nines). Then he revises his estimate and says, "must be more . . . 19 . . . or more . . . 19 and a half!"

I couldn't see well enough to tell if he had anticipated the cuff as 18, simply measuring 9 and then looking at what was left over, or whether he actually measured the whole thing.

"Now shirt," J. says, which breaks the series of measurements into two parts. G. writes the second set, leaving some space after the trouser measurements. J. measures and says, "back 21." He means across the shoulders. Then J. measures from shoulder to wrist, bending the man's arm, and says (without naming what he's measured), "24." J. measures from back of neck to buttocks, "28." J. acts as if that is all he intends to do, and both G. and V.G., another tailor who has been watching, say, "measure his chest and waist!"

The two watching tailors served as a check on and also a memory aid for J., who followed their instructions, getting a chest measurement of 39, and a waist of 38, just below the customer's potbelly. J. then started to close the transaction, assuring the customer that the job would be finished quickly:

> "The suit will be done at 11 tomorrow," [J. says,] just as M.P. brings in the Higher Heights suit from across the way and shows the customer buttons. The customer nods yes, the buttons are OK. J. says, "I charge you $18.50. This is higher than the vague price first offered, of "about $18." The customer comes back with, "You say this ready made suit $25. I brought my own cloth. . . . Then you tell me $18.50?"

Of interest in this exchange is how throughout the bargaining process, the two parties wove in and out and came back to the same issues. J. first made a quite speedy offer about how long the job would take—until "11 tomorrow"—following it up immediately with a high price. It should not be surprising, then, what his comeback was to the customer's pointing out he'd brought his own cloth: "I'm very busy right now." (Read: "I won't get it done by 11 tomorrow." Or "speed is one reason I'm charging a price you think is too high.")

There was more bargaining talk, which was too low for me to catch. Then J. asked, "O.K., how much you pay?" The customer replied, "I got $10." This was not a response to the question of what he would be willing to pay, but a new move, whereby he was trying to make the amount he was willing to pay in advance a lever in establishing the final price.

> J. then talks about how many expenses he will have in making the suit: the cost of stiffening and buttons—it will take ten buttons, he says. And pressing is $1.50. This is not true. All the tailors, apprentices as well as masters, know that suit pressing costs $1. "So, it will cost a lot to make the suit."
>
> [The customer says,] "Pressing—that's your business." Then he says, "OK, I pay $15."

As soon as the customer agrees to pay $15, he starts urging J. to start on the suit immediately. Next he says how important and non-negotiable the deadline is because he has important business tomorrow in Grand Bassa. So he has come up slightly in price, but is trying to get J. to provide services—the bargaining is not over yet. The customer gives J. $10, then looks at J.'s I.D. card to see if he is who he says he is. J. agrees to the time—"Come back at 11 in the morning." The customer, in his turn gives something. He says, "If you make it well, I'll come back again," offering future business contingent on the quality of the current job.

Meanwhile, during the conversation between J. and the customer, M.P. had measured the cloth again, this time in order to cut it in two pieces. I missed how J. and M.P. negotiated the agreement that they would work together, and how they were going to divide up the work. It would likely be understood, if they agreed to work together, that J. would do the trousers and M.P. the jacket, since M.P. was quite skilled and J. was not. The two tailors would need two pieces of cloth, one for the pants, one for the jacket.

> G. tells M.P. to measure "one and a quarter [yards] of cloth and four inches" for J.'s share of the cloth, and [comments], "This is good 'cause man is fat!"
>
> M.P. takes the $10 the customer gives J. and goes off with it to buy stiffening and lining, while the customer sits and talks about his business dealings to J. who sews on a [pair of] trousers he was working on before the customer came in. M.P. comes back. M.P. and J. check the change to see if it is right. The customer helps count the change that is spread out between them.
>
> J. says he will write down expenses in his school notebook. He says out loud as he writes: "stiffening, lining . . ." After one more item he stops. This list is never completed or referred to again. Neither M.P. nor the customer responds to the idea of making a list. J., discouraged, quits. School math is discouraged in the shop setting. There are some final leave-taking remarks, and the customer leaves.
>
> J. says to M.P.: "The balance money is what we share."

That is, J. tried to persuade M.P. to wait until the customer finished paying for the suit before dividing the money. But M.P. wanted to divide up what was left of the initial payment immediately. After buying the lining and stiffening, there was $8.60 left—a five-dollar bill, three silver dollars, and sixty cents in change.

> J. goes on, "We won't spend any of the profits until it all finish." M.P. takes 10 cents, J. writes it in his notebook. G. laughs at J's exaggerated account keeping routine. M.P. clearly wants to divide the money. J. compromises: M.P. and J. end up each taking 30 cents, that is, they divide the change equally between them. J. wraps the $5 [bill] and the 3 silver dollars in a piece of paper and puts it in his pocket. G. says to me, "Maybe J. will spend some tonight." M.P. leaves to cut and sew the coat at home.

G. comments, "They won't carry equal." Then with heavy sarcasm he adds, "Maybe M.P. carry more 'cause making the coat is harder." But we both know that J. is ruthless and not very honest, that M.P. is a gentle, unassertive person, and that M.P. is likely to get cheated by J.

The next morning at 10 a.m. M.P. is working on the front of the jacket, and it is not very far along. J. is not yet in. J.K., another tailor in the shop, takes the suit jacket from M.P.'s machine, looks at the details carefully, and hands it back to M.P. M.P. goes on working on it. At 10:50 G. arrives. As he passes M.P.'s machine, he picks up a sleeve of the coat and looks at it carefully. He puts it back (again, no comment). J. comes in. J. and another tailor, J.B., look over the trousers to the suit. J.B. points out an uneven place in the hem. J. shrugs.

I was out of the shop when the customer came to claim the suit. G. told me about it later:

"J. says each man carry $5.75 (and J. give J.K. and me each 50 cents)." I asked G. why J. gave them the money. He shrugged, "I don't know, maybe because we helped with measuring the man." Perhaps he was trying to keep them from complaining on behalf of M.P. For after all, as G. said at the end: "J. cheat M.P.—jacket harder than trousers."

The making of the Higher Heights suit illustrated some features of (my still school-shadowed view of) arithmetic problem solving in the midst of other ongoing activity. The process was interactive. Calculations were carried out as part of a broader strategy for making a profitable sale of a suit. Not only was calculation not an end in itself, but when I asked another tailor who had been a coparticipant in the project to sum up the transaction with the customer, he gave a detailed history of the changing inputs to the calculation over the thirty-hour period, as the fortunes of the various players waxed and waned. He seemed more interested in these shifts than in following out various calculations to their solutions.[1]

Mundane Math

Two issues seemed pressing for analyzing and interpreting what I was seeing in the tailor shops. On the one hand, I needed some way to describe quantitative relations that did not immediately impose a school-based theory of problem solving on what might or might not be "schoolish" sorts of activities in tailor shops. On the other hand, what were the tailors doing, if not math as in school? I thought that in the tailor shops precise calculation of the answer to an arithmetic problem might be a last resort, only undertaken when all else failed, and I began to speculate about why this could be so.

In an attempt to articulate what I was seeing in "non-schoolish" terms, I invented a scheme for analyzing "mundane math." It began with the idea that where one procedure for problem solving required more effort and another procedure required less, it seemed reasonable that tailors would generally prefer the latter. The less precise the calculation, the less effort required; a memorized solution required the least effort; and it would often be less work to recruit someone else to carry out a calculation than for a tailor to do it himself. Second, the fact that most arithmetic problems arose in the midst of social interaction increased the likelihood that arithmetic calculation would be low priority, for calculation would require temporary withdrawal from interaction or disrupt conversation. Social strategies for gathering inputs for arithmetic calculations and for obtaining solutions to arithmetic problems seemed less disruptive to ongoing interaction than precise calculation. Third, we should therefore expect to see lots of alternatives to calculation as an end in itself. If this turned out to be true, it would place mundane math activity in the tailor shops at odds with conventional assumptions about a constant, transferable math practice with a constant purpose, salience, and value. Certainly some of these notions were apparent in the example of the fat man's Higher Height's suit.

These assumptions allowed me to start making sense of what tailors did with quantitative relations in the tailor shops in somewhat different terms than the comparative education model of school math. I began to see that the tailors often used old results, carried out updates and comparisons, used specialized meters for specialized content domains, and made specialized calculations, generated on the spot, often associated with "tables" of inputs and their associated solutions. The tailors shared customary presuppositions about how precise the solutions for different kinds of problems needed to be. Money transactions were meticulously precise while constraints on generating other kinds of quantities were often less stringent than those connoted by "precise calculation," reducing the amount of effort required to solve problems.[2] Further, because arithmetic problem solving was usually quick (compared to the time it took to negotiate and complete the sale of a Higher Heights suit) and because it was only one among many things going on in most situations where math was involved, some features of particular calculational activity seemed to arise from its subordination or incorporation in more important and more broadly defined issues for the tailors. This was a crucial possibility. It implied that general features of arithmetic problem solving were not sufficient to predict specific features of calculational activities. In order to understand why particular relations of quantity got treated as they did, it would be necessary to go outside the characteristics of arithmetic calculation to find out what other concerns shaped particular problem-solving procedures.

The rest of this chapter explores these ideas, moving from the more specific focus on doing calculating in the tailor shops to exploring social relations of calculational work, and finally to letting go of the notion of math problems as things in themselves, in a discussion of calculation as part of more pressing concerns.

Calculating

CONTEXTUAL RESOURCES

For the tailors, the alley was a rich setting in which to pursue their daily work and its attendant calculations. A great deal of what they needed to know could be found near at hand. There were a dozen tailors in the shop whose daily lives transpired in a common place in very similar ways, but whose specific knowledge differed, and who could be called upon for help. Access to other peoples' knowledge was socially organized. The tailors operated with the tacit assumption that anyone present with appropriate knowledge would volunteer it. (The Higher Heights suit example was full of such moments.) One tailor often didn't even need to know what another tailor knew in order to gain access to it.

The shop down the alley where sewing notions were sold served as a powerful interactive organizer of memory. For example, B.S. set off to get a buckle for a belt and some buttons, and he came back with an additional purchase—eyelets in the belt for the buckle to attach to. The tape measure was a metering device that stored information, and because of its standardized nature, it made information about other tailors' craft practice more accessible. And perhaps most important, the openness of the tailor shop, where tailors had ready access to each other's activities, meant that craft and trade information could be seen and overheard, gossiped about, and exchanged, copied, and acted upon. Clearly, problem-solving strategies did not depend exclusively on information stored in the tailors' heads. Problem-solving strategies involved the local setting and very often a reliance on the unfolding of events to produce new information or to produce circumstances that made it clear that new information was needed or additional action required. Calculations might well end up stored in the daily life of the shop as well—whether in a pattern piece for hat sections or in a distant customer's body (he could be measured again if he ever came back).

PRECISION CONSTRAINTS

Shared, customary precision constraints bracketed every familiar, repeatedly encountered, arithmetic problem. But these constraints varied, sometimes more precise and sometimes less, depending on the requirements for accuracy in different settings. They were not always symmetrical around the target figure—think of how one figures how much gas is *left* in the tank—but by being appropriately broad they reduced the amount of calculation required.[3]

In making ready-to-wear trousers and shirts, the tailors' precision for waistband size had about a three-inch range, evenly spread around some target measurement. Replies to two of my questions in the shop may serve as examples:

> I asked J. earlier for the sizes of the different trousers that he had hanging up outside the shop to sell. We go out to look at them. He says "30" for the first pair, then looks uneasy. Then when I pursue the sizes of others he stops me and says, "I don't know what sizes. When I sew them they not all the same. But 28, 30, 31 is what I try for." V.G. says that he makes his shirts 17 or 18 at the shoulders.

> G. is cutting out trousers for B.S. to sew. "What size?" I ask. G. says, "Well, I don't know. I will cut them 29, 30, 31. But he (B.S.) sew it, to him." [The final measurement will depend on how B.S. sews it].

All of the tailors used the tape measure to construct the pattern for trousers on the cloth when they were cutting them out. Measuring and cutting determined the waist size within two or three inches. But the finished size depended on how the trousers were sewn, in particular how the seat seam was adjusted, given that the side seams had already been sewn. In the making of a series of thirty-five pairs of trousers, the tape measure was employed during the sewing process in only two cases. In both instances, the trousers were being made for customers who had been measured. The contrast is a good illustration of what is meant by precision constraints. A custom-made pair of trousers was made to fit the customer, but customers who came looking for ready-to-wear trousers fit themselves into the variety of sizes available.

There were one-sided precision constraints as well. If an error was made in sewing trousers for a customer, it was clearly better to make them too big than too small. This was reflected in questions the tailors asked customers:

> G. gets ready to cut trousers. "What waist size?" I ask. G: "I don't know. But when finish, not more than 37." He measures the usual pieces to cut

out. "You want the waist 38 or 37?" The larger number, given first, is an invitation to the customer to request that the trousers be conservatively large. The tailor continues, "You want them all over big?"

Bargaining also involved relatively loose precision constraints. For instance, bargaining never proceeded in units smaller than half a dollar if the asking price was five dollars or more. For hats and small items whose asking price was under five dollars, bargaining sometimes proceeded down to the level of twenty-five cents. But essentially neither buyer nor seller expected finer tuning.

On the other hand, it would appear from the learning transfer experiments that finer precision in figuring prices and in dealing with quantities was required in the shop than in school-like situations. In the shop, there was little tolerance for errors, for example, by an apprentice bringing back change for a forty-cent purchase for his master. Another way to put the same thing is to say that in the shop there was tolerance only for small errors. And even the term "error" here may be inappropriate if school precision constraints were being applied in a situation where different precision constraints were customarily in effect. A thirty-four-inch waistband when the tailor intended thirty-three would be an error by school precision constraints but not by shop standards. In contrast, in school a large error was penalized to the same degree as a small error.

OLD AND NEW INSTANCES OF THE SAME PROBLEM

Old and standard results. Some arithmetic problems in the tailors' shop occurred frequently. The kinds of inputs to such problems were well known, as were the operations to be performed. On many occasions, the only thing that was new was the particular value of an input. One implication was that old results were often good enough if precision constraints were relatively loose. If a tailor sewed trousers for the same customer several times, he remembered the measurements and didn't bother to measure the customer again the next time. The cost of pressing trousers rose slowly. So did the cost of fabric. Therefore, using prices from the last trip to the laundry or cloth merchant's to decide how much money to send along with the apprentice making the trip was close enough. Old results had a very important role in bargaining. Again, think of the man bargaining for the Higher Heights suit. Without knowing the usual price, it would have been very difficult for him to bargain effectively.

Many problems were solved as soon as the difference between even one old input and a current input was known. Thus, much more of the tailors' problem-solving activity was directed at establishing those differences, and at establishing their implications, than in carrying out calculations. Using relations between old and new instances of a problem as a basic problem-solving strategy was a very common alternative to calculating the solution to a problem. It followed that people had rather general knowledge of the principles of arithmetic, on the level of recognizing that if a particular amount was added to any input in an addition problem, the solution would increase by the same amount. Subtraction would have the reverse effect. Similar principles existed for multiplication and division.

Decisions instead of solutions. Another implication of the proposition that some problems of quantity were familiar, that the representation of a problem was mainly a matter of recognizing what it had in common with earlier ones, becomes clear in the following transaction: Two men were bargaining over the sale of a dozen hats that they intended to resell on the street. The last hat was not ready at the time a price was agreed to, and the buyers went off for a couple of hours on other errands.

> While B.S. starts sewing hats fast, G. says that the new, cheap cloth he has just bought is $1.50 a yard. The blue denim they used before (out of which the eleven hats on the table are made) was $2.50 a yard: five hats, one yard. Sell each for $1.50, or for lots of hats $1.25. He doesn't complete the calculation of profit. He has given me enough information so that I could figure either the break-even point in sales, or the average expected profit. After the rest of the exchange, however, I came to the conclusion that G. had given me the information he was working with, the information that had gone into his calculation.
>
> Meanwhile, B.S. sews hats very fast, and does not sew facings into the ones he is making now. Gradually their strategy becomes clear. If they make several hats out of cheap cloth before the two men get back, they can mix them with the more expensive hats the men thought they bought, and make more profit. The two tailors mix them in, alternating types of hats, until they have six of each. The men, when they come back, accept the stack. Success. All G. and B.S. needed to "calculate" was that $1.50/yard is less than $2.50/yard, and that they would make more by selling the cheap hats than expensive ones.

The price the men paid didn't change; the number of hats didn't change. All that changed was one input into a profit calculation, the price of materials. Because problems like this were well-known and only input values changed, alternative strategies to precise calculation focused on relations between old or standard inputs and current ones, rather than operating on new inputs to produce a new result.

The outcome of such a process was very often a decision about a problem rather than a solution to a problem. That is, G. and B.S. decided to extract as much profit from the customer as possible. This decision was made without going through a calculation of expected profit on six cheap and six expensive hats. It did involve a knowledge of relations between inputs and solution, that is, that cheaper inputs result in higher profit.

One reason for emphasizing the comparison of old and new inputs is that it helped to account for what, observing math activity in the shop, I described to myself as "lots of single numbers floating around." There weren't very often verbally described problems, and the answers weren't very often the numbers I heard. More common were single numbers, both because a changed input was sufficient to point to an appropriate decision, and because input figures were hard-to-find, problematic parts of daily quantitative dilemmas. In the example of the fat man's Higher Heights suit, it took twenty-four hours to get figures for M.P.'s profit calculation. It may be that skill in math in the tailor shops was focused more on extended activities for generating appropriate inputs to calculations than on doing those calculations in a schoolish sense. Given the difficulty associated with finding inputs, it made good sense to concentrate on relations between old and new inputs and to use old ones (or differences between old and new ones) as a basis for making decisions.

Friendly number facts, lists, and tables. One way in which comparison of old and new inputs manifested itself was in the lists and tables of stable inputs and solutions to standard problems that the tailors used frequently.

V.G. says, "Fifty cents for twelve [buttons]. I want to buy all [of a sack] for $3.50 but a customer sell them to me for $2.50. Twelve dozen [buttons]. Each shirt take five button.

"Each shirt take three button, then four shirt take one dozen button. But some shirts five button. Then dozen take two shirts, two button over. Four shirts then one dozen buttons, one dozen buttons take two shirts and two left over."

I ask, "If you buy a dozen at a time, how much would you pay for the whole sack?"

The answer comes quickly, "$6."

"How do you know?"

"Ten dozen, $5," he says, with an "any fool would know that" inflection. "So twelve dozen, $6."

This exchange provides evidence for what I think were, in effect, tables. V.G. was using at least two closely related tables. One was the cost of x number of dozens of buttons. The other included how many shirts with different numbers of buttons (including at least three and five) could be completed with a unit purchase of buttons (one unit = a dozen). Moving up a list of button-dozens from one to six was a way of using old results to generate new ones. The focus was on systematic relations between inputs that belonged in the same problem.

A second characteristic of the tailors' tables and lists was that they were specialized. That is, they could be viewed as crystallized instances of old inputs to recurring problems. Because of their interrelation with specific problems, they were clearly defined, there were lots of them, they were relatively small in size, and the tailors seemed able to move from one to another with little effort. A break-even calculation was a typical table.

> One yard cloth, $2.50. Get five hat from it. Sell them $1.50 to one person to wear [i.e., not wholesale]. One more hat covers thread and yellow rubber fabric [to trim hats]. So two hats are to you.

A break-even calculation told the tailor at what point in a series of sales the money taken in was profit over and above the amount invested in materials. In contrast, a total expected profit for the sale of, say, a number of pairs of trousers made in one spate of work, was rarely calculated. I asked a tailor how many hats he could make with a yard of cloth:

> He says, "Five hats. I sell for $1.25 because four hats, $5." I think he arrived at this total by addition—it wasn't memorized because it took too long. At one point I hear him say "$3.75," which would be three hats. This supports the idea that he was adding.

In general the tailors refused to speculate about expected sales, pointing out that since they bargained over the selling price they didn't sell all garments for the same amount and they could not figure out how much they would make. I pushed M.P. on the subject one day:

> He is making seventeen shirts today. He says he will sell one for $2.50. I ask him how much he will get when he sells all? He replies, "I sell them one, one [not wholesale]. "Someone pay $2, someone have $2.25, maybe." I ask, "But if you sold each one $2.50?" M.P. uses his fingers to represent the number of shirts, I think. His movements are small and don't seem systematic enough to be more than a very rough memory aid. He says he'll have to figure it out. Then after maybe thirty seconds he says $42.50. I ask him to explain how he figured it out. "Two shirts, $5. Two shirts, $5.

So four shirts, $10. Eight shirts, $20. And eight shirts more, $20 dollars, sixteen shirts, $40, and one shirt more, $42.50.

The tailors complained often that they didn't know how much they were making or spending over a month. In discussions about why some tailors were moving from self-employment in the tailors' alley to work in the garment factory, different tailors offered more regular income as a reason. That is, although they thought they would make less money if they worked in the factory, they would regularly get paid a salary. They would at least know how much they were earning each week and could make decisions about how to spend it better.

The problem of cash flow and the contrast between common break-even calculations and rare total-sales calculations were the same: the difficulty of maintaining an ongoing calculation over long periods of time. Break-even events happened more quickly and involved fewer sales than finishing the sale of a whole run of shirts. A problem that could be worked comfortably in a minute or less became much more difficult if it took more than two days. Record keeping was one way to beat the time problem. But it would be a mistake to characterize the ability to write down inputs or solutions to arithmetic problems as a crucial factor in changing the cognitive characteristics of people's minds. It seems obvious that the contribution of literacy in this case was to increase the information available in Happy Corner. Literacy probably had its greatest impact on the information available in the environment and only secondarily on how people searched the environment and under what circumstances. But these practices seemed different to me from the kinds of effects literacy was hypothesized to have on cognitive skills.[4]

Social Strategies: Calculational Division of Labor and Its Limits

It followed from my discussions with tailors about problem solving that there might well be a calculational division of labor in the relatively sustained settings of their shops, where they had ready access to each other. A tailor often found it easier to get someone else to solve a problem than to do it himself, though there were other reasons for taking the opposite tack. And because in many cases, calculation was required at precisely the time that attention needed to be directed to an ongoing social interaction—such as negotiating a sale with a customer, when withdrawing would be unsociable, even antisocial—every tailor was likely to call on other tailors for help with calculations. Partly owing to the openness of the tailor shop, tailors also readily volunteered aid to each other. All of these circumstances

helped to produce the shifting and fluid nature of the division of calculational labor. This was not a setting in which one tailor functioned as trouser-
construction diagnostician or chief cashier. It was accepted by all in the tailor shops that a certain kind of mathematical literacy could be learned in
school. But while in fact literate tailors acted informally as scribes (reading
legal documents, writing letters), there were virtually no appeals to those
who had been to school to use their arithmetic skills on behalf of those who
had not attended school. All the tailors in the shop had, by their own standards, an adequate knowledge of their various arithmetic systems to handle
the problems they encountered in the tailor shop.

At various times, tailors used bystanders to solve problems, asked colleagues for information about problem inputs, got help unsolicited from all
tailors in the vicinity of a problem, and fixed problems so that a less experienced apprentice could solve them.

> B.S. needs "hardware" in order to finish four pairs of trousers, including
> press snaps for the waist, and fly buttons. One pair has a cloth belt and
> needs a buckle. G., who will pay for the hardware, asks B.S. how much
> each item will cost. G.: "Buckle?" B.S.: "30 cents." G.: Press button? B.S.:
> "15 cents, one." (G., like all the tailors, already knows the cost of trou-
> ser buttons.) G.: "Buy four press buttons, 10-cents trouser buttons, 35-
> cent buckle." (Apparently he mishears B.S.'s "Buckle 30 cents" remark.)
> "That's 1[dollar] and 5 [cents]. I got a dollar." B.S. goes out for a 30-cent
> buckle and the buttons, taking G.'s dollar. He comes back with press but-
> tons, and trouser buttons, but not a buckle. B.S. says, "30-cent buckle too
> small." G. then turns to another master tailor, L.M., and asks, "What size
> buckle do I need?" The other tailor says, "50-cent buckle." G. interpolates
> and decides to try a 40-cent buckle. (I miss what happens about the ad-
> ditional money. B.S. has already spent 70 cents and needs 10 cents more
> to buy the buckle. Maybe he just contributes it out of his own pocket?)
> B.S. goes off to get the buckle, taking the cloth belt with him. B.S. returns
> with the 40-cent buckle and also has gotten metal eyelets put on the belt,
> which G. had forgotten. B.S. tells G. that two eyelets cost 5 cents and the
> belt needs four eyelets. G. gives B.S. a dime and sends him back to pay the
> shopkeeper who did the eyelets.

The calculations in the problem changed as information increased. Requests
for help and volunteered help both led to additional useful knowledge.

Social strategies varied in relation to the subject matter of calculations.
Taking in money was something tailors preferred to do privately. So the tailors generally conducted bargaining with customers in front of the tailor

shop rather than inside, where other tailors could easily hear and watch transactions. There were prohibitions on asking fellow tailors what price they had sold things for. Thus, G. commented that M. wouldn't tell him what he sold trousers for, even if G. asked him. Spending money was different. Here the more information the better, especially in bargaining situations. The man bargaining for a Higher Heights suit managed to make his offer stick mainly because he knew the asking price for a ready-to-wear Higher Heights suit in the shop across the alley and the price of the cloth he had brought himself. When he didn't know the price of pressing a suit, he rejected that cost as an issue in the bargaining. He was very good at managing information. The buckle example above underscores the information-, and misinformation-rich setting of the tailors and especially the sometimes conflicting social strategies employed in finding inputs for mundane problems.

The example of the fat man's Higher Heights suit contained instances of a calculational division of labor as M.P. and G. measured the cloth and decided how much should be used for making the trousers and how much for the jacket while J. continued to bargain with the customer over the price and delivery time. But given the characteristics of mundane problem solving, the kind of cooperation possible between people trying to solve the same problem was limited. There were not many situations in which one person said "five plus," another said, "three equals," and a third finished, "eight." I can think of but one example of this kind of interrelated exchange in the tailor shop, between G. and M.P. talking about measurements, and they had worked in the same shop for a long time:

M.P. says in English, "28 inches." Then, "31 inches."

G. says, "Three and a half yard. One and three quarter each. One and one quarter [is too] small. One and three quarter."

M.P. immediately nods and says, "Three and a half yard."

G. quickly says, "$10.50" (the price for three and a half yards of trouser cloth).

Mostly cooperation was limited to checking and confirming activities. That is, the necessity of attending to a calculation made cooperation in calculation a limited strategy. Two people could solve the same problem in parallel with each other, but with a few exceptions such as the one above, could not actually work on the same calculation cooperatively. In particular, checking operations seemed to be social processes in which consensus was the criterion for correct calculating. In the case of the Higher Heights suit, J. counted the change that M.P. brought back after buying stiffening and lining for the suit. As he checked M.P.'s transaction, all three participants (J., M.P., and the customer) became silent and focused on the moving coins. Little M. brought back change and B.S. counted it, repeating the problem-solving process as a means of checking.[5] Also in the Higher Heights suit example, G. watched as M.P. first measured thirty-six inches on the cloth, then folded it in thirds. As he finished, G. said, half to M.P., half to himself, "Three yards." He had been working the problem also. And, of course, the tailors could count on each other to act as prompters and volunteers of information during their easily observable transactions, as when several tailors told J. about measurements he had forgotten to make.

In any situation in which two people attempted to solve the same problem, either to help each other out or for opposing reasons when, say, bargaining, buying, and selling, there was some advantage in using the procedure it was assumed that the other person was using in order to make communication easier if either was called on to explain or defend the result. A good deal of the effort that goes into simplifying problems—"I'll sell you one pair of trousers for $8.50, two for $8 each"—as well as effort to make it easy for two people to use the same calculation process, probably grew out of concern for maintaining the trust of the other person. It was to the tailor's advantage to make the problem simple enough that the customer could solve it accurately and easily, for this helped to establish the tailor's trustworthiness and goodwill. Using congruent methods for solving problems contributed to this same goal.

Social pressure toward the use of congruent methods was a major factor in why tailors did not use school math in the tailor shops. Certainly on the two occasions during the negotiations for the Higher Heights suit when J. tried to write down elements of the monetary transactions, a process that could not be duplicated by either of the others, he was ignored and was unable to proceed with this method of keeping track of the money.[6] Even tailors who had fairly extensive schooling said that when working in the shop they used arithmetic like everyone else.

Calculation as Part of More Pressing Concerns

A number of considerations shaped the value of calculations for the tailors—that value often being minor or subordinate to other concerns. One such consideration was the desire for symmetry in garment construction. Another had to do with the resolution of disagreements within the tailor shop in a way that played off the tailors' serious bargaining, a style that might be called "caricatured bargaining."

SYMMETRY

The goal of making a symmetrical pair of trousers was clearly much more important to the tailors than making a precisely sized pair of trousers. A tailor could sell trousers with a waist of 29 3/16 inches, or 35 5/9, but not trousers with one leg longer than the other or with the back seam two inches off center. Therefore procedures for making many size calculations were made to accommodate desires for symmetry. If symmetry were of no concern, the measurement calculations might have been done quite differently.

> M.P. doubles the tape and doubles a bunch of nested strips of cloth and holds the tape along one side, in order to cut out collars for shirts. This ensures that the collars will be symmetrically cut, although it gives up some accuracy in size. (Also, notice that this procedure reduced the need for calculation: by knowing only the desired finished length for the collars, and folding the tape so that the zero point met the desired length, he avoided having to halve the finished length in his head.)

The processes used to ensure symmetry led to unusual procedures for measuring. If linear measurement were the only concern, such measurements could be made more accurately and with less effort by measuring the desired distance on the cloth and subsequently folding it the required number of times. But in making salable trousers, the subordination of measurement to symmetry seemed sensible. The use of the tape measure here was interesting. It was used as an analog device for performing doubling and halving operations. A tailor could double by folding the tape at a number and reading off the number at the point where the end of the tape reached. He could halve by folding the tape over to a certain point and using the folded portion as the standard of measurement.

CONFLICTING INTERESTS

Caricatured bargaining also incorporated arithmetic procedures in other concerns. Among tailors in the shops who knew each other well, caricatured bargaining was the only appropriate kind of bargaining. A bargaining process between friends was complex and different from bargaining with others. Serious bargaining, which was the reference process for this friendly bargaining, was carried out with customers, with street sellers, and occasionally with tailors who were not close associates. It was the process of caricatured bargaining that shaped the calculations involved, however.

Caricatured bargaining helped to establish reciprocity in the social world of the shop, where the tailors' extremely casual intrusion on each other's space, services, and resources was the order of the day. Although goodwill was assumed, the participants were nonetheless self-employed craftsmen with meager incomes, trying to make ends meet. They faced the daily dilemma of regulating, mostly curtailing, each other's rights to help themselves to things they needed while maintaining friendly relations that implied helpfulness and generosity. Typically, in-house bargaining took place over resources and services that had economic consequences for the tailors but on which no price was customarily set.

F. and B.S., both young master tailors, are bargaining over a small piece of red cloth B.S. has and F. wants. Intertwined with conversation about several other things, B.S. responds to a request for the cloth, saying, "50 cents." F. shoots back, "10 cents." Talk drifts to other things. Then B.S. thrusts the red cloth at F. who puts two nickels down on top of it. B.S. says, "$1." F. puts a dime down with the two nickels and takes the cloth.

B.S., the original possessor, opened with an absurd price for the red cloth, and both parties knew it. Furthermore, he shortly afterward doubled that price, and did so as a late move in the bargaining. This was also absurd, for he should have been moving closer to the offer rather than further away from it. F.'s response was also ridiculous. He responded with a figure so much smaller than B.S.'s that it, too, could not occur in a serious bargaining situation. The process was open ended; there was never an agreement or dramatic punctuation, for in these interchanges the "seller" never indicated whether he accepted or approved of the last offer. He just passively let the item go. The first tailor, B.S., doubled his price to a dollar after F. put down ten cents. In response, F. doubled his own offer to twenty cents. B.S. managed to convey what he wanted in an exaggerated style that made it possible to appear not to be serious about the bargain.

M. asks G. if he can use G.'s iron (and electricity) to press trousers.
    G: "How many trousers?"
    M: "Six." They argue about how much for pressing each one.
    G. says: "$1" (for all). (This is not much, compared to the price at the cleaners of 75 cents for one pair of trousers. It is a quarter of the month's electric bill, which G. pays.)
    M. doesn't suggest another price. Just says, "Too much"—and goes out to get his trousers to press. They both know that once having asked, M. will press his trousers. But it seems probable that unless G. initiated a caricatured bargain routine M. would treat use of the iron as a favor.

Once G. initiates bargaining, M. is very likely to pay G. something. Negotiations proceed vigorously and deadpan.

I ask G., "What will happen?"

G: "Well, he didn't make another price. He will fix trousers, then give me 25 cents maybe, or else something else."

A few minutes later: G. and M. have a long argument over how much M. should pay G. to use the iron. The bargaining expands so that they talk about whether M. should just pay for the current transaction or whether he should pay by the month. They agree on $2 a month. This is half of the month's electric bill.

M. then shifts the issue to pay $1 now, $1 later. That is, time advantages are now negotiated.

G. finally accepts $1 but says, "This is for the pressing right now!" $1 was his original asking price. The solution is a beautifully multi-purpose face-saver for M., allowing him to capitulate on the $1 but to do what he wanted about the monthly payment. Meanwhile M. starts to press the waistband stiffening onto a waistband. He is interrupted and goes out. G. just picks up the iron and starts pressing for him.

All the characteristics of caricatured bargaining present in the first example were present in the second. Numbers were used ambiguously as part of covert negotiations. Both the exchanges between F. and B.S. and those between M. and G. illustrate the way in which quantities become ambiguous parts of complex social encounters. The very best solutions to everyday arithmetic problems solved several problems and condensed several kinds of meaning at the same time. They could blunt conflict by meeting the differing interests of the participants in a calculation. They were more like poems than facts. So, in the example of the red cloth, B.S. got what he wanted while appearing not to want it. In the second example, the solution payment (for ironing privileges) served conflicting goals for G. and M. and at the same time allowed them to reach apparent or actual agreement.

These incidents, and many others in which relations of quantity were part of the ongoing fabric of the tailors' daily lives and fortunes, were very different from the tailors' engagement with math problems in the experiments, where the manipulation of quantities was the first priority and the outcome uncomfortably subject to scrutiny and evaluation—requiring a head-on focus on solving math problems. The situations themselves—experiments on the one hand, and daily life in the tailor shops on the other—had different characters and different configurations of meaning as well as different relations with other situations of the tailors' lives. The ways in which relations of quantity were constituted were qualitatively different.

Commentary

Having laid out a picture of math practice in tailor shops, it is now possible to broaden the scope of analysis to consider the possibilities for comparing the same participants engaged in math practice in two social settings that furnish quite different problem-solving circumstances. (This is roughly opposite to the strategy of experimental research on learning transfer, since such experiments compare two groups of participants with different educational backgrounds in a single setting.) But establishing the analytic terms for comparison raises difficult issues: I've been arguing all along that pervasive school-centric binary theory makes it exceptionally difficult to generate an analytic apparatus with which to make even roughly evenhanded comparisons. How, then, are we to approach a comparison of problem solving-circumstances in experiments and tailor shops?

As described at the beginning of this chapter, early on I employed school-derived criteria for identifying problems requiring arithmetic solutions in the tailor shops. It quickly became obvious that those implicitly comparative conventions didn't adequately capture relations of quantity in the shops. The mundane math model did a better job, taking the institutional arrangements of everyday life into consideration (though by no means completely divesting the exploration of math in the tailor shops from the shadow of school expectations). The mundane math model was a hybrid concoction, for its initial assumptions came from the culture of experiments (cognitive-economic rationalism, e.g., means/ends relations and efficient use of energy), while the analytic tools that followed from its application in the tailor shops (e.g., contextual resources, relations between old and new results, decisions instead of solutions, and caricatured bargaining) reflected problem-solving circumstances in the shops. Perhaps the most interesting result of exploring math in the tailor shops was to come to see, although very partially, the *doing* of quantitative relations (rather than searching for math *problems*.)[7]

Suppose from a perspective more grounded in the tailor shops, we try to compare the doing of math there with the doing of math in experiments. How similar or different are problem-solving circumstances in experiments (as surrogates for school effects, among other things) to problem-solving circumstances in the tailor shops—when we use the mundane math model as the yardstick for comparison?

The most radical differences between the experiments and tailor shops involved means-ends relations. In the experiments recounted in chapter 4, each problem was predetermined and the tailors had to be deal with it as it stood. Solving arithmetic problems was turned into an end in itself. It might

TABLE 4. A comparative model of arithmetic problem-solving circumstances

Comparative model of problem-solving circumstances	Experiments	Tailor shops
1. Means-ends relations	Problem solving as an end in itself	Problem solving as a means to many other ends
2. Arithmetic problem solving is effortful and requires attention	Yes	Yes, a drawback, requiring inventive social circumvention
3. What constitutes a problem?	Prescribed Fixed precision Error cost fixed	Flexible Variable Socially and economically defined
4. Problem solving is relatively quick (no interruptions)	Yes, all information	Yes and no
5. Social strategies for problem solving	Not permitted	Frequent

seem that relations between means and ends would thus be clearer under experimental circumstances. Not so. Participants in my experiments did not know how the experimental situation was related to other situations in which they were routinely involved, and my attempts to create (some) problems that were meaningful to the tailors in the first round of experiments did not address the tailors' probable puzzlement concerning the meanings of the experiments as social situations.[8] Further, experiments create arbitrary changes in the social conditions of activity. Most of the "cognitive" skills typically addressed in experiments are transformed from incidental means into ends in themselves as they move from everyday situations into experimental ones.

In the tailor shops, problems could be coped with as they arose, one way or another. As means to some other end, arithmetic problems could be simplified (e.g., if you buy two, it'll be eight dollars each), or they could be handed over to someone else to solve, and sometimes they could be rejected entirely. Precision constraints were expected to vary because arithmetic served many different purposes. In contrast, precision constraints were expected to be uniform in the experiments, since solving problems was the only goal. In problem solving in the tailor shops, the cost of errors was defined in relation to varying precision constraints, and the precision constraints were themselves the product of, among other things, assessments of the social and economic costs of an error. In the experimental situation, where problem solving was intended to be an end in itself, error was defined in terms of correct answer / incorrect answer only, so error costs didn't vary.

Two other features of the mundane math scheme would hold for both experiments and shops, namely, that arithmetic problem solving required attention and was therefore effortful, and that it was, all things being equal, relatively quick. However, this assumed that arithmetic problems took the form of school problems, while part of the transformative effect of looking at everyday math in the shops was to arrive at a more complex understanding of what was problematic about relations of quantity in shops as opposed to experiments.

Social strategies for problem solving were frequent in the shops; experiments disrupted the customary division of calculational labor because social strategies simply weren't allowed. So there was a strong contrast in the use of these methods between the two situations. The tailors evaluated the handling of quantitative relations in the tailor shops in terms of social and economic considerations more pressing than the math. Experimenters generally evaluate experimental results in terms of differences between individuals' performances, and evaluate individuals as if they *were* their test scores. Other contrasts are also salient. For example, designations of problem giver and problem solver blurred into irrelevance in the tailor shops, while the experiments kept them rigidly apart. (Distinctions discussed in chapter 3 between situated and didactic instruction resonate here.) Answers were checked by consensus in everyday situations, a social criterion. In experiments they had to be checked by an additional arithmetic operation, since social checking was not available as a strategy.[9]

Therefore, from the perspective of the mundane math scheme, the experiments were unstable and unlikely places to try to capture tailors' everyday math practices. But of course, this perspective takes us further, for if situational differences in math practice are significant, experimentalists' claim to be capturing universal cognitive processes must be profoundly in doubt.

The problem of comparison has been one of the two central issues concerning critical ethnographic practice in this chapter. The discussion of settings, situations, and "circumstances of problem solving" raises the second key issue. My ongoing observations of the tailors' interactions described in this chapter initiated my earliest efforts to explore math practice in situations as far removed from the hegemonic shadow of schooling as possible (cf. Lave 1988). It is clear that conceptions of situations and situated practice are crucial to such an effort. But the Liberian project opened a number of issues that it did not resolve. Consider the limitations of the argument so far. Looking intensely at quantitative relations in tailor shops and experiments and underlining their differences was not conducive to addressing questions about relations *between* situations. This brings us back to the question raised in chapter 4 by the experimental work on learning transfer. If there is no "general learning transfer" from school or anywhere else, do we live in a world of disconnected situations? My work was in danger of suggesting so.[10] At the same time, more felicitously, the differences I found also suggested that participation in math activity might be different in one situation than in another situation because in every case it is complexly imbricated in social, cultural, and historical relations. As I concluded in chapter 4, "If we think of the world as composed of a variety of places, locations, and institutional arrangements for life's activities, we must ask what holds them together and interconnects what goes on in one with another."

That question remained unanswered at the conclusion of the Liberian project, but the direction of a resolution was visible, contrasting sharply with the binary politics of formal and informal education with its polarized assumptions about "situations," and penchant for treating contexts as forms or containers for knowledge (cf. McDermott 1993). At one pole were formal educational sites holding/producing in individuals "decontextualized," abstract, general knowledge, and at the other pole informal educational sites holding/producing context-bound, particular knowledge that shouldn't "generalize." I've touched on another version of that polar theory in an old debate over contrasting characteristics of experiments and everyday life—the first treated as a special site for exposing general cognitive characteristics, the latter as the general site for context-bound particular knowledges.[11] Neither characterization of "situation" holds up in the face of critical ethnographic inquiry. I started to move away from this conventional approach by reframing the differences between experiments and tailor shops in terms of problem-solving "circumstances." Problem-solving circumstances included institutional arrangements that furnished different resources and conditions for solving problems. Those circumstances also included characteristics of problem solvers and their relations with each other. The mundane math model suggested that characteristics of persons' activities, social relations, and institutional arrangements *together* constituted the "circumstances of problem solving." The mundane math model is therefore ambiguous about *how* subjects and the social world are related. It mixes together practice, participants, and locations, though without acknowledging this or laying out a theory of their relations. In chapter 6, I'll argue that this was a cheeringly productive muddle.

This brings us to the question of the "partiality" of critical ethnographic practice.[12] In my view, there are modestly useful resources for change in attempting to reform rather than reproduce polar assumptions—although reproducing them is the most likely outcome of critical research in the naïve sense. They do, in measured, sometimes unexpected ways, generate new, if not radically new, questions, because they emerge from critical shifts in the social location of inquiry. As a way station in a process of struggle to reach a break with the conventional problematic and search for a different critical theoretical-empirical practice, there are interesting consequences of turning an ethnographically informed theoretical stance upside down (like a pair of trousers) and shaking it to see what falls out. For instance, questioning the hierarchical difference in value assigned to formal and informal education opened the value-laden meaning of its numerous claims to different lines of inquiry, anchored in a somewhat different political-social location (e.g., about learning as a matter of learners doing). The scattered "pocket change" so gathered revealed ideas and incentives for exploring the possibility of a theoretical break. The move from two to multiple "poles" was helpful as well, for as differently situated math practices were encountered in practice, it became more difficult to look for conventional bipolar types. It became more important to look carefully and in detail for what constituted instructively different social situations and persons in activity—different scopes of analysis than binary comparison usually dictated. It opened up considerations, in short, that could recommend changing theoretical problematic (cf. Lave and Packer 2008).

Looking back on the project as a whole, several things stand out. First of all, I admired the Vai and Gola tailors' apprenticeship, while, according to the values embedded in the theory of formal and informal education, I should have reserved my admiration for schooling. This opened the value-laden meaning of each part of the theory to new critical interpretations and the possibility of new conclusions. Why was the tailors' apprenticeship an appealing kind of educational practice? I had happened upon a case of effective education, relatively benign and accessible. The result, for very poor people who might have been expected to experience their lives and themselves as miserable in several senses of that word, was a strong sense of their worth and dignity. They were without a doubt poor, and they were able, respected, and self-respecting, with a "take" on the world that had a considerable penetration of the real conditions of their lives. Eighty-five percent or more who started a tailors' apprenticeship finished it and continued their practice as tailors. In short, given dualist beliefs about apprenticeship in contrast with schooling, the asymmetrical value I had placed on the two sides shifted to a view that valued apprenticeship positively.

Second, I discovered that following the *doing* of learning was a more fruitful basis for a conceptual understanding of learning and situated instruction than focusing on (didactic) teaching as the cause and condition of possibility for learning. Contemplate one last time the master ostentatiously instructing the apprentice for my benefit that the fly goes on the front of the trousers. Teaching, especially as situated instruction, certainly is an object for analytic inquiry, but not an explanation for learning. Taking learning to be at the heart of the matter invites a change of perspective: Suppose we began to theorize about learning, and its associated varieties of instruction, from the position of learners engaged in learning.

The work pursued here on situated quantitative relations, combined with earlier analyses of apprenticeship, of situated learning and situated instruction, of multiple number systems and their associated arithmetics, and of the ephemeral, unpersuasive trace of learning transfer, led to the most important conclusion of this chapter and the principal forward step of the project as a whole: to the *situated* character of participation in social life. This conclusion gathered force as all the strands of the project came to speak to each other. And of course, the tailors' apprenticeship as a whole was an elegant example, for no matter what aspect of their lives I turned to, the tailors were participants in changing practice in the ongoing world of which they were also a part.

But hold on! There was nothing theoretically transformative, nor even revisionist, about arguing for the context-embedded (or better, the situated) character of apprenticeship and the practice of tailoring in Happy Corner. After all, this was the bedrock assumption separating the "informal" from the "formal" in the binary comparative theory. Thankfully, this wasn't my argument. Instead, the situated, embedded character of mathematical practice—the practice of quintessentially "formal," "abstract," "decontextualized" knowledge in conventional theory—made possible a much stronger proposal: Suppose it was not just some designated "informal" side of life that was composed of intricately context-embedded and situated activity. Suppose there is nothing else?

I have gone on supposing this ever since. But this assumption is thoroughly, definitively incompatible with the binary comparative theory. We have arrived at one of those uncrossable gaps envisioned by Favret-Saada. For if all activity is spatially, materially, and historically situated, this directly contradicts pristine conventional divisions between subject and world and between mind and body, to name two very fundamental assumptions defining the binary problematic. From the point of view of a theory of situated practice, claims for polar distinctions appear to be merely historical-political contrivances, while "cognitive universals" and "theoretical generalities" must be understood as local political practices. Through this and the previous three chapters, I have been trying to show how the process of ethnographic research in Liberia led to conclusions like these. But I have also tried to show how the ethnographic practice moved toward a different theoretical stance—not to just any alternative problematic but to the relational commitments of social practice theory. The concluding chapter explores those relations.

6 Research on Apprenticeship, Research as Apprenticeship

This book has traced a struggle to relocate research on tailors' apprenticeship in Liberia in a relational problematic. We are now ready to address questions about what such a problematic might look like, and especially, how we might understand critical ethnographic practice as the research praxis of a relational problematic. In seeking answers, we'll consider one last time the several processes of apprenticeship intertwined throughout the book—in relational terms.

The Liberian Project and Its Discontents

The ethnographic project in Liberia began in commonsense conventional terms to explore a series of specific claims generated through a bipolar logic of inquiry (laid out in figure 1 in chapter 1). These claims concerned different educational contexts, contents, modes of teaching, presumed ways of learning, and potential for learning transfer. Each new segment of the project started off with commonsense description, whether of the tailors' alley, of master-apprentice relations, of the changing learning trajectories of tailors' apprentices, of learning transfer tasks and experiments, or of math problem solving in tailor shops.

This project was critical ethnography in the direct sense: It kept front and center specific doubts about the sufficiency of commonsense/conventional theory (given the institutional pillars supporting it) as the basis for analyzing ongoing practice in other institutional settings. The project involved turning initial ethnographic efforts into objects of analysis. It stood in opposition to the political commitments built into conventional theory that maintain and justify the status quo. It has worked to unpack claims to pristine separation between places, people, practices, ideas, and their "high" and "low" value and power—the politics of binary extremism. The commentaries in each chapter addressed a number of other shortcomings deriving from this theoretical stance. This has led to a different theoretical account of critique as a part of critical ethnographic practice.

The level of disagreement between the analysis of tailors' apprenticeship on the one hand and contrastive orthodoxies about schooling and "informal" education on the other grew stronger as the project went on: The ethnographic research on apprenticeship did not support value-loaded contrasts between formal and informal education, raising doubts about the meaning of the distinction itself. Experiments based on a detailed inquiry into a specific educational practice—not some vague residual "non-schooling"—revealed no significant superiority in learning transfer between tailors who had been to school and tailors who had not. Most powerful in raising doubts about the binary theory itself were lines of inquiry about the tailors' everyday working lives focused on socially situated processes of production—of trousers, of tailors, of apprentices, of math problem solving, and of research. Finding that people's activities around quantitative relations in experiments were different from those that incorporated quantitative relations in tailor shops made salient the situated nature of the activities and drew into question the validity of broad extrapolations about individual minds from the behavior of persons in experimental situations. This in turn raised critical questions about the assumptions shaping cognitive experiments—assumptions that only juxtaposed minds with different social contexts. Again, in turn, these doubts led to substantive questions about what different tailors did differently and why. The experiments drew on ordinary cross-cultural psychological research practice, only to turn that practice into an object of analysis as I gradually came to recognize that experiments were socially situated exotic events. Similarly, while apprenticeship was originally an exemplar of informal education, the ethnographic work furnished a critical basis for questioning the binary theory of formal/informal education. Then, as apprenticeship turned from a docile example into an unruly object demanding analysis in its own right, it became a key to the theoretical/ethnographic crafting of a conception of situated practice.

Likewise, the significance of math for the whole project started out, as we saw in chapter 4, as merely a handy subject enabling comparisons of schooled and other tailors in the first experiments. But looking closely at the results raised critical objections to any simple universal conception of arithmetic. Math then became an analytic tool through inquiry into Vai and Gola number systems that made it possible to proceed with the analysis of the second round of learning transfer experiments.[1] Chapter 5 traced how math in the tailor shops turned into the object of study, recast through the mundane math model as part of the fabric of everyday life. Eventually, Western assumptions about math provided a worst-case scenario in critical support of the argument for the situated character of (mathematical) practice and the constitutive importance of the social contexts of the tailors' working lives. This so violated the conventional theoretical division between subject and world that it became difficult to figure out how to go on conceiving of social being in these deeply divided terms. The most basic assumptions underlying that theory no longer seemed to reflect the realities I was trying to comprehend or the ways I was trying to comprehend them.

This way of stepping through segment after segment of the project paints a picture of forward movement, but each segment goes back to old starting points as well. In fact, with a naïve agenda rooted in Western abstract prescriptions for what should constitute evidence, I went back to square one every time I started to inquire into a new facet of apprenticeship, or math practice, or psychological experiments. But also, not once, but over and over, a detailed descriptive account led in unexpected directions of inquiry to changing conclusions, to ideas for next segments, and to questions about the theoretical limitations of the enterprise. These shifts in direction sometimes followed sharp breaks—"aha" moments—but the breaks themselves were made possible by a lot of hard slogging. This is how one comes to inhabit a particular kind of ethnographic practice, at once an empirical and a theoretical endeavor. This process is part of what I mean by apprenticeship in critical ethnographic practice, and it also helps to explain why ethnographic research is iterative, open ended, partial, and long term. I might not have noticed or taken as significant the starting at both ends, moving forward and backward through ethnographic research, if I hadn't inquired into the ways in which Vai and Gola tailors come to inhabit their craft (think about the process of learning to make trousers, for instance, recounted in chapter 3).[2]

Any theoretical perspective makes some aspects of inquiry easy, some difficult, and some impossible. The strictures of commonsense positivist theory led me, in spite of a critical stance, to suppress some things going on with the tailors that were important, that should have been developed, and that instead remained unclear, muffled, or missing. Some of these can be found in awkward little sections that didn't fit well in the chapter arguments. Other things were said in passing that came to be much more significant in later readings in other contexts. Perhaps the most startling was the way references to participation, legitimate participation, and peripheral participation appeared here and there, only to become central in later work (Lave and Wenger 1991). Likewise, clues about critical issues of identity, including a discussion of the trajectory of apprenticeship as a matter

of "maturity," went almost unacknowledged, along with a recognition that
the apprentices were developing into master tailors, in complex relations
of gender and power (not merely becoming "producers of garments"). I detailed in chapter 4 my difficulties in trying to lay "learning transfer" to rest
even after experiments supported my objections to both the concept and
to standard methods of investigating it. Another issue seems to me now to
have been suppressed in spite of an invitation from the ethnographic material to push further: the conflictual, political-economic relations shaping
master-apprentice relations and practices of learning, making, and doing
in Happy Corner. Suppressing analysis of relations of power is habitual under conventional theory, and I failed to oppose conventional theory in this
respect.[3]

These developments, both the project's direct challenges to commonsense theory and challenges that remained partially suppressed, raised dis-
contents (some immediately, others later) that went beyond technical problems resolvable through more empirical investigation or by massaging
theoretical tenets. I was face to face with the limitations of my argument,
in disagreement over basic theoretical assumptions, institutional arrangements, and their hegemonic effects on and through commonsense theory. I
needed a different problematic.

What Is a Problematic?

The idea of a theoretical/empirical problematic (cf. Geras 1972) comes from
a historical-materialist social-theoretical tradition, of which social practice
theory is one strand.[4] This tradition does not assume that "theory" is the
end result of a research project that has employed an atheoretical "method"
to that point. Nor does it apply the term "theory" to small fragments of human activity, as in learning transfer "theory." It is impossible in this view to
excise bits of human activity for study without distorting them beyond recognition, and no one-body-part-at-a-time "theory" is sufficient to constitute a theoretical problematic. Instead, one looks at a specific aspect of social life in its relations made with, in, and through other objects, persons,
institutional arrangements, contexts, and events. This requires establishing how specific aspects of social life are part of other human activity in a
"world" that is historically construed. A problematic includes assumptions
(an ontology, an epistemology, an ethics) about relations between persons
and world, the nature of human being and how it is produced, in what terms
we can know it and the nature of knowledge. These are deep assumptions
that together underlie—from start to finish—the more specific working assumptions embodied in the practices of different institutionalized genres of

research. When a social practice theorist tries to identify a researcher's theoretical stance, she is inquiring into those deep assumptions that generate and are expressed in the researcher's varied working methods, logic of inquiry, findings, and ways of drawing conclusions. To change from one theoretical problematic to another means changing the basis of one's research so as to be working from a distinctly different set of premises about subject-world relations, history, knowledge, and power, employing distinctly different analytic tools, concepts, and questions. Further, different kinds of relations between the empirical and the theoretical are crafted differently as part of different problematics.

A social-theoretical problematic can be thought of most fundamentally as a claim about reality and how we know it. Exploring nuanced distinctions and relations between conceptions of reality and conceptions of ways of coming to know it has been the work of philosophers for centuries and social theorists more recently. At the risk of risible oversimplification, a first approximation to mapping different problematics might be a simple table of two columns and two rows, with cross-cutting answers to two questions: "Where does reality lie?" (inside or outside the observing subject) and "How do we know it?" (as a project of empirical description and classification or as a project of analytic search for the workings of generative principles of social life). In this vastly simplified scheme, there are four quite different social-theoretical problematics that are at base mutually exclusive. The deep, spare claims entailed in different problematics furnish different worldviews. Different metaphysical commitments get extensively elaborated through other assumptions and entailments. They differ in many other ways, including interrelated conceptions of learning, research preparation and practice, and knowledge, as Kvale proposed (see table 1 in chapter 1), and with respect to politics, ethics, and social change.

Does critical ethnographic practice always seek to move from one problematic to another? Yes and no. The conventional positivist problematic of the twentieth and early twenty-first centuries in the United States is a descriptive enterprise aimed at revealing a reality "out there," independent of the observer. We live our lives, including our working lives, in a world fashioned in the institutional arrangements for, and in the name of, this view of reality. The struggle to treat binary comparative theory and its politics critically as an object for analysis must be ongoing. There is nothing in a conventional descriptive problematic that insists on such a stance—it does not take a critical stance with respect to itself. This stands in contrast to a relational theoretical problematic (of which social practice theory and its instantiation in critical ethnographic practice is an example). Given these circumstances, a project of changing one's problematic seems important as well as always partial and always in need of work. Second—the case for no—the change sought through critical ethnographic practice is not that of moving from one problematic to another. The object of critical ethnographic practice is to work within a considered stance that expresses one's strongest intuitions about the nature of reality, the capacity to inquire into it, a political-ethical stance in the broadest sense, and convictions about how to engage in the most rigorous and illuminating research. If the politics of commonsense comparative theorizing doesn't do it for you, then it takes work to come to inhabit that different problematic.

Social Practice Theory

Elaborating a historical-materialist problematic—one whose roots lie in Marxist theory of praxis—by rights requires another book.[5] Meanwhile, it is possible to lay out key assumptions underlying social practice theory and to sketch the logic by which they hang together and offer the critical ethnographer a way to approach inquiry into social being and doing.

First, to focus on the world as it presents itself assumes that the lived-in world is in process and in change and that this changing process is historical in character.

Next, the notion of situated activity assumes that subjects, objects, lives, and worlds are made in their relations. That is, the contexts of people's lives aren't merely containers or backdrops, nor are they simply whatever seems salient to immediate experience. Persons are always embodied, located uniquely in space, and in their relations with other persons, things, practices, and institutional arrangements. They come to be located differently, where they are, doing what they are doing, as part of ongoing historical process. The researcher is no exception, and so ethnographic labor must be included, critically, as part of what needs to be analyzed.

If people are always actively making the places and practices of their world—in the reciprocal relations by which those places and practices make them—then bodies are neither operating nor operated on separately from minds, but again each is made in their relations.

Praxis encompasses all of these assumptions about social life—people making their lives together in various historically forged institutional arrangements, not exactly as they choose. If we accept that it is the basis of social being, then social life is not reducible to knowledge or even to knowing, but to collective doing, as what being is, as part of the lived-in world. Reducing activity to mental activity—acquiring, transferring, creating, transmitting, internalizing knowledge is not inclusive enough to identify where, how, or with what meaning the stuff we call "knowledge" is part of social life. Knowledgeability is always part of situated social, historical being. Thinking or knowing or knowledge is always only part of praxis, captured through notions of identity, personal—of course social-relational—and collective with respect to various social arrangements (Dreier 2003, 2008; Holland et. al. 1998).

If one accepts this position, every problematic is imbued with the politics of the historically, political-economically structured social-cultural world as it exists at present—call this the "conjuncture." Living (including research on and as apprenticeship) is embedded in political arrangements, hegemonic projects, and diffuse relations of power. This both raises the stakes and complexity of carrying out rigorous research and makes clear the need for an ethical stance by researchers so engaged. So the political stance of social practice theorists is understood in terms of historical, political-economic forces and arguments, and on-the-ground conflict and struggle for change.

If things, persons, world, and praxis are made in their relations, how is comparison possible in the problematic of social practice theory? The answer requires a digression to consider once more the vexing issue of comparison.

I have pointed out through one chapter after another the ubiquitous, hierarchical, deck-stacking character of comparative claims derived from the commonsense problematic. By the end of the work described in chapter 4, the alternative with respect to education, math, and learning transfer was to say that there was more than one number system and more than one valuable way of engaging in math—call this the "relativistic" alternative. Certainly it ran counter to the commonsense binary to say that Vai and Gola math are differently constituted but perfectly sensible mathematical systems and practices, with different histories and social locations than Western school math. As recounted in chapter 5, I started out with Western school math as the reference point—looking for "well-formed math problems." So long as I followed that path of inquiry, whatever I "discovered" in the tailor shops was still defined in relation to Western math. This too was problematic as a method of comparison, and by no means a relational one. The relativist version of comparison sustains the hegemonic political enterprise, for the ethnographer must still perform translation work in order to be able to say that talking about *x* here compared to *y* there refers to sufficiently "the same thing" to allow a valid comparison. And this strategy of inquiry cannot escape the practical locus of the whole exercise in Western universalist (positivist commonsense) categories, practice, and assumptions that establishes the ball park and says, in effect, If yours is different, it is different *from this*.[6]

I only partially and gradually moved toward a relational account of quantity in the tailor shops. This happened when I began to consider that practices in which relations of quantity were constituted in the tailor shops were composed in and as different sorts of social relations than those assumed to be canonical to the practice of Western school math.

In my experience there are at least three compelling temptations for ethnographers to settle for comparisons in relativist terms. One is the satisfaction of demonstrating that, for example, apprenticeship or Vai and Gola number systems are different from Western ones—but comparably complex and productive. Second, there are the difficulties of communicating to, say, experimental psychologists or human subjects boards, in relational terms when such terms are neither recognized nor understood. It is then exceedingly difficult to avoid taking the psychologists' theoretical assumptions, issues, practice, and politics as the yardstick by which to define "difference," as "difference from *their* practice"—rather than explaining difference in incommensurate relational terms. Finally, paradoxes of translation more generally mark the logic of inquiry of ethnographic practice as a whole, as ethnographers inquire into some world, however conceived, with questions and reasons brought from and to the non–field based trajectories of their (working) lives.

Relational theory is a way to move away from these political dilemmas of comparison by changing the way in which comparison is understood, by analyzing things as their relations, in practice. Gillian Hart explains it this way:

> Instead of starting with a presumption of pre-existing bounded entities—whether spatial, social, or individual—a relational approach attends explicitly to ongoing *processes* of constitution. This processual understanding, in turn, is grounded in a theory of praxis that asserts the inseparability of situated practices and their associated meanings and power relations. (Hart 2002, 296)

Rather than saying that to get to the truth of human being we must figure out its most basic elements and build up from there, relational ethnography recognizes that the truth of human being is its historical processual coming to be and that we can only get at it by starting with our existing, given, social life, that is, with social practice in the historical present, in its political-economic, cultural-institutional arrangements in the conjuncture, working backward and forward in time and space rather than up and down a chain of abstractions.

If social being is a matter of its constitutive relations, it seems crucial to work out carefully just what sort of relations these are. How might we proceed, having rejected claims for the pristine divide between mind and body or formal and informal education by insisting that subjects and world make each other? Complex, contradictory relations do not lie between nodes in networks; they *are* what things are. Relations that make things what they are with respect to each other are multiple, historical, and contradictory. The issues are complicated. The relations are dialectical. Coming to inhabit them takes a lot of practice (cf. Ollman 1976; Hall 2003). In social practice theory, there is a term for bringing theoretically informed empirical work and empirically shaped theoretical practice into a constitutive relation: "rising to the concrete" (Hall 2003, 131). That this apparently paradoxical phrase stands in contrast to conventional belief in the value of ever-greater abstraction is no doubt intentional. The notion of "rising to the concrete" acknowledges the historical, relational character of changing social life, and hence the need for efforts to craft historical, relational understandings that are at once empirical and theoretical.

If everything is its relations, how can we take social life apart to analyze an object or facet or issue in relational terms without destroying it?[7] It is a delicate matter, a matter of looking at one thing *through* another in order to understand how it works through/in social life. This is the craft of rising to the concrete, of engaging in empirical-theoretical practice. Another way of describing critical ethnographic practice, then, is to say that social inquiry is always a matter of looking at any object of analysis as its relations, that is, *with respect to* whatever else we are interested in that makes it what it is.[8]

Apprenticeship: A Relational Concept

This whole project began with that impulsive decision to see what apprenticeship was about among Vai and Gola tailors in Liberia. Let's go back for a moment to the earliest period of field inquiry in the study of the tailors' apprenticeship, to a question central to chapter 2.[9] What is (this Vai and Gola tailors') apprenticeship? Esther Goody, with a theoretical stance similar to the one with which I (and many other ethnographers of apprenticeship) started, asked herself this question in her capacity as reviewer and synthesizer of a number of apprenticeship ethnographies:

> Like most of the contributions to this collection, my substantive papers on apprenticeship were written without specifically examining how it should be defined. Several different definitions are in fact used in these

papers, and this did force me to confront the question: What is apprenticeship? I think all would agree with the broadest of these; "an apprentice is someone who doesn't know, learning from someone who does." (1989, 234)

From a relational perspective, I would now say, quite to the contrary, that we are all apprentices, engaged in learning to do what we are already doing. The differences between these two definitions are significant. To begin with, the distinction between one who knows and one who doesn't invokes the binary comparative theory and its epistemological politics. More interestingly, to *learn* to do what you are already doing is a contradiction in terms; it implies that there is always more than one relation of knowing and doing in play—knowing and not knowing, doing and undoing, understanding theoretically but not empirically and vice versa, starting from both ends of processes of production and coming together in the middle in (relational, concrete) ways that transform conceptions of the ends. It surely implies that apprenticeship is a process of *changing* practice. Further, learning to act on the basis of any craft, and for that matter, any problematic, requires practice to come to inhabit the practice and its conception of the world. Such relations also characterize research practice, whether empirically (theoretically) in the project in Liberia or theoretically (empirically) in a problematic of social practice theory. Part of producing a concrete conception of apprenticeship has been considering crafts and theoretical problematics in everyday, processual, relational terms as parts of one relation.

What has been learned by following the process of producing the ethnographic research in Liberia about tailors' apprenticeship on the one hand and exploring apprenticeship in critical ethnographic practice on the other? Reading each with respect to the other has changed how I have come to understand each one. This process treats them not as identical, but considers each as produced in and through the other—research on apprenticeship, research as apprenticeship. Indeed, what we have been doing is rising to a concrete relational conception of apprenticeship and in the process becoming apprentices to our own future practice.

NOTES

Chapter One

1. The most immediate academic context of the project was the radical experiment in interdisciplinary social science begun at the University of California, Irvine, in 1965. In the interest of breaking down disciplinary boundaries, we turned to the language(s) of models and mathematics. Colleagues Michael Cole, Duane Metzger, and Charles Lave in the School of Social Sciences were active collaborators and interlocutors in the Liberian project. Cf. Michael Cole's *The Cultural Context of Learning and Thinking* (1971) and Charles Lave and James G. March's *An Introduction to Models in the Social Sciences* (1975). I now see the school's efforts to establish a universal, ahistorical, interdisciplinary social science as hugely contradictory. On the other hand, that intense environment of interdisciplinary interchange transformed the direction of everything I have done since. Many of the early faculty and students who passed through the School of Social Sciences would say the same, I think.

2. To reflect their inseparability, the term "ethnographic practice," rather than "theory and practice" or "fieldwork and theory," is employed throughout—making it difficult, I hope impossible, to forget the theoretical character of empirical inquiry and the empirical character of theoretical inquiry. Even when discussion focuses on one or the other, it is never about only one or the other.

3. Snow, Morrill, and Anderson (2003) cite numerous anthropological and sociological discussions that establish a division between empirical and theoretical work—between accounts of ethnographic work that start with going into the field and end when the ethnographer departs (e.g., Adler and Adler 1987; Wax 1971; and Weber 2001) on the one hand, and accounts of anthropology as writing ethnography (e.g., Clifford and Marcus 1986; Van Maanen 1990; and Denzin 1992) on the other. Myriad fieldwork manuals, as well as critiques of ethnographic writing, walk up to this divide from one direction or the other and in the process reify lines between field and academy, and between method and theory. (See, e.g., Robben and Sluka 2007, an encyclopedic assembly of anthropologists' reflections on fieldwork. It scarcely mentions writing ethnographies, nor does it deal with theory, theoretical problematics, or theoretical formation and analysis.)

4. Strathern's inquiry into the 1980s argument appears here to accept the primacy of "the organization of text" without reservation. But rather than arguing for Clifford's all-embracing textualism, I believe she is making a narrower point: that the use of particular anthropologists as *emblems* of the discipline comes about because of their textual

innovations. By this argument "Clifford" and "Marcus" have become in their turn reduced and flattened emblems in the early twenty-first century.

"Textual innovation" is not a convincingly robust explanation of the production of disciplinary icons. Surely it takes a historical conjuncture, luck, and political work, not to mention a social arena and supportive institutional arrangements.

5. Meyer Fortes, a major figure in British anthropology in the mid-twentieth century, and influential in America as well, gave the first Lewis Henry Morgan Lecture in 1963: "Kinship and the Social Order: The Legacy of Lewis Henry Morgan" (Fortes 1969). Fortes was a participant and witness during the period under discussion, and he would not agree with Clifford's views. He argued that "fieldwork in the empirical mode remains the *sine qua non* both for the testing of theory and, what is more important, for the making of new discoveries" (1978, 26). Fortes doesn't refer to the ethnographic monograph as the site of either the testing or the discoveries. This omission would support Clifford's (and Strathern's) thesis. On the other hand, their thesis erases the complex, dedicated practice of field research attested to by many "functionalist" anthropologists like Fortes without engaging in the heavy lifting required to explain its supposedly passive relation to ethnography-as-text.

Fortes had definite views about relations between fieldwork and theory. He explained his views in "An Anthropologist's Apprenticeship" (1978, 3), a fascinating account of the anthropologists, theories, and debates in the period of his early days as an anthropologist in the 1930s (and later in his career). He takes us from seminars at the London School of Economics to his first fieldwork, thence to the lessons of fieldwork, and from there into discoveries and debates over central issues in anthropology, kinship institutions, politico-jural institutions, and more. About relations between field experience and general findings he has this to say:

> Consider some of the findings of general import that emerged in the process of presenting and analyzing my field materials under the influence of Radcliffe-Brown and Evans-Pritchard. And though I want particularly to stress the empirical basis of these findings, I want equally to stress their place in the process of cumulative alternation of theory and fieldwork that confirms to me the scientific status of social anthropology. (11)

He is silent here about the material locus of analysis and theory. There is room for disagreement over his theoretical stance (and its assumptions about relations between the empirical and the theoretical), but it seems less easy to object to his assertions about the active contribution of field study to debates in anthropology.

Fortes's opposition to theory with a capital "T" is vividly reflected in his characterization of apprenticeship, reminding us that there is more than one way to understand apprenticeship as a matter of its relations (a point that will have relevance to our discussion of Kvale's work shortly). He begins "An Anthropologist's Apprenticeship" by observing that philosopher A. J. Ayer once divided philosophers into "pontiffs" and "journeymen," a distinction he finds applicable to anthropologists as well,"

> though perhaps not exhaustively, when we consider the ever-growing army of phenomenological, semiological, Marxist and other exploiters of anthropological data

to represent their personal world views or intellectual or moral or political commitments. Professor Ayer declares himself to be a journeyman philosopher: and I happily place myself in the corresponding category of anthropologists.

The Oxford English Dictionary informs us that a journeyman is "one who having served his apprenticeship to a handicraft or trade is qualified to work at it for days' wages"; "a qualified mechanic or artisan who works for another." . . . A journeyman's eyes are on his material, not on higher things. His aim is to turn out a particular product at a time using the best tools at his disposal. What he has by way of skill and technique are directed strictly to the job at hand, to making the most of the material he has to work with in the light of whatever good ideas happen to be appropriate to his task. It is as a journeyman in this spirit that I have always approached my vocation as an anthropologist. (1–2)

Fortes goes on to quote a description of his work by John Barnes:

The ethnographer arrives in the field with a theory and an analytic toolkit which proves to be inadequate for coping with the ethnographic facts that crowd upon him. He modifies his theory and develops new tools in the traumatic situation of first fieldwork, or in the sometimes equally traumatic situation of wrestling with his data to produce an analysis that will stand up to the scrutiny of his colleagues. (Barnes 1971, 263–64

Fortes concludes, "I think this justifies my describing myself as a journeyman in contrast to the pontiffs" (1978, 2).

6. Strathern comments: "It will be apparent that I use the contrast between modernism and postmodernism to indicate a shift within anthropological writing—one might or might not wish to subsume it all under the term 'modern'" (1990, 108n36; see also 110–11n40).

7. Marcus, for example, has a curious, rather ventriloquistic manner of writing. He announces that "ethnography wants this" or "it does that"—and then he equates the discipline of anthropology with his version of ethnography (e.g., 1994, 44). Its antitheoretical stance (see Comaroff and Comaroff 2003, 153) may make it difficult for proponents of the reflexive turn to comprehend their perspective as only one of a number of theoretical possibilities within anthropology.

8. Strathern expresses doubts on this subject (e.g., 1990, 111–12). Malkki (Cerwonka and Malkki 2007) makes an elegant analysis of why ethnographic work is always an improvised practice and at the same time is in no way a matter of free play.

9. Examples of professional involution from Marcus 1994:

Ethnography within anthropology now has the possibility of redefining its position within Western intellectual discourses. . . . and [can] exemplify a discipline that not only heeds the continuing critique of its practices and discourses, but embraces such critique as the very source of its projects of knowledge. (42)

[Ethnography] functions well and creatively without a sense that it needs a positive theoretical paradigm—that is, conventional social theory—to guide it. Instead, it breeds off the critique of its own rhetoric. (44)

10. Margery Wolf gave the Morgan Lecture in 1983: "China and the Anthropology of Women." Her later book, *A Thrice Told Tale* (1992), is a critical feminist meditation on the 1980s arguments about ethnographic writing. It deserves special mention, not because it is uniquely critical—many feminist anthropologists joined the debate—but because she did so in a manner and spirit close to that of the present book. With the intention of speaking to apprentice ethnographers, she explores the ethical and political complexities of the ethnographer's craft, including the effects of differences in the writer's voice and authority, through different accounts of her own early fieldwork. In exploring commonalities and differences in feminist and postmodern critiques of ethnographic practice, the differences seem to emerge from that "certainty of context" and purpose (alluded to by Strathern) that comes from her stance as a feminist anthropologist:

> There is a curious postmodernist politics that condemns us for our individual colonialist attitudes but remains aloof from the often bloody results of oppressive governments, of the left and the right. . . . The power that accrues to being first world in a third-world country cannot be denied and yet cannot be used without alienating somebody. Postmodernism gives us little guidance here. (1992, 6)

She urges ethnographers not to privilege issues of (written) form in a retreat from "the admittedly messy stuff of experience." (58):

> I hope that feminist anthropologists don't become distracted by postmodernism's preoccupation with form . . . to the neglect of our political agenda, which depends on our discovering all we can about the diversity of women's lived experience. (118)

11. One way Willis and Trondman draw a line between the 1980s and their vision is to identify what they call the "postmodern fallacy,"

> not in its recognition of diversification and individualization at the cultural level, but in the cutting of the latter's social moorings. Only because it effectively declares the end of "the social" can postmodern thinking and analysis establish culture as a "floating signifier." (2000, 9)

This is similar to Wolf's and Strathern's observations on differences between feminist anthropology and anthropology as a "postmodern" enterprise.

12. Remember Strathern's observation that "what must be laid to Malinowski's door . . . is the proclamation of the kinds of spaces that had to be made to convey the 'new' analytical ideas" (1990, 98). Here, the notion of "space" is embedded in a new set of relations. Gupta and Ferguson (1992) argue that "recent notions of 'cultural critique' depend on a spatialized understanding of cultural difference that needs to be problematized" (in Robben and Sluka 2007, 343, referring to Marcus and Fischer 1986). They challenge the we/they relations that informed debates in the 1980s and Strathern's analytic scheme for contrasting the '80s with earlier incarnations of ethnography as well. The world is not composed of distinct cultures; population flow around a profoundly interconnected world makes an equation of a geographical territory with a culture or people impossible; and every nation-state is a profoundly heterogeneous polity. Yet, Gupta and Ferguson continue,

> cultural critique assumes an original separation, bridged at the initiation of the anthropological fieldworker. . . . What is needed is a willingness to interrogate, politi-

cally and historically, the apparent "given" of a world in the first place divided into "ourselves" and "others." (343)

13. The Comaroffs argue that it is possible to concentrate on the deep concerns embodied in everyday practice in a particular location and still pursue the broad, overlapping, and complex relations they produce and that produce them. There are other approaches to these issues, in the name of "multisited ethnography." These are theoretically diverse. Caution is necessary in sorting out their different implications for field research (e.g., Marcus 1995; Hannerz 2003; cf. Robben in Robben and Sluka 2007, 331–36).

14. The section of Malkki's essay called "Critical Theoretical Practice" goes beyond first notions of the "critical." She discusses several relations that inhere in such a stance. Ethnographic "objects" are taken to be empirically and theoretically constructed at the same time (rather than separately and in sequence as in a positivist/empiricist stance). She emphasizes the simultaneously empirical and theoretical nature of "fieldwork" (Cerwonka and Malkki 2007, 171). She focuses on systems of relations rather than a positivist measurement using standard units, for example, "the individual." And critical theoretical practice is improvisational, a spiral or back-and-forth way in which observations and theoretical conceptions change each other. Malkki doesn't quite say that all of this together is what she means by critical theoretical practice, but that surely is her intention.

15. Murphy captures the idea retrospectively in writing about his book *The Dialectics of Social Life* (1972):

> In calling for a critical anthropology, the book was an extended argument for the indissolubility of praxis and thought, of deeds and words, of social activity and its cultural construction . . . in a union that is primordially dialectical in nature. (1994, 57)

16. Faubion identifies "the death of theory" as a serious issue with respect to the 1980s critique of ethnography (Faubion and Marcus 2009, 154ff.)

17. For instance, Snow, Morrill, and Anderson (2003, 183–84) draw attention to analytic work—but they see this as a link, indeed a missing link, between empirical fieldwork and theoretical work. They argue that analysis could and should bring them together through unpacking analytic relations more carefully than is usually found in the work of anthropologists—or archeologists (cf. Lucas 2000).

18. I have been trying to convey a feel for theoretical problematics and their irresolvable differences by discussing debates over different visions of ethnographic practice (the next section of the chapter offers another illustration). Chapter 6 will address the concept directly, as part of an account of social practice theory. But briefly, social practice theory belongs to a family of relational Marxist theories that begin with a concept of praxis, the idea that human beings make their lives together, in a complexly structured, historically and materially changing world. One commitment that separates the broad family of practice theories, with their emphasis on relations and process, from other social theories is a reversal of the usual separation and priority of thought over action in the production of social life. Given that praxis is about human being as activity, you might imagine that it singles out a specific level of analysis, a kind of athletic psychology, as the right subject matter for social research. But praxis is central to all aspects of social life—to analyses of political economy, consciousness, value, history, and more (Bernstein 1971, 62). The theoretical stance that grows out of a conception of social life as praxis is therefore complex

and also comprehensive (though this is not to be read as complete). There are many approaches to social research, psychological research, social theory, and philosophy that involve praxis-like concepts, some close to my concerns, others taking conceptions related to praxis in disparate directions. But my understanding of social practice theory has been most strongly shaped by reading Marx's work through Gramsci, Stuart Hall, Willis, and others who pursued a critical social direction at the Birmingham Center for Contemporary Cultural Studies in the 1970s, and through the work of theorists such as Lefebvre, Ollman, and Dorothy Smith. The deep influence of close colleagues includes the powerful theoretical craft of critical psychologist Ole Dreier; the work of Ray McDermott on pragmatists William James and John Dewey; Dorothy Holland's work, especially her incorporation of Bakhtin's theory into social practice theory; the work of Mariane Hedegaard, Seth Chaiklin, Michael Cole, and others on Vygotsky and Soviet activity theory; and the work of social practice theorists Gill Hart and Alan Pred, colleagues in the geography department at UC Berkeley.

It should be noted in the context of the Morgan Lectures that Marx read Morgan's *Ancient Society*. He made extensive notes on it as well as on other ethnological literature, Lawrence Krader tells us. He also warns us that Marx's reading of this literature, including Morgan's work, was unfinished at the end of his life:

How Marx had intended to present his work, whether as a book on an ethnological subject, or as part a work on another subject is unclear; his work cannot be said to have taken a particular form, it was rather in the process of gestation. (1974, 7)

19. The result, as Comaroff and Comaroff observe, is that

anthropology has, for the most part, remained unrelentingly positivist in spirit. Much of its shared wisdom consists in generalizations about the particular that are also particularizations of the general; empirical aggregates, in short, not abstract propositions or explanatory schemata. . . . The epistemic consequences that follow are plain enough: a committed relativism, and a form of relativism that sits uneasily with "general" theory grounded in history, philosophy, political economy, or whatever. True, there have always been counter tendencies: those who have espoused evolutionary, Marxist, sociobiological, or psychoanalytic approaches, for instance, have been more partial to higher-order abstraction, generalization, explanation. But this minority has tended to be the exception that proves the rule. (2003, 153–54)

20. Bourgois reminds us in deeply critical terms of some of the historical forces at work in producing our commonsense binary politics:

The crypto-puritanical, upwardly mobile, immigrant heritage of the United States imposes an unusually polarized understanding of politics and practice. It invites us to view individuals and actions as either all bad or all good, sinful or virtuous, noble or ignoble. Most importantly, individuals . . . must be judged to be autonomous agents responsible for the moral worth and implications of all their actions. Our righteous and highly individualistic way of thinking [is] rooted deep in the fundamental categories of our national culture. (2002, 222)

21. Another reason that apprentice ethnographers today may bring with them a pos-

itivist sensibility is that they sometimes come from disciplines—cognitive psychology, management, education, information technology, sociology, and social psychology—where ethnography is not automatically a method of choice and where positivist assumptions are more officially central than in anthropology. The first question for a broad spectrum of apprentice ethnographers, then, may not be the one debated here about which ethnographic approach makes better sense, but rather, why ethnography at all. This book is not an attempt to defend ethnography to positivist officialdom (see Cerwonka and Malkki 2007 for a useful discussion; Willis 1980 gives an elegant account of the limitations of positivist, quantitative, objectivist research).

22. Multiple levels of dualism are in operation here—this is not a matter of choosing a straw opponent in the guise of theoretically unsophisticated genres of work in the field of anthropology generations ago (even if it operated in the 1970s, as I will shortly show). Theorizing in dichotomous, polar terms *is* deeply ingrained in positivist common sense (see Jenks 1998 for an encyclopedic survey of "Core Sociological Dichotomies"; see also note 20 above).

Allen Newell, influential cognitive scientist, argued that dualism is the standard logic of research in experimental, including cognitive, psychology in a paper called "You Can't Play 20 Questions with Nature and Win" (1973). There is surely a dualist logic behind the idea that after carrying out an experiment using a method with "no theoretical bias" the outcome will help decide between nature/nurture—or for that matter formal and informal education. He described cognitive psychology as generating, through elegant experimentation, evidence for an increasing number of specific psychological phenomena (the fifty-nine he lists include, for example, recency, rotation, warm up, and clustering in recall). He went on to suggest, critically, that this is not a taxonomy but only a simple list. And such a list is a cause for worry. For the middle-level theory that could indicate how these phenomena fit together isn't there. Instead, according to Newell, there are a number of dichotomously phrased issues such as nature versus nurture, or visual versus discrete information storage in long-term memory. To illustrate this point further, he offers a list of twenty-four binary oppositions in psychology (288, fig. 2). The existence of a new psychological phenomenon is taken (only) as evidence for one side or the other in one of these highly abstract controversies that are conceived of as "theories." Herbert Simon responded in "How to Win at 20 Questions with Nature," disagreeing with Newell's "pessimism," but missing the point when he conceded, "We cannot have theory-building without binary (or n-ary) oppositions" (1980, 539).

Stallybrass and White (1986) offer an exposition and critique of what they call "the politics of binary extremism." Whereas most objections to dualist theory emphasize the *epistemological* inadmissibility of binary social logic, they set out to analyze the *politics* of dualist practices and their rhetoric. Their argument suggests an interesting way to set ethnographic inquiry in motion, as they sketch a logic of research that helps us see how ethnographic research practice may have critical effects. They argue that dualist theories that separate subject and social world (or science and craft, or formal and informal education) claim that the two do not partake of one another, but instead are polar opposites. Such claims deny their interdependence, and thereby suppress their connections. This politics of binary extremism comes from and sustains social hierarchy from the locus of those in power. This involves not only efforts to separate and deny relations between high and low poles, but to suppress the low, make it taboo, depoliticize the division and naturalize it. Furthermore, this encourages a habit of treating social phenomena representing the poles only one at a time. Stripped of contradictions and the contexts of their mutual production, it is easy to treat either as simply good or bad (as we shall see that Fortes approaches Tallensi education). Yet it is crucial to recognize that dualist theorizing as a template for research is always a comparative enterprise with these particular characteristics.

In addition to the arguments of Jenks and Simon, Bourgois, and Stallybrass and White, we should not forget that there are structural features in the logic of ethnographic and other culture-crossing research practices that require attention to specific levels and kinds of dualistic practices. Strathern mentions several in her 1990 paper: "concentration . . . on single cultures [that] opened up the possibility of exploiting the dualism of the relation between observer and observed" (101) and "cross-cultural comparison which rests on an elucidation of similarities and differences but always implies the distinctiveness of units so compared" (102).

23. I wouldn't assign an end date yet: Quantitative evidence might lie in a recently noted 1,740,000 hits on Google for "formal and informal education." See also Davis and Hogarth's "Rethinking Management Education" (1992), in which Chicago Business School faculty reproduce the logic and the typical distinctions dividing formal and informal education styled as "the university" and "the workplace."

24. Middleton placed traditional and industrialized societies in direct contrast with one another, and suggested correspondences between these forms of social organization and particular types of education:

> In . . . "traditional" societies, those with a minimum of observed social change, with most recognition given to ascribed and formal statuses, and with little importance given to social mobility and the achievement of higher social positions, the education given to children and adolescents is devoted mainly to such matters as kinship, mythology, and cosmological values and moral sanctions that are the heart of their various cultures. Training in physical and vocational techniques is largely incidental and regarded merely as a sign of normal growing up. (1970, xiv–xv)

> In . . . Western industrialized nations, most statuses are achieved; social mobility is both necessary and valued, . . . We should expect the main thrust in our education to be in technical, vocational, and professional training. Education in non-vocational matters (with learning one's social organization, values, beliefs, and assumptions that are also part of our culture) is regarded as of less educational importance. (xiv)

The differentiation of educational from other kinds of social institutions was part of the meaning of "complex," as opposed to what Middleton called "simply organized" societies. It followed that the more differentiated and (technically) specialized the educational institutions, the more explicit should be the pedagogy and the more formal the teaching. Less continuity between educational work and play or less emphasis on the social contribution of learners to the work of adults was seen as an indication of advances in discontinuity between educational forms and the settings of daily activities.

25. In the intellectual ambience of the 1970s, neither anthropologists nor psychologists looked to ethnographies of apprenticeship for clues about the comparative validity

of claims distinguishing formal from informal education. The ethnographies were mostly silent about their implications for comparative theories of education, not least because anthropologists treated issues of apprenticeship qua learning as incidental to accounts of craft practices themselves. There are now a number of ethnographies of apprenticeship, mostly since the 1970s (but see Spier 1924; Reichard 1936). The interests of the ethnographers are extremely heterogeneous, making it difficult to sum up their collective impact on the issues at hand, but a few points stand out (cf. Lave 1995; Lave and Wenger 1991; Herzfeld 2004). A number of anthropologists have experimented with apprenticing *themselves* as part of their fieldwork, as a way to derive a more intimate understanding of local practice (e.g., Reichard 1936; Coy 1989; Cooper 1980, 1989; Keller and Keller 1996; Kondo 1990; Marchand 2001). Given Kvale's insistence on the interrelations of processes of research training and processes of research activity, this should not be too surprising. It offers an interesting reversal of the terms of debate about ethnographic inquiry into apprenticeship. Both Goody (1989) and Lave and Wenger (1991) assumed that ethnographies of apprenticeship were routinely "about" learning. On a closer reading, this turned out not to be true: few ethnographies of apprenticeship are directly focused on this issue. They nonetheless depend on *assumptions* about learning, education, and knowledge in a comparative framework, often in positivist commonsense terms. They offer even unintentionally a challenge to the sort of theorizing that sharply delimits its field of operation to schooling, limits its view of learning to psychological accounts of classroom teaching, and reduces its assumptions about knowledge to its diffusion or circulation (cf. Latour 1987, chap. 3, part C). The ethnographers of apprenticeship exhibit a cheerful lack of interest in those stubbornly institutionalized boundaries and distinctions, and end up imbricating minds, learning, and education in political-economic, historical, cultural, and social relations—relations usually excised from research on learning and schooling in order to give theoretical credence to the decontextualized, the universal, and the abstract. The problem is to take these ethnographers up on the resources they offer us. *Situated Learning* (Lave and Wenger 1991) argued that if you began with ethnographies of apprenticeship and then set out to design a theory of learning (one that formed questions even about schooling with an inquiring spirit), you could arrive at a usefully different theoretical/empirical agenda than if you started as usual from accounts of "formal education." Serious work on the implications of craft practice and apprenticeship for theorizing learning include Keller and Keller 1996, Ingold 2000, and Marchand 2001 as well as Lave and Wenger 1991 and my own later work.

There is one further way in which ethnographies of apprenticeship disturb the conventional enterprise of comparative theorizing about education/learning as they explore apprenticeship as a matter of specific, historical, political-economic relations. They indirectly challenge the assumption of universality underlying much theorizing about learning, knowledge, and research practice. When ethnographic studies of apprenticeship are brought together, they reveal the historical variability of class location, relations with other educational institutional practices, and ideologies of technology in apprenticeship/craft practices (Lave and Wenger 1991, chap. 3). They are neither a timeless form of labor or preparation for labor (see Singleton 1998, on Japanese national tradition; Marchand 2001, on the unique historical traditions in Yemen; and McNaughton 1988, on craft castes and apprenticeship in the Mande Empire). There are accounts of changing practices of craft/

apprenticeship in historical struggles in Europe over shifts from mercantile to industrial capitalism (Goody 1982), agonistic relations under colonial regimes in the nineteenth and twentieth centuries among competing educational practices, schooling and apprenticeship in Egypt (Mitchell 1988) and in Kenya (King 1977), and critical ethnographies of contemporary attempts to co-opt craft practices into state/NGO/neoliberal economic arrangements in Egypt (Elyachar 2005), in France (Terrio 2000), and in Crete (Herzfeld 2004).

These ethnographies provide evidence that crafts and apprenticeship practices are constituted in different historical and cultural relations. A broad conclusion surely follows: If we try to excise those relations of research training and activity, knowledge and learning from their political-economic, historical, and social relations, we do so at our peril. There are no doubt other ways to arrive at this conclusion, but the ethnographies of craft/apprenticeship, taken together, make the point forcefully.

26. As the Liberian project unfolded, there was much to be desired of mathematical sophistication in my argument. New resources for exploring mathematics in relational theoretical terms are now at hand in the work of Helen Verran (2001). Discussion of her work begins at the end of this chapter and goes on throughout the book. Since my partial review of earlier cross-cultural work on mathematics in *Cognition in Practice* (1988), the anthropology of mathematics has expanded and increased in sophistication in the hands of Verran, Eglash (1999), Guyer (2004; Guyer, Khan, and Obarrio 2010), Maurer (e.g., 2005, 2006, 2008), and others.

27. Michael Cole and Sylvia Scribner had already begun the Vai Literacy Project in Liberia when I first went there. Mike encouraged the tailors' apprenticeship project, and he and Sylvia were supportive throughout. We all began, driven quite considerably in reaction to existing cross-cultural experimental studies (see chapter 4, note 1, below), but also by Mike's critical concerns about his own earlier efforts (e.g., Gay and Cole 1967; Cole et al. 1971) and by sustained collaborative teaching and collegial interaction among the group of psychologists and anthropologists he drew together at UC Irvine and later at Rockefeller University. We were trying to develop new approaches to cross-cultural research. Other anthropologists were involved, notably Jack Goody (e.g., Goody, Cole, and Scribner 1977).

28. Hobsbawm, in his introduction to a Verso edition of *The Communist Manifesto* (Marx and Engels 1998, 3), offers an example that could not be more appropriate to the present discussion. He points to a disconcerting historical connection between the craft of tailoring and Marx's theory of labor as praxis:

> In the spring of 1847 Karl Marx and Frederick Engels agreed to join the so-called League of the Just . . . , an offshoot of the earlier League of the Outlaws . . . , a revolutionary secret society formed in Paris in the 1830s under French Revolutionary influence on German journeymen—mostly tailors and woodworkers.

29. Williams does not address how institutions of colonial domination, including trade in slaves, were implicated in those multiple historical distinctions about knowledge and practice. But deep colonial assumptions have surely contributed to the binary logic of asymmetrical comparative research that made Africa a popular test bench for anthropologists and cross-cultural psychologists. As Moran (among myriad others) points out, "Africa in general has long been constructed in the Western imagination as the opposite of the West" (2006, 27).

30. Moran (2006) contrasts pre-and post-1980 Liberia:

The seventies had been characterized by considerable political openness as the ruling one-party state responded to increasing demands for greater participation in government by intellectuals, rural people, and those of indigenous background. (8)

In Liberia, where group identity had historically been fluid, localized, and situational, politicized "tribalism" emerged only after 1980. (16).

By her analysis, it was only the sudden precarious alignment of political power and the state with one ethnolinguistic group after the Samuel Doe coup that set the stage for civil war in Liberia in tribalist terms—an eventuality that seemed very unlikely to me in the mid-1970s.

31. There are a number of ethnographic studies of craft apprenticeship in West Africa, including Allan 1982 (Nigeria); Deafenbaugh 1989 (Hausa weavers in Nigeria); Argenti 2002 (woodcarvers in Cameroon); Dilley 1989, 1999 (Tukolor weavers in Senegal); Dorjahn 1967 (tailors, carpenters, and leather workers in Sierra Leone; Goody 1982 (cloth weavers in Ghana); Lancy 1980 (Kpelle blacksmiths in Liberia); McLaughlin 1979 (wayside mechanics in Ghana); McNaughton 1988 (Mande blacksmiths in Guinea and Mali); Mustafa 1997 (tailors in Senegal); Pokrant 1982 (tailors in Kano, Nigeria); Peil 1970, 1979 (tailors in Accra); and Verdon 1979 (based on Terence Smutylo's 1973 data on Ghanaian artisan workshops in Accra). They variously focus on pre-Western craft production and apprenticeship (e.g., McNaughton), and post-Western colonial capitalist effects (e.g., Goody, McLaughlin, and Mustafa).

32. Elizabeth Brenner, who carried out her dissertation research in Vai math classrooms in Robertsport in 1980, returned to Liberia three years later. She found that

apprenticeship continued to be a viable training opportunity for many young people [while primary, and especially secondary, schooling had mostly collapsed during the civil war]. Goldsmiths, carpenters, tailors and drivers in the city all had apprentices, although many complained that business was not the same because of Liberia's economic recession. In the rural areas, the more traditional skills such as mid-wifery, carving and music were also being taught to a small number of young people in an apprenticeship-style manner. For rural children, learning a trade had generally entailed moving to the city to live and work with a master craftsman. This continued to be the practice in 1988. (1990, 10)

33. Historian Sean Hanretta, Stanford University, e-mail communication, April 30, 2009.

34. "Mande, Manding, and Mandingue have all been used, inconsistently, to identify the civilization that now encompasses the western third of Africa's great northern savanna and large sections of the coastal forests" (McNaughton 1988, xvii).

35. By the mid-fifteenth century, Portuguese ships had begun stopping at the coast, initiating trade in European wares for gold, ivory, and pepper from the interior for which the Vai were intermediaries (Person 1962, 59). Trade in slaves began at the end of the seventeenth century. They were captured by forays into the interior or from inland groups and

sold through intermediaries like the Vai to British and French slavers. Slave taking was abolished by the British in 1807, gradually diminishing until about 1850 (Holsoe 1967).

36. According to Hlophe,

> At the height of their hegemony, between the eleventh and sixteenth centuries, the African Sudanic kingdoms had become the major world suppliers of gold and salt. . . . The fortunes of long-distance trade facilitated the consolidation of state power, the spread of Islamic learning . . . and the formation of a class of professional traders, within the Malinke ethnic group commonly referred to as the Djulas. . . . It was under this Manding supremacy . . . that the empire of Mali attained eminence, as the centre of commerce, religion and learning. (1979, 26)

Corby says that

> trade along the route from southern Guinea to the Atlantic flourished well into the twentieth century and this enabled the Manding to keep in communication with Musadu, the principal Muslim center in southern Guinea. The Manding created an important Islamic corridor in the last third of the eighteenth century which extended from the Muslim center of Musadu to the Loma and Bandi people, then along the trails used by the traders through the Gola Forest to Bopolu and the Condo confederation, and finally to the coast at Cape Mount. . . . At Cape Mount they encountered the Vai. . . . In Vai country the Poro society, always inimical to Islam, was not as powerful as among the Gola and the Mende in the hinterland (1988, 47).

37. Sean Hanretta, e-mail communication, April 30, 2009.

38. Compared to, say, contemporary blacksmiths in Mali and Guinea, the urban Vai and Gola tailors' craft seems to have taken on rather narrow occupational boundaries. McNaughton (1988) examines two puzzling relations that crucially define Mande blacksmiths' endeavors and place in the world. These go well beyond the notion of "occupation" on which Western analyses of apprenticeship rest, offering a mind-boggling contrast to the historical European assumptions about craft production, life, work, power, knowledge, and art laid out by Raymond Williams. One has to do with the relations of the blacksmiths to the rest of Mande society. They are reviled and feared, live apart as near outcasts, and yet are crucial advisors and mediators in major political affairs both locally and much more broadly. The other puzzle has to do with what else the blacksmiths do: They are blacksmiths, making and repairing household and farm implements on a day-to-day basis, true. But they are also community sorcerers, healers, sculptors, performers of circumcision, and often heads of initiation societies. As McNaughton explains, "Their services are so pervasive in Mande society and so embedded in the Mande world view that they literally infuse the culture with much of its character" (1988, 5). Pursuing both puzzles, McNaughton argues that it is not the production of commodities, but the social control of power in special ways in which bards, blacksmiths and leather workers are engaged: "Many blacksmiths are deeply involved in the articulation of Mande social and spiritual space" (40).

39. The idea that critical ethnographic research is always partial has several layers of meaning. First, the double meaning of partial is intended: the results of critical research never achieve a complete or totalizing account of social life. But also, critical ethnographic

research, its practice and its products, stand *for* something, and reflect, analyze, and criticize connections of value and power that adhere in rigorous, reflexive inquiry. Second, as is demonstrated in chapters to come, critical ethnographic practice is characterized by partiality as a way station in one's own changing practice as old established relations become partial in new ways over time. Third, as we are participants in the world we study, unable to step completely outside it for an unobstructed bird's-eye view, research critical of commonsense theoretical practices goes on being part of the problem and requires effort to continue to change.

40. See note 10 above.

41. The way in which mathematics figures in our projects is both strategically similar and substantively different. Verran, philosopher of science and anthropologist, is a profound critic of colonial practices with respect to theorizing number. We share a view that research on number offers a rich field for the study of the politics at the heart of different logics of inquiry. Her close study of Yoruba numbering, and the differences between foundational and relational accounts of numbering, focuses on number as emerging in embodied ritualized generalizing performances, collective goings-on, and relations between language and logic. She points out that in my work I "black box" number (Verran 2001, 259n2). Her point is well taken. In turn, I worry that Verran may "black box" historical forces, complex social relations and institutional practices as she zooms in on "microworlds" of gestural practice. I return to Verran's work in later chapters.

Chapter Two

1. One way to confirm these impressions of the tailors is to compare them to a random sample of urban and rural Vai. These samples were developed by Scribner and Cole in their Vai Literacy Survey, as part of their monumental five-year study of practices of Vai, Arabic, and English literacy among Vai people in Liberia (Scribner and Cole 1981). It appears that the tailors were drawn from families with slightly more craft occupations (among their fathers) than Scribner and Cole's sample of Vai in general. Many in their urban and rural subsamples had some Qur'anic training (in Arabic), though rarely study of the language itself. Many had learned the Vai script, and possibly attended school. The tailors looked much like Scribner and Cole's rural sample with respect to Qur'anic training. Scribner and Cole's urban sample averaged half as much Qur'anic training. The pattern for school attendance was just the opposite: the urban Vai sample showed greater average schooling, both in terms of grades completed and literacy scores, than the rural Vai or the tailors. Eighty-four percent of the rural sample never attended school, as opposed to 70 percent of the tailors and 57 percent of the urban Vai—the tailors were more likely to go to school than if they lived in rural settings but not as likely as other urban Vai. Essentially all members of the two urban samples spoke English. Certainly among the tailors, only the very youngest apprentices spoke little English. The tailors and urban Vai spoke—perhaps more accurately, understood—three languages on average, and the average for the rural sample was only slightly lower. In cosmopolitan West Africa, most people are multilingual, and some of those surveyed could understand as many as five languages.

2. The export of second-hand clothing from the West to third world countries is, as Karen Hansen shows, "an immense, profitable, but barely examined worldwide trading

network that exports millions of dollars worth of used clothing in a commodity trade that has grown more than sixfold worldwide over the last fifteen years" (Hansen 2000, 100). Most people who donate clothing to charities like the Salvation Army or Goodwill Industries or, in the past, Caritas assume the clothing is either given away or sold at nominal prices, but they donate so much that charities can't handle it (103, 104). Instead,

> the purchase and sale of used garments from charities relieves consumers of unwanted clothing, charities obtain much-needed funds, textile recyclers find a reliable supply of clean used clothing, and people in developing countries—where much of the clothing goes—have the opportunity to purchase affordable garments. (101).

It is possible that the bales of clothing I observed were contraband of a sort—Hansen describes several ways this could happen. In the worldwide trade it would have been a tiny fraction of the business.

Hansen's remarkable study of the second-hand clothing trade focuses on Zambia, but what she has to say applies in many respects to Liberia as well. What I saw as the likely end of craft tailoring in Liberia in 1978 might have been too pessimistic, if we go by changes in response to second-hand imports in Zambia. Hansen says that although by 1995 (when second-hand clothing was ubiquitous) there were fewer tailors in Zambia than in the 1980s (when second-hand clothing started to become widespread), tailors still operated in niche markets, "repairing and altering secondhand clothing and sewing garments to order" (145, 165, 173, 176). Hansen explains: "While I have monitored these trades [second-hand clothing imports] had not 'killed' the small-scale tailoring craft, as some feared when I began exploring these issues in 1992" (176–77). As in Liberia, clothing factories may have fared worse than small-scale tailoring endeavors:

> At the end of the 1990s, hardly any garment manufacturers were left in Zambia, save for small-scale tailoring workshops and individual tailors. In fact, the number of small-scale workshops appears to be growing, confronting the . . . import by turning to niche production of garments in styles . . . and sizes not readily found in the second-hand clothing markets. (237)

3. Partly, also, I was laying groundwork for later learning transfer experiments. It seemed important to make sure that the experimental findings were not an effect of sampling bias that could arise if there were strong selection pressures on some strikingly unusual group of Vai and Gola boys to become tailors, or for some apprentices to leave apprenticeship with dispatch if unsuccessful.

4. I asked many of the Vai and Gola tailors whether they thought it would be better to apprentice *their* children to a close relative, a distant relative, or to someone who was no relative at all. A few argued for close relatives, and 80 percent for strangers. There were clearly different opinions about the importance of indulgent parenting compared with stern inculcation of craft standards. Those I talked with who actually had apprenticed children had followed their own advice with surprising consistency.

5. Caroline Bledsoe, who delivered the Morgan Lectures in 1999, writes specifically about the Kpelle of Liberia as engaging in a "wealth-in-people" system that binds people to their superiors in ties of marriage, clientship, and filial obligation: "I will argue that all [Kpelle] people, men as well as women, try to sever their own ties with superiors when

possible, but try to keep subordinates bound to them in ties of obligation" (1980, 1). She speculates that these points might apply widely across West Africa. This would include, of course, master/apprentice relations, a kind of relation of clientship, for the Vai and Gola as well as the Kpelle. Moran concurs, but with reservations (2006, 31).

6. This was common practice until 1978, when a number of the masters made hats for the Independence Day celebration. Reasons for this shift included competition in trousers but not hats from the second-hand clothing import business and inflation that led to greater customer demand for less expensive items such as hats.

7. Mr. B.'s account is quite a close fit with the apprenticeship process described in chapter 3. The picture he paints with respect to teaching is more problematic. His biographical account offers clues about points in the apprenticeship process where instruction from more knowledgeable tailors and apprentices is most likely. Also consider that Mr. B.'s account may enumerate virtually every meaningful formal pedagogical interchange with his master, while being silent about the other 99 percent of the process. The point of this observation will become clearer in chapter 3.

8. The process could be organized in radically different ways. In the garment factory, a tailor carried out a single operation and was known, for example, as either a "cutter" or a "sewer." But in the tailor shops, the garment types were the organizers of major periods of learning. Operations (e.g., cutting and sewing) organized time and effort within shorter periods. See chapter 3.

9. Hansen explains: "Negotiating both clothing needs and desires, consumers are influenced by a variety of sources when they purchase garments. Above all, clothing consumption implicates cultural norms about gender and authority" (2000, 196)—to which tailors must respond, no doubt. "A good deal of clothing competence is entailed in . . . identifying tailors who are able to deliver a finished product to the satisfaction of customers" (204). There is considerable work on the rich and complex intertwined political, cultural, and economic relations of clothing, concerning, for instance, what Misty Bastian identifies as, "what it means to be clothed, to experience clothing on one's body, and to clothe others—in short, what might constitute the embodied practice(s) of clothing" (1996, 100). Bastian discusses conflict with and among Nigerian tailors as well as their clients over women's play with bodily, gendered, and class stereotypes in their clothing practices. Lukose (2009) analyzes the politics around the invention of "demure modern" dress among women college students in Kerala in South India, and Hudita Mustafa (1997) explores artisanal garment production and fashion in Dakar. A number of other studies on "clothing and difference" are gathered together in Hendrickson 1996. All of this work develops dimensions of clothing practices that I could barely conjure at the time.

10. I repeated the struggle in research in the United States on everyday math practices. It takes persistent effort not to formulate research projects, analytic questions, and concepts in academic ethno-, school-centric terms. I concluded *Cognition in Practice* with the critical view that our struggle to escape these assumptions was only very partially successful, and that to the extent that it was, we began to see, and evaluate, relations of quantity in everyday life quite differently than a school template would dictate (Lave 1988).

11. We will see in chapter 4, for example, that imagining the world in terms of distinctions between form and content pervades positivist commonsense theory even at the minute level of individual arithmetic problems as well as at the larger scale discussed here.

12. Verran has a similar reaction:

> My contention, so passionately held that it motivates my long struggle to write this
> book, is that laughter, which can easily turn to a visceral groan, this disconcertment,
> source of both clear delight and confused misery, must be privileged and nurtured,
> valued and expanded upon. These fleeting experiences, ephemeral and embodied, are
> a sure guide in struggling though colonizing pasts, and in generating possibilities for
> new futures. (2001, 5)

Paul Willis talks about coming to a place where "conventional techniques cannot follow
the subjects of subjects themselves," a point where the cultural/symbolic/material systems of the subject and the ethnographer diverge:

> Why are these things happening? Why has the subject behaved in this way? Why do
> certain areas remain obscure to the researcher? What differences in orientation lie be-
> hind the failure to communicate
>
>   It is here, in the interlocking of human meanings, of cultural codes and of forms,
> that there is the possibility of "being surprised." And in terms of the generation of
> "new" knowledge, we know what it is precisely *not* because we shared it—the usual
> notion of empathy—but because we have *not* shared it. It is here that the classical can-
> ons are overturned. . . . It is time to initiate actions or to break expectations in order to
> probe different angles in different lights. Of course, this is a time of maximum distur-
> bance to researchers, whose own meanings are being thoroughly contested. It is pre-
> cisely at this point that the researcher must assume an unrestrained and hazardous
> *self-reflexivity.* (1980, 92)

Chapter Three

1. Burton, Brown, and Fischer's work was based on a conception of "microworlds" moving in the 1970s from the Artificial Intelligence Lab at MIT to center stage in the AI world.
Key figures included Minsky and Papert, Abelson, and Sussman and Winograd (cf. Dreyfus 1981 for a critical review; Honing 1993 for a brief overview). Papert and his associates
criticized common school methods of teaching math and physics. They turned to Piaget
and observations of children's learning outside school in order to develop a pedagogical
application of "microworlds" (i.e., the self-contained world of TURTLE geometry). This
was intended to create contexts in which children could become "the architects of their
own learning."

> Children get to know what it is like to explore the properties of a chosen microworld
> undisturbed by extraneous questions. In doing so they learn to transfer habits of ex-
> ploration from their personal lives to the formal domain of scientific theory construc-
> tion. (Papert 1980, 117)

Burton Brown, and Fischer (1984) applied these ideas in their paper on learning to ski.
Brown was part of the loose synergistic group in and around the School of Social Sciences
at UC Irvine in its early years. Burton, Brown, and Fischer's work on ski instruction was
published in Rogoff and Lave 1984.

2. Papers by Erik Axel (2003, 2009) and Klaus Nielsen (2006, 2007) develop this idea through their research on a complex building construction project in Denmark.

3. In the midst of the fieldwork, I did not attach sufficient importance to relations among the apprentices. I suspect I missed rich and subtle occasions on which all parties learned a great deal about work, skills, and details in the shops—at night while the masters were gone, and the apprentices were together in the shops.

4. I find it fascinating that Helen Verran also turned to a concept of "microworlds." I am trying to grapple in this chapter with the relations between pedagogy and learning on which educational adaptations of the notion of "microworlds" rest. There are critical differences between Burton, Brown, and Fischer's conception of microworlds and my conception of practices of situated learning and of situated instruction in the tailor shops. Verran takes the concept in a different direction and applies it to a close analysis of how Yoruba children generalize. Her conception of "microworlds" is a key and very complex point in her argument about the logic of the culturally situated character of "natural number." She takes off from a notion of microworld given a Foucauldian twist "linking sites of interrogation, normalization and tracking" by Joseph Rouse in his 1987 book *Knowledge and Power* (Verran 2001, 257n2). Rouse in turn got it from the same sources as Burton, Brown, and Fischer (i.e., from Minsky and Papert). I find it difficult enough to imagine a marriage of AI microworlds to Foucault, but the more interesting question may be why Verran would take on such a disjunctive concept at all. Briefly, in her terms microworlds are

specific materially arranged times/places where rituals, repeated routine performances, occur [like two kids exchanging peanuts]. In the structuring of the performance, a vast amount of irrelevant complexity is excluded, and momentarily, ongoing collective life becomes extremely simple. (159)

What goes on "inside" the microworld so constituted is the subject of a complex analysis by Verran about the nature of generalization and ontological politics (2001, chap. 8, 159–62, 173). If Papert (1980, 120) is trying to show that *he* can program simplified microworlds to support children's practices as natural learners, which in his view (buttressed in more sophisticated terms by Piaget's) is to "relate the new to something you already know, then play with it," Verran might be said to be trying to show that *children's* banal everyday practices of generalization are processes of making microworlds (though her microworlds are things like the word "three" in a conversation).

Papert and Verran's interest in the making/learning of science—logics of numbering, or problems in conveying a grasp of Newtonian physics—might not immediately provoke questions about "the outsides" of their micoworlds, but questions about the world of which microworlds are a part are as crucial here as they have been in the broader history of AI theory and practice. The flaws revealed through questions raised about "the context problem" in artificial intelligence proved fatal, specifically with respect to microworld-based research on intelligence (Dreyfus 1979, 1981). I believe a certain practical bracketing of historical forces, institutional arrangements, and the long-term organization of common goings on characterizes Verran's project, though she is not intent on a residualizing dismissal of history and context in principle (the AI problem).

5. Notice the school-like character of this arrangement. Arguably the preoccupation

with autocorrection was motivated in part by the institutional arrangements of schooling—the many-to-one relation of pupils to teacher.

6. Bourdieu's critique of anthropologists' predilection for synoptic diagrams is surely appropriate here (1977, chap. 3).

7. It is also an illustration of the theoretical inadequacy of form/content divisions. The discussion of such divisions at the end of chapter 2 applies to the present discussion as well.

8. Much of the argument here is deeply influenced by Ole Dreier's work (e.g., 2008) and our ongoing discussions.

9. Think about the difference between notions of "way-in" processes by which apprentices initiated new steps, and Burton, Brown, and Fischer's notion of "entry points"—designated by others.

10. Think of Foucault's analysis (1977) of timetables, postures, regimented activities, and rigid routines imposed absolutely as a matter of everyday practice, or of Saba Mahmood's account (2002) of the daily discipline of Egyptian women who undertake to help themselves and each other to become better practitioners of piety. Bourdieu and Passeron (1977) started with the premise that instruction and learning were matters of power and politics. Their analysis addressed teaching as inculcation, as symbolic violence, forced (with legitimacy) on novice learners, though they thereby reduced learning to only a mystified misrecognition of the arbitrary character of acts of pedagogy.

11. To anticipate where this story is going in the longer run, note that conceptions of learning transfer do not acknowledge social practice as we have been looking at it in chapters 2 and 3. If you start with a rough translation of the question that "learning transfer" tries to address—"How does knowledgeable practice move and change across the situations of people's lives?" (cf. Dreier 2008)—a critical ethnographer would follow apprentices across the varying situations of their everyday lives. If you stop reducing learning to individual mental exercise, it becomes possible to open the issue of transfer to broader questions concerning the complex conveyance of "knowledge on the move." But the project in Liberia had a long way to go before reaching this view.

Chapter Four

1. Elizabeth Brenner (n.d.) reviewed cross-cultural experimental psychological research at the time, searching two decades' worth of journals, including the *Journal of Cross-Cultural Psychology*, *International Journal of Psychology*, *British Journal of Educational Psychology*, *Child Development*, *Africana Psychologica*, and *Human Development*. She analyzed in great detail fifty-seven cross-cultural experimental studies (the earliest 1962, the latest 1978) in which schooling was somehow implicated. It made its appearance almost without exception in the form of "school attendance" as a major independent variable (yes, no, number of years of schooling, grades completed). The vast majority of these studies (forty-one) were set in sub-Saharan Africa, most frequently West Africa. The results of her analysis can be briefly paraphrased. Most cross-cultural studies were adaptations of psychological experiments developed in Western countries, and the studies were superficial if not silent about the effects of cultural differences between the experimenter and the experimental subjects. The studies were silent about social class, cultural, and other differences among groups of

children they compared (exceptions included Goodnow 1962 and Serpell 1969). The studies rarely located their experimental tasks or the children themselves in the contexts of their activities. None compared schooling to any other specific form of education. The studies were mostly vague about just how schooling was supposed to affect cognitive performances, it just did—or it didn't (most authors presented their data as the mean number of right responses on experimental tasks). The effect, Brenner observed, appeared to be "an ethnocentric attitude that the only interesting information is whether other people are like us but it doesn't matter what they actually do." Piagetians and the Cole-Scribner group were most likely to look for different strategies for carrying out experimental tasks, although this approach was also common in memory studies (Doob 1965; Wagner 1974, 1978). Brenner pointed out that the studies were completely unrevealing about *schooling*, for "*x* years of schooling" figured only as an attribute of subjects. What schools are, how they work, what children do in school—similarly or differently in West Africa than in Western Europe or the United States—were not addressed even indirectly.

Issues of language, specifically, the use of interpreters and translators, were especially confounding. Brenner observed that in only seven cases had the experimenters learned the local language well enough to administer experiments themselves; and of those seven, four were done by Greenfield, who learned Wolof, and her assistant Childs, who learned Tzotzil (e.g., Greenfield and Childs 1977). Most experimenters hired research assistants who spoke the local language. Brenner pointed out that there was not enough information in the studies to judge the competence of local assistants or translators when more than one language was involved. Looking at just the twenty-three Piagetian studies, she compared their results with their language arrangements. Of the nine studies "finding no difference between schooled and unschooled subjects, four were done by native speakers of the local language and in two the foreign experimenter had learned the local language well enough to administer the tasks." Two others used translators, and one involved a nonverbal task. Of the eleven studies that did claim to demonstrate positive school effects, all the experiments were administered by local research assistants. (Three more showed mixed results, of which two involved a research assistant.) Cross-cultural experimental results appeared to be more clearly an effect of differences between experimenters than differences in subjects' "education."

Across the experiments as a whole, the evidence for and against school effects were at best deeply equivocal. Amalgamating the results task by task from within studies, there were twenty-six tasks in which "schooled" children were more successful. Countering assumptions about the superior effects of schooling, for twenty-nine tasks there was no difference between schooled and "unschooled" children, and nine other tasks where the latter scored higher than those who attended school. Against this background, an ethnographically based study involving a theory of how schooling and other educational practices are supposed to operate (differently) looked like a move in the right direction.

The cross-cultural experimental studies looked at school effects mainly as a background to questions about just what kids who didn't go to school were (and were not) able to do. And yet schooling was on the table at all times, whether directly of interest or not. Why? The real question here is not "Why school?" but "Why Africa?" A long answer would analyze the history of colonial domination, Western claims about schooling and scientific achievement, social evolutionary theories featuring literacy as a crucial element in reaching a "civilized" state, notions about primitive thought by the likes of Lévy-Bruhl, from whence come psychologists' categories of thought (classification, memory, logic) and developmental stages supposed to recapitulate phylogeny or the history of knowledge (Piaget). This state of affairs drew both researchers who were in uncritical agreement but also those intent on critical resistance to this ethnocentric historical, political-economic morass.

Experimentalists might also have given a second answer to the "Why Africa?" question: In instrumental mode, bracketing out all of the above, in a place where schooling is the exception, researchers could find a "naturally occurring experiment" that was not possible "at home," where schooling was virtually universal. Cognitive development could be examined independently from "school effects." The Vai people in Liberia, with their century-old syllabic script, were of special interest to Scribner and Cole (on the critical side) because it was further possible to separate the effects of literacy on cognition when that literacy was not transmitted through schooling and, further, was learned and used in the context of Arabic and English literacy practices as well (cf. Scribner and Cole 1981).

2. This limited menu still lies deep in the commonsense problematic: Parallel distributed processing (PDP) arose in the 1980s as the second of two central theories of artificial intelligence, opposing a theory of connectionism to a theory of central processing units (CPU) engaged in hierarchical tree structuring. To model changing "intelligence," central processing theory focused on generalization of formal structures, PDP on the formation of associations. Hubert Dreyfus became a defender of PDP connectionism, leading him to reject the old theory of learning (novices start out as intuitive actors and as they become experts become more and more Judd-like rule-guided knowers), in favor of his "new" account, in which learning has just the reverse trajectory, from rigid and naïve rule-guided activity to complex intuitively connected expertise (Dreyfus and Dreyfus 1986). Together, these theories of information processing and learning reproduce precisely the distinctions central to the Judd/Thorndike debate over learning transfer.

3. In the earliest incarnation of this book, I worked through the experimental data via multiple regression analysis. Charles Lave advised and encouraged Scribner and Cole and me in this endeavor. For present purposes, I have set this level of detail aside.

4. See Sharp, Cole, and Lave (1979) and Scribner and Cole (1981, 250) for discussions of this practice.

Jane Guyer, in her Morgan Lectures book, *Monetary Transactions in Atlantic Africa*, is appropriately critical of initial survey work:

> Anthropologists generally steer clear of standardized surveys, where the framing of the problematic and the choice of concepts strongly shape the findings toward specific policy purposes.... Possibly the respondents were interpreting the questions from their own vantage points. People say *something* true about themselves, but on assumptions that probably differ from those of the investigators.... They are saying something, but perhaps something *else*. (2004, 131)

I have worried similarly about the interview/survey work I did in the early days in Happy Corner. Some of my questions were surely poorly designed to elicit reasonable local responses. Some answers may have been produced by tailors who had to guess what I "really" wanted to know. Analysis tends to categorize and compartmentalize people, their characteristics, activities, and relations in ways that fit, for example, modernization theory or sociological notions about social mobility, but not local practices. For all of these reasons, I trusted some of my interview questions and their responses more than others, but none of them completely. Malkki also discusses anthropological concerns about surveys critically and helpfully (e.g., Cerwonka and Malkki 2007, 167–69).

5. The term "school" is often applied unreflectively to situations that seem even vaguely analogous, including sites of drawn-out initiation ceremonies, like Poro, or Qur'anic training. But their quite different institutional arrangements and everyday practices require careful analysis before deciding to group them together (or not).

6. I was not alone in drawing limited conclusions from equivocal or negative findings. Scribner and Cole concluded their book on the Vai Literacy Project with this observation:

> In this book we have made a seemingly relentless descent from the general to the specific. We began with grand and ancient speculations about the impact of literacy on history, on philosophy, and on the minds of individual human beings; we ended with details of experiments on mundane, everyday activities that would, under other circumstances, probably escape our notice or our interest. Instead of generalized changes in cognitive ability, we found localized changes in cognitive skills manifested in relatively esoteric experimental settings. Instead of qualitative changes in a person's orientation to language, we found differences in selected features of speech and communication. If we were to regard only general consequences as worthy of serious attention, we would have to dismiss literacy activities among the Vai as being of little psychological interest. (1981, 234)

Their critical concerns about the state of the field were based in part on a theoretical perspective based on notions of "practice" and "social practice." I was as surprised by this language, in going back to *The Psychology of Literacy* after some years, as I was by paths crossed by Verran and artificial intelligence researchers over the idea of "microworlds" in chapter 3. By a practice Scribner and Cole meant

> a recurrent, goal-directed sequence of activities using a particular technology and particular systems of knowledge. We use the term "skills" to refer to the coordinated sets of actions involved in applying this knowledge in particular settings. A practice, then, consists of three components: technology, knowledge, and skills. . . . tasks that individuals engage in constitute a social practice when they are directed to socially recognized goals and make use of a shared technology and knowledge system. (236)

Their view of practice still lay in the theoretical ballpark of cognitive theory, but it propelled them beyond general notions of literacy and their reputed consequences ("alphabetic literacy fosters abstraction") into persistent questions about what people *do* with literacy in specific contexts for specific purposes. They concluded with respect to Vai and Arabic literacies that each led to narrow skills deriving from rather specifically related practices. This might not surprise, but their conclusions included school / English literacy as well:

> Some investigators have concluded that "attendance at school stimulates growth of overall cognitive competence" . . . but school effects in our studies are not consistent enough to support that generalization. . . . The one [confirmed] hypothesis about

> schooling effects . . . is the observation that school fosters abilities in expository talk in contrived situations. . . . All primary influences of schooling in the present research fit this description. (244)

However, they ended by noting an asymmetry between "school and script effects: English schooling contributes to performance on most tasks that we devised to model Vai script practices. . . . But script literacy shows no such similar spread to the general ability tasks that historically have demonstrated the influence of schooling" (253). Although they said in passing that they relied on "the experiments which historically have been used to examine intellectual consequences of schooling, and which formed our initial cognitive batteries" (257), nowhere did they mention the possibility that experiments themselves, as social practices, were far more intelligible in terms of school classroom practices than any other, and might well account for the asymmetry that they attributed instead to different literacies. I bring this up, because I explore this point here and in chapter 5.

Scribner and Cole's care and caution led to appropriately narrow results; they called for ethnographic studies of schooling and highlighted the need to unpack "urbanization" in their experimental findings. All of this—including their call for arduous tasks not suited to the psychologists' forte at "cycles of hypothesis testing" (at which Scribner and Cole were wizards), may well have contributed to reducing enthusiasm for cross-cultural psychological studies in the 1980s as Verran suggests (2001, 241–42n20; though see Greenfield 2004). There were many other forces at work in West Africa, not least the civil wars in Liberia and Sierra Leone. I do not believe that the issues involved have become less salient as they have moved to, or continued on in, other arenas (Lave 1988).

7. See also chapter 5, note 9, below.

8. When next in Liberia, I asked Vai and Gola friends about the customary use of written numbers. Anyone literate in English (or Arabic) would use numerals in writing dates on letters and for numbers appearing in the text of letters. This is true in Vai script documents as well. I went through the Vai manuscript collection of the Rockefeller project and found many examples of this practice, confirming my informants' statements. Furthermore, informants stated that essentially all Vai and Gola adults can read Arabic numbers, whether they are otherwise literate or not.

From the Rockefeller Vai manuscript collection, the following observations emerge. The Vai appear to have shifted from a British monetary system using pounds, shillings, and pence in the early 1950s. Lists of people are numbered in Arabic numerals; pages are also numbered in this way. Sums of money are written in columns of entries, for example, for dues to self-insurance clubs. Dates are written in Arabic numerals. Occasionally placeholding conventions for addition and subtraction or decimal notation for money occur in the middle of lines of script. Occasional problems are written in Vai with only the numbers in Arabic script.

9. There was a little evidence in the performance data that at first appeared to support the Western assumption that school math ought to replace shop-learned math. Looking only at scores of tailors who sometimes employed the base-ten, written Arabic arithmetic system, it was fairly easy to sort the tailors' scores into three groups that reflected how much schooling they had had. But there was one anomalous group: tailors with a moderate amount of schooling and at the same time a moderate amount of tailoring experience

did less well than the group with a similar amount of schooling and *either* a little or a lot of tailoring experience. This moderate schooling, moderate tailoring experience group improved in score at a much slower rate than other groups. The tailors with 3–6 years of tailoring experience and 1–4 years of schooling did no better than tailors who had not been to school at all. The effect was not due to small differences in average amount of schooling: both those with 1–2 years of tailoring experience and those with 3–6 years of experience averaged 1.7 years of school. This middle group was younger than most groups—perhaps they had not had as much time to learn basic arithmetic skills. But they were only half a year younger than those with 1–2 years (that is, less) tailoring experience, who did much better on the arithmetic task. The effect seemed to be a finding, not an artifact of sampling.

It seemed possible that we were seeing snapshots of a years'-long process of a shift to a syncretic system combining some features of the spoken Vai arithmetic system and the base-ten system being taught in Liberian schools. A syncretic system certainly was not taught in schools. Elizabeth Brenner's dissertation research in Vai schools in Robertsport (1985a) showed that Vai children arrived at school with a knowledge of a Vai number system and its everyday uses; they entered schools that taught base-ten arithmetic in English. She discovered that in the classroom (but not elsewhere) they created a synthetic approach combining the two, and used the others differently in other times and places. The syncretic Vai/Arabic place-holding math was not used in the tailor shops (as we'll see in the next chapter).

10. I have been careful to use the term arithmetic "experiment" or experimental "task" in writing. But I thought about them interchangeably as the "arithmetic test." Schools and tests, experiments and tasks—the familiarity of each for the other testifies to the shadow of schooling on the cross-cultural experimental enterprise (Lave 1986).

11. I went on in the 1980s to explore and analyze learning transfer critically with colleagues Michael Murtaugh and Olivia de la Rocha in the Adult Math Project and to write a book based on that project, *Cognition in Practice* (Lave 1988). Despite a constant stream of theoretical and practical objections throughout its history, the notion of "learning transfer" remains a key enabling justification in research on schooling (see Lobato's 2006 review of recent work). Packer (2001) gives a powerful critical analysis of these debates. Dreier (2008) moves the conversation to focus on the conduct of everyday life, on people moving among, connecting, separating, and influencing the multiple contexts of their lives. Such an approach would analyze the everyday practices attendant on the institutionalized sequestration that defines schooling as part of people's trajectories through those multiple daily contexts. An exclusive preoccupation with "knowledge" traffic out of school is quite unlikely to illuminate relations between schooling and other contexts, in my view.

12. Chapter 3 of Verran's *Science and an African Logic* (2001) is a powerful analysis of number concepts and practice. She offers an intricate account of Yoruba number names, the recursions that make them generative, and a grammatical and in-talk analysis of how they act as nominalized verbs that give the mode of "presenting: particular arranged manifestations." She goes on:

> Whereas Yoruba number names imply a second-order form of modifying, English language numerals are a form of second-order qualifying.

It is this characteristic of working through modes that has an analyst like Hallpike classifying Yoruba numeration as primitive. On his universalist account of quantifying, processes that proceed in ways that fail to evoke the abstract element of qualities are primitive. Similarly, Carnap's positivist account has the evoking of qualities as central in the development of quantitative concepts. Here we see the significance of a relativist account of number like Bloor's (1991). This has social practices of ordering [numbering] as constituting the foundation for the domain of number, and allows for the possibility of numbers being modes as easily as it accepts the possibility of their being qualities. We begin to recognize the possibility of there being many separate logics of generalizing, each recognizable only as relative to others. (70)

Chapter Five

1. Guyer (2004, 59) quotes Belasco (1980, 32): "Uncertainty among the Yoruba is not fixed on the unpredictability of profit in a market enterprise, but rather it is concerned with the possibility of existential reversals."

2. Here, the term "precise calculation" is used as a gloss for school-based assumptions that there is a fixed, given problem to be worked through from representation to solution followed by checking. The answer should be calculated exactly if in whole numbers, or to one or two decimal places, matching the accuracy displayed in the problem (Säljö and Wyndhamn 1993).

3. The term "estimation" used in the transfer experiment analysis in chapter 4 is not employed in this discussion because it had too many possible meanings: guessing, approximating a length or angle without a metering device when such a device exists, simplifying inputs and/or arithmetic operations to produce a solution less accurate than that recommended by customary precision constraints, making use of less accurate inputs than usual because better information is not available, a process attributed to someone else if their customary precision constraints are looser than the speaker's. The word "estimation" has connotations of inaccuracy—the modifier "accurate" has to be added to express the notion of estimation very close to a target point—but the accuracy-in-relation-to-a-point may be very high, and consistently so. For example, the tailors were extremely accurate (from the point of view of my customary precision constraints) at estimating linear distances up to a yard or four feet within 5 or 10 percent of the distance involved, often much closer.

4. Anthropologist Hugh Gladwin suggested an excellent example (personal communication): A good analogy to Sumerian commercial records or Mayan code multiplication tables is the telephone directory. The purpose is to increase the amount of information in the environment. We don't expect a child's cognitive functions to change as a result of consulting the telephone directory.

5. One common, interesting checking routine involved use of the tape measure in cutting out trousers. The tailor almost always guessed the distance he was aiming for, then used the tape measure to check it, rather than using the tape first.

6. Further, Arabic place-holding arithmetic notation is a spatial scheme for representing numbers, most useful where it can be written. There were two problems with this in the tailor shops: paper and pencils were not part of the tailors' usual inventory of tools—

among other things, they were too expensive. Furthermore, privacy was difficult to sustain in the tailor shops, and written monetary records in a tailor's storage box would be easily accessible when he was not in the shop.

7. In the examples of doing relations of quantity, the social events in which they are embedded may give numbers a poetic ambiguity, while the numbers themselves remain unanalyzed. For a glimpse of how Verran (2001) might explore their innards as ritually produced microworlds, see above, note 4 in chapter 3 and note 12 in chapter 4.

8. A lot of effort went into making it roughly as easy for tailors who had not been to school to guess what was wanted of them during the first experiments, as it was for the tailors who had been to school. Given the close relationship of school tests and experimental tasks, that was a tall order, indeed I suspect an impossible one.

9. Comparisons such as those discussed here were pertinent to an ongoing argument in the late 1970s and early 1980s about the relative complexity posed by experiments in general in contrast with everyday life in general. The conventional logic argued that experiments tested and probed, pushing for the limits of capacities that were not to be seen in the supposedly simple and uncomplicated efforts of everyday life. Led by the Laboratory for Comparative Human Cognition, this dualist claim was in the process of flipping over to a more respectful appreciation of the complexities of everyday life. The tailors project spoke to this debate (e.g., Lave 1980). In subsequent years, I've come to think that although I claimed that my scheme referred to some general and unspecified notion of "everyday life," in fact its power lay in the familiar institutional arrangements and practices of the tailor shops.

10. I think of this as the "lily pad" problem. Conceiving of people as merely hopping from one situation to another still refuses to address the more profound questions of how situations and their differences make each other and how participants shape and are shaped by their trajectories of practice. Ole Dreier's 2008 exploration of "the conduct of everyday life" offers a theoretically powerful antidote.

11. See note 9 above.

12. See chapter 1, note 39, above.

Chapter Six

1. A concept of "analysis" has proved to be indispensable to the tailors project and to the book—laced through the discussion from beginning to end. This complex concept, composed of questions, categories, and other tools of inquiry, should by rights be the subject of careful analysis itself. Certainly care is required in using the term—for "analysis" often seems to contrast with notions of description or interpretation (among others) as the leading kind of work of inquiring in different problematics. It is not used with rigorous consistency even when it is a central term for "doing inquiry." I sketch a relational concept of analysis briefly in note 7 below after discussing relational concepts more generally.

2. Likewise, some years later, notions of reading problem and solution through each other was central to the conception of "gap-closing" arithmetic processes in our research in Orange County, California (Lave 1988, 19 and, more amply, chap. 5).

3. The concept of "communities of practice" in Lave and Wenger 1991 was an attempt

to address this problem, though that might surprise readers who have encountered the notion in other settings.

4. See also chapter 1, note 18, above.

5. I am working on this project in a book forthcoming under the title *Changing Practice*.

6. Verran (2001) offers complex, sustained analysis of these issues.

7. What, for instance, is involved in "doing analysis" in relational terms? On the one hand, analysis is a process of empirical (theoretical) inquiry, looking for patterns, connections, disconnections, contradictions, tensions, and generative logics of practice. On the other hand, theoretically, analysis furnishes theoretical tools for engaging in a process of rising to the concrete, making historical relational comparisons, and working with relational concepts. Analysis is in fact a dialectical process. It is surely empirical and theoretical at the same time; it is the work of tracing and transforming apparently separate social objects and concepts in their relations. It requires keeping after the notion that nothing is only "itself," and keeping front and center the idea that its relations are multiple and contradictory. Paul Willis describes this as

> the possibility of a circular development between a progressively more specified "theoretical confession" and the reconstituted forms of theory and back to the specifics of the fieldwork relation. This is the project of producing, finally, a fuller explanatory presentation of the concrete. (1980, 93)

8. What it is possible to understand historically-relationally about the world will be different when worked through other relation(s). "Apprenticeship" is not the only interesting relation of which the tailors' world, critical ethnographic practice, or social practice theory may be a part.

9. That is, go back to "that concrete empirical reference, a privileged and undissolved 'moment' within a theoretical analysis without thereby making it 'empiricist'" (Hall 2003, 128).

REFERENCES

Adler, Patricia A., and Peter Adler. 1987. *Membership roles in field research.* Newbury Park, CA: Sage Publications.

Allan, Rob. 1982. Capitalist development and the educational role of Nigerian apprenticeship. *Comparative Education* 18 (2): 123–37.

Argenti, Nicolas. 2002. People of the chisel: Apprenticeship, youth, and elites in Oku (Cameroon). *American Ethnologist* 29 (3): 497–533.

Axel, Erik. 2003. Theoretical deliberations on regulation as productive tool use. *Outlines* 5 (1): 31–46.

———. 2009. What makes us talk about wing nuts? Critical psychology and subjects at work. *Theory and Psychology* 19 (2): 275–95.

Barnes, John A. 1971. *Three styles in the study of kinship.* London: Tavistock.

Bastian, Misty L. 1996. Female "Alhajis" and entrepreneurial fashions: Flexible identities in southeastern Nigerian clothing practice. In *Clothing and difference: Embodied identities in colonial and post-colonial Africa,* ed. Hildi Hendrickson, 97–132. Durham, NC: Duke University Press.

Bateson, Gregory. 1972. *Steps to an ecology of mind.* Chicago: University of Chicago Press.

Becker, Howard. 2000. Response to the "Manifesto." *Ethnography* 1 (2): 257–60.

Belasco, Bernard. 1980. *The entrepreneur as culture-hero: Preadaptations to Nigerian economic development.* New York: J. F. Bergin.

Bernstein, Richard J. 1971. *Praxis and action: Contemporary philosophies of human activity.* Philadelphia: University of Pennsylvania Press.

Bledsoe, Caroline H. 1980. *Women and marriage in Kpelle society.* Stanford: Stanford University Press.

Bloor, David. 1991. *Knowledge and social imagery.* 2nd ed. Chicago: University of Chicago Press.

Bourdieu, Pierre. 1977. *Outline of a theory of practice.* Cambridge: Cambridge University Press.

Bourdieu, Pierre, and Jean-Claude Passeron. 1977. *Reproduction in education, society and culture.* London: Sage Publications.

Bourgois, Philippe. 2002. The violence of moral binaries: Response to Leigh Binford. *Ethnography* 3 (2): 221–31.

Brenner, Mary Elizabeth. 1985a. Arithmetic and classroom interaction as cultural practices among the Vai of Liberia. PhD diss., University of California, Irvine.

———. 1985b. The practice of arithmetic in Liberian schools. *Anthropology and Education Quarterly* 16 (3): 177–86.

———. 1990. Education and the Vai: School and alternatives. Talk delivered to the American Educational Research Association, Boston, MA.

———. n.d. A review of cross-cultural experiments on cognition. School of Social Sciences, University of California, Irvine.

Burton, Richard R., John Seely Brown, and Gerhard Fischer. 1984. Skiing as a model of instruction. In *Everyday cognition: Its development in social context*, ed. Barbara Rogoff and Jean Lave, 139–50. Cambridge: Harvard University Press.

Cerwonka, Allaine, and Liisa H. Malkki. 2007. *Improvising theory: Process and temporality in ethnographic fieldwork.* Chicago: University of Chicago Press.

Clifford, James. 1986. On ethnographic self-fashioning: Conrad and Malinowski. In *Reconstructing individualism*, ed. T. Heller, D. Wellburg, and M. Sosna, 140–62. Stanford: Stanford University Press.

Clifford, James, and George E. Marcus, eds. 1986. *Writing culture: The poetics and politics of ethnography.* Berkeley and Los Angeles: University of California Press.

Clower, R. W., and G. Dalton, M. Harwitz, and A. A. Walters. 1966. *Growth without development: An economic survey of Liberia.* Evanston, IL: Northwestern University Press.

Cole, Michael, John Gay, Joseph A. Glick, and Donald W. Sharp, with Thomas Ciborowski, Frederick Frankel, John Kellemu, and David F. Lancy. 1971. *The cultural context of learning and thinking: An Exploration in experimental anthropology.* New York: Basic Books.

Cole, Michael, Lois Hood, and Raymond McDermott. 1978. Ecological niche picking: Ecological invalidity as an axiom of experimental cognitive psychology. Unpublished manuscript. Laboratory of Comparative Human Cognition, University of California, San Diego.

Colson, Elizabeth. 1985. Using anthropology in a world on the move. *Human Organization* 44 (3): 191–96.

Comaroff, Jean, and John Comaroff. 2003. Ethnography on an awkward scale: Postcolonial anthropology and the violence of abstraction. *Ethnography* 4 (2): 147–79.

Conrad, David C., and Barbara E. Frank. 1995. Nyamkalaya: Contradiction and ambiguity in Mande society. In *Status and identity in West Africa: Nyamakalaw of Mande*, ed. David C. Conrad and Barbara E. Frank, 1–26. Bloomington: University of Indiana Press.

Cooper, Eugene. 1980. *The wood-carvers of Hong Kong: Craft production in the world capitalist periphery.* Cambridge: Cambridge University Press.

———. 1989. Apprenticeship as field method: Lessons from Hong Kong. In *Apprenticeship: From theory to method and back again*, ed. Michael W. Coy, 137–48. Albany: State University of New York Press.

Corby, Richard A. 1988. Manding traders and clerics: The development of Islam in Liberia to the 1870s. *Liberian Studies Journal* 8 (1): 42–66.

Coy, Michael W., ed. 1989. *Apprenticeship: From theory to method and back again.* Albany: State University of New York Press.

D'Azevedo, Warren L. 1959. The setting of Gola society and culture: Some theoretical implications of variation in time and space. *Kroeber Anthropological Society Papers* 21:43–125.

———, ed. 1973. *The traditional artist in African societies*. Bloomington: Indiana University Press.

———. 1980. Gola Poro and Sande: Primal tasks in social custodianship. *Ethnologische Zeitschrift Zürich* 1:13–22.

Davis, Harry L., and Robin M. Hogarth. 1992. Rethinking management education: A view from Chicago. Selected Paper 72, University of Chicago, Graduate School of Business.

Deafenbaugh, Linda. 1989. Hausa weaving: Surviving amid the paradoxes. In *Apprenticeship: From theory to method and back again*, ed. Michael Coy, 163–80. Albany: State University of New York Press.

Denzin, N. K. 1992. *Symbolic interactionism and cultural studies: The politics of interpretation*. Oxford: Blackwell.

Dilley, Roy M. 1989. Secrets and skills: Apprenticeship among Tukolor weavers. In *Apprenticeship: From theory to method and back again*, ed. Michael Coy, 181–198. Albany: State University of New York Press.

———. 1999. Ways of knowing, forms of power. *Cultural Dynamics* 11 (1): 33–55.

Doob, L. 1965. Exploring eidetic imagery among the Kamba of central Kenya. *Journal of Social Psychology* 67:3–22.

Dorjahn, Vernon R. 1967. Tailors, carpenters, and leather workers in Magburaka. *Sierra Leone Studies* 20:158–72.

Dreier, Ole. 2003. *Subjectivity and social practice*. Center for Health, Humanity and Culture, Philosophy Department, University of Aarhus, Denmark.

———. 2008. *Psychotherapy in everyday life*. Cambridge: Cambridge University Press.

Dreyfus, Hubert L. 1979. *What computers can't do: The limits of artificial intelligence*. New York: Harper and Row.

———. 1981. From micro-worlds to knowledge representation: AI at an impasse. In *Mind design: Philosophy, psychology, artificial intelligence*, ed. John Haugeland, 161–204. Montgomery, VT: Bradford Books.

Dreyfus, Hubert L., and Stuart E. Dreyfus. 1986. *Mind over machine: The power of human intuition and expertise in the era of the computer*. New York: The Free Press.

Eglash, Ron. 1999. *African fractals: Modern computing and indigenous design*. New Brunswick: Rutgers University Press.

Elyachar, Julia. 2005. *Markets of dispossession: NGOs, economic development, and the state in Cairo*. Durham: Duke University Press.

Faubion, James D., and George E. Marcus, ed. 2009. *Fieldwork is not what it used to be: Learning anthropology's method in a time of transition*. Ithaca: Cornell University Press.

Favret-Saada, Jeanne. 1980. *Deadly words: Witchcraft in the Bocage*. Trans. Catherine Cullen. Cambridge: Cambridge University Press.

Fortes, Meyer. 1938. Social and psychological aspects of education in Taleland. First published as a supplement to *Africa* 11 (4). Reprinted in *Time and social structure*, ed. Meyer Fortes (New York: Humanities Press), 201–39.

———. 1969. *Kinship and the social order: The legacy of Lewis Henry Morgan*. Chicago: Aldine.

———. 1978. An anthropologist's apprenticeship. *Annual Review of Anthropology* 7:1–30.

Foucault, Michel. 1977. *Discipline and punish: The birth of the prison.* New York: Pantheon Books.

Fraenkel, Merran. 1964. *Tribe and class in Monrovia.* Oxford: Oxford University Press.

Gay, John, and Michael Cole. 1967. *The new mathematics and an old culture.* New York: Holt, Rinehart and Winston.

Geertz, Clifford. 1988. *Works and lives.* Stanford: Stanford University Press.

Geras, Norman. 1972. Althusser's Marxism: An account and assessment. *New Left Review* 71:57–86.

Ginsburg, Herbert. 1977. Some problems in the study of schooling and cognition. *The Quarterly Newsletter of the Institute for Comparative Human Development* (Rockefeller University) 1:7–10.

Goodnow, Jacqueline J. 1962. A test of milieu differences with some of Piaget's tasks. *Psychological Monographs* 76 (36), whole no. 555.

Goody, Esther. N. 1982. Daboya weavers: Relations of production, dependence and reciprocity. In *From craft to industry: The ethnography of proto-industrial cloth production,* ed. Esther N. Goody. Cambridge: Cambridge University Press.

———. 1989. Learning, apprenticeship and the division of labor. In *From theory to method and back again,* ed. Michael W. Coy, 233–56. Albany: State University of New York Press.

Goody, Jack. 1977. *The domestication of the savage mind.* Cambridge: Cambridge University Press.

Goody, Jack, Michael Cole, and Sylvia Scribner. 1977. Writing and formal operations: A case study among the Vai. *Africa* 47 (3): 289–304.

Greenfield, Patricia Marks. 2004. *Weaving generations together: Evolving creativity in the Maya of Chiapas.* Santa Fe: School of American Research Press.

Greenfield, Patricia Marks, and Carla P. Childs. 1977. Weaving, color terms, and pattern representation: Cultural influences and cognitive development among the Zinacantecos of southern Mexico. *International Journal of Psychology* 11:23–48.

Gupta, Akhil, and James Ferguson. 1992. Beyond "culture": Space, identity, and the politics of difference. *Cultural Anthropology* 7 (1): 6–23. Reprinted in *Ethnographic fieldwork: An anthropological reader,* ed. Antonius Robben and Jeffrey A. Sluka, 337–46. Oxford: Blackwell.

———. 1997. Discipline and practice: "The field" as site, method, and location in anthropology. In *Anthropological locations: Boundaries and grounds of a field science,* ed. Akhil Gupta and James Ferguson, 1–46. Berkeley and Los Angeles: University of California Press.

Guyer, Jane I. 2004. *Marginal gains: Monetary transactions in Atlantic Africa.* Chicago: University of Chicago Press.

Guyer, Jane I., Naveeda Khan, and Juan Obarrio. 2010. Number as inventive frontier. *Anthropological Theory* 10 (1): 36–61.

Hall, Stuart. 2003. Marx's *Notes on method*: A "reading" of the 1857 introduction. *Cultural Studies* 17 (2): 113–49.

Hannerz, Ulf. 2003. Being there . . . and there . . . and there! Reflections on multi-site ethnography. *Ethnography* 4 (2): 201–16.

———. 2004. *Foreign news: Exploring the world of foreign correspondents*. Lewis Henry Morgan Lecture Series. Chicago: University of Chicago Press.

Hanretta, Sean. 1991. The development of caste systems in West Africa. *The Journal of African History* 32(2): 221–50.

Hansen, Karen Tranberg. 2000. *Salaula: The world of secondhand clothing and Zambia*. Chicago: University of Chicago Press.

Hart, Gillian. 2002. *Disabling globalization: Places of power in post-apartheid South Africa*. Berkeley and Los Angeles: University of California Press.

Hendrickson, Hildi, ed. 1996. *Clothing and difference: Embodied identities in colonial and post-colonial Africa*. Durham: Duke University Press.

Herzfeld, Michael. 2004. *The body impolitic: Artisans and artifice in the global hierarchy of value*. Chicago: University of Chicago Press.

Hill, Matthew H. 1972. Speculations on linguistic and cultural history in Sierra Leone. Paper presented at the Conference on Manding Studies, SOAS, London.

Hlophe, Stephen. 1979. *Class, ethnicity and politics in Liberia: A class analysis of power struggles in the Tubman and Tolbert Administrations from 1944–1975*. Washington, DC: University Press of America.

Holland, Dorothy, and Jean Lave, eds. 2001. *History in person: Enduring struggles, contentious practice, intimate identities*. Santa Fe: School of American Research Press.

Holland, Dorothy, William Lachicotte Jr., Debra Skinner, and Carol Cain. 1998. *Identity and agency in cultural worlds*. Cambridge: Harvard University Press.

Holsoe, Svend. 1967. The cassava leaf people: An ethnohistorical study of the Vai people with a particular emphasis on the Tewo Kingdom. PhD diss., Boston University.

———. 1976. The Manding in western Liberia: An overview. *Liberian Studies Journal* 8 (1): 1–12.

———. 1977. Slavery and economic response among the Vai. In *Slavery in Africa: Historical and anthropological perspectives*, ed. Suzanne Miers and Igor Kopytoff, 287–303. Madison: University of Wisconsin Press.

———. 1984–85. Vai occupational continuities: Traditional to modern. *Liberian Studies Journal* 10 (2): 12–23.

———. 1987. The dynamics of Liberian Vai culture and Islam. *Liberian Studies Journal* 12 (2): 135–48.

Honing, Henkjan. 1993. A microworld approach to the formalization of musical knowledge. *Computers and the Humanities* 27:41–47.

Ingold, Tim. 2000. *The perception of the environment: Essays on livelihood, dwelling, and skill*. London: Routledge.

Jenks, Chris, ed. 1998. *Core sociological dichotomies*. London: Sage Publications.

Johnson, Norris Brock. 1984. Sex, color, and rites of passage in ethnographic research. *Human Organization* 43 (2): 108–20.

Jones, Adam. 1981. Who were the Vai? *Journal of African History* 22 (2): 159–78.

King, Kenneth. 1977. *The African artisan: Education and the informal sector in Kenya*. London: Heinemann / New York: Teachers College Press.

Keller, Charles M., and Janet Dixon Keller. 1996. *Cognition and tool use: The blacksmith at work*. Cambridge: Cambridge University Press.

Kondo, Dorinne K. 1990. *Crafting selves: Power, gender, and discourses of identity in a Japanese workplace.* Chicago: University of Chicago Press.

Krader, Lawrence. 1974. *The ethnological notebooks of Karl Marx.* Studies of Morgan, Phear, Maine, Lubbock. Assen: Van Gorcum.

Kvale, Steinar. 1997. Research apprenticeship. *Nordic Journal of Educational Research* 17 (3): 186–94.

———. 2006. Interviewing between method and craft. Paper presented at the Second International Congress of Qualitative Inquiry, Urbana-Champaign, Illinois.

Kvale, Steinar, and Svend Brinkmann. 2008. *InterViews: Learning the craft of qualitative research interviewing.* 2nd ed. Thousand Oaks, CA: Sage Publications.

Lageman, Ellen. 1989. The plural worlds of educational research. *History of Education Quarterly* 29 (2): 185–214.

Lancy, D. F. 1980. Becoming a blacksmith in Gbarngasuakwelle. *Anthropology and Education Quarterly* 11 (4): 266–74.

Latour, Bruno. 1987. *Science in action: How to follow scientists and engineers through society.* Cambridge: Harvard University Press.

Lave, Charles, and James G. March. 1975. *An introduction to models in the social sciences.* New York: Harper and Row.

Lave, Jean. 1977. Tailor-made experiments and evaluating the intellectual consequences of apprenticeship training. *Quarterly Newsletter of the Institute for Comparative Human Development* 1 (2): 1–3.

———. 1980. What's special about experiments as contexts of thinking. *Quarterly Newsletter of the Laboratory of Comparative Human Cognition* 2 (4): 86–91.

———. 1986. Experiments, tests, jobs and chores: How we know what we do. In *Becoming a worker*, ed. K. Borman and J. Reisman. Norwood, NJ: Ablex: 1986.

———. 1988. *Cognition in practice: Mind, mathematics and culture in everyday life.* New York: Cambridge University Press.

———. 1992. Wor(l)d problems: A microcosm of theories of learning. In *Context and cognition: Ways of learning and knowing*, ed. P. Light and G. Butterworth, 74–92. Hemel Hempstead, Hert.: Harvester Wheatsheaf.

———. 1995. Ethnographies of apprenticeship. Unpublished manuscript.

———. 1996. The savagery of the domestic mind. In *Naked science*, ed. Laura Nader, 87–100. New York: Routledge.

———. Forthcoming. *Changing Practice.*

Lave, Jean, and Ray McDermott. 2002. "Estranged labor learning." *Outlines: The Journal of Scandinavian Social Science* 4 (1): 19–48. Reprinted in *Critical perspectives on activity: Explorations across education, work and everyday Life*, ed. Peter Sawchuk, Newton Duarte, and Mohamed Elhammoumi (Cambridge: Cambridge University Press, 2006), 89–122.

Lave, Jean, and Martin Packer. 2008. Towards a social ontology of learning. In *A qualitative stance: In memory of Steinar Kvale, 1938-2008*, ed. Klaus Nielsen, Svend Brinkmann, Claus Elmholdt, Lene Tanggaard, Peter Musaeus, and Gerda Kraft, 17–47. Aarhus: Aarhus University Press.

Lave, Jean, and Etienne Wenger. 1991. *Situated learning: Legitimate peripheral participation.* New York: Cambridge University Press.

Law, John. 2004. *After method: Mess in social science research.* London: Routledge.

Liebenow, J. Gus. 1987. *Liberia: The quest for democracy*. Bloomington: Indiana University Press.

Lobato, Joanne. 2006. Alternative perspectives on the transfer of learning: History, issues, and challenges for future research. *Journal of the Learning Sciences* 15(4): 431–49.

Lucas, Gavin. 2000. *Critical approaches to fieldwork: Contemporary and historical archaeological practice*. New York: Routledge.

Lukose, Ritty, 2009. *Liberalization's children: Gender, youth and consumer citizenship in globalizing India*. Durham: Duke University Press.

Mahmood, Saba. 2002. Feminist theory, embodiment, and the docile agent: Some reflections on the Egyptian Islamic revival. *Cultural Anthropology* 6 (2): 202–36.

Manganaro, Marc, ed. 1990. *Modernist anthropology: From fieldwork to text*. Princeton: Princeton University Press.

Marchand, Trevor H. J. 2001. *Minaret building and apprenticeship in Yemen*. Richmond, Surrey: Curzon.

Marcus, George. 1994. After the *Critique of ethnography*: Faith, hope, and charity, but the greatest of these is charity. In *Assessing cultural anthropology*, ed. Robert Borofsky, 40–52. New York: McGraw-Hill.

———. 1995. Ethnography in/of the world system: The emergence of multi-sited ethnography. *Annual Review of Anthropology* 24:95–117.

Marcus, George E., and Michael M. J. Fischer. 1986. *Anthropology as cultural critique: An experimental moment in the human sciences*. Chicago: University of Chicago Press.

Marx, Karl, and Frederick Engels. 1847/1998. *The Communist manifesto*. Ed. Eric Hobsbawm. London: Verso.

Maurer, Bill. 2005. *Mutual life, limited: Islamic banking, alternative currencies, lateral reason*. Princeton: Princeton University Press.

———. 2006. The anthropology of money. *Annual Review of Anthropology* 35:15–36.

———. 2008. Re-socialising finance? Or dressing it in mufti? Calculating alternatives for cultural economies. *Journal of Cultural Economy* 1 (1): 65–78.

McDermott, Raymond P. 1993. The acquisition of a child by a learning disability. In *Understanding practice: Perspectives on activity and context*, ed. Seth Chaiklin and Jean Lave, 269–305. Cambridge: Cambridge University Press.

McLaughlin, Stephen Douglas. 1979. *The wayside mechanic: An analysis of skill acquisition in Ghana*. Amherst: Center for International Education, University of Massachusetts, Amherst.

McNaughton, Patrick R. 1988. *The Mande blacksmiths: Knowledge, power, and art in West Africa*. Bloomington: University of Indiana Press.

Middleton, John, ed. 1970. *From child to adult: Studies in the anthropology of education*. Garden City, NY: American Museum of Natural History, the Natural History Press.

Ministry of Planning and Economic Affairs. 1987. *Population and housing census of Liberia summary results, 1984*. Monrovia, Liberia.

Mitchell, Timothy. 1988. *Colonising Egypt*. Cambridge: Cambridge University Press.

Moran, Mary H. 2006. *Liberia: The violence of democracy*. Philadelphia: University of Pennsylvania Press.

Murphy, Robert F. 1972. *The dialectics of social life: Alarms and excursions in anthropological theory*. London: Allen and Unwin.

———. 1990. The dialectics of deeds and words, or anti-the-antis (and the anti-antis). *Cultural Anthropology* 5 (3): 331–37.

———. 1994. The dialectics of deeds and words. In *Assessing cultural anthropology*, ed. Robert Borofsky, 55–59. New York: McGraw-Hill. Originally published, in slightly different form, in *Cultural Anthropology* 1990 5 (3): 331–37.

Mustafa, Hudita. 1997. Practicing beauty: Crisis, value and the challenge of self-mastery in Dakar, 1970–1994. PhD diss., Harvard University.

Nakamura, Jeanne, and Mihaly Csikszentmihalyi. 2002. The concept of flow. In *Handbook of positive psychology*, ed. C. R. Snyder and Shane J. Lopez. Oxford: Oxford University Press.

Newell, Alan. 1973. You can't play 20 questions with nature and win. In *Visual information processing*, ed. W. G. Chase, 283–308. New York: Academic Press.

Nielsen, Klaus. 2006. Learning to do things with things: Apprenticeship learning in bakery as economy and social practice. In *Doing things with things*, ed. Alan Costall and Ole Dreier, 209–24. Aldershot: Ashgate Publishing.

———. 2007. Learning in a changing practice. Paper presented at the International Society for Theoretical Psychology Conference, June 18–22, York University, Toronto, Canada.

Ollman, Bertell. 1976. *Alienation: Marx's conception of man in capitalist society*. 2nd ed. Cambridge: Cambridge University Press.

Packer, Martin. 2001. The problem of transfer, and the sociocultural critique of schooling. *Journal of the Learning Sciences* 10 (4): 493–514.

Papert, Seymour. 1980. *Mindstorms: Children, computers and powerful ideas*. New York: Basic Books.

Peil, Margaret. 1970. The apprenticeship system in Accra. *Africa: Journal of the International African Institute* 40 (2): 137–50.

———. 1979. West African urban craftsmen. *Journal of Developing Areas* 14 (1): 3–22.

Person, Yves. 1962. Tradition orale et chronologie. *Cahiers d'études africaines* 2 (7): 462–76.

Petitto, Andrea. 1979. Knowledge of arithmetic among schooled and unschooled African tailors and cloth-merchants. PhD diss., Cornell University.

Pokrant, R. J. 1982. The tailors of Kano City. In *From craft to industry: The ethnography of proto-industrial cloth production*, ed. Esther N. Goody, 85–132. Cambridge: Cambridge University Press.

Posner, Jill 1978. The development of mathematical knowledge among Baoule and Dioula children in Ivory Coast. PhD diss., Cornell University.

Rabinow, Paul. 1986. Representations are social facts: Modernity and post-modernity in anthropology. In *Writing culture: The poetics and politics of ethnography*, ed. James Clifford and Robert E. Marcus, 234–61. Berkeley and Los Angeles: University of California Press.

Reed, H. J., and Jean Lave. 1979. Arithmetic as a tool of investigating relations between culture and cognition. *American Ethnologist* 6 (3): 568–82.

Reichard, Gladys A. 1936. *Navajo shepherd and weaver*. Glorieta, NM: Rio Grande Press.

Robben, Antonius C. G. M., and Jeffrey A. Sluka, eds. 2007. *Ethnographic fieldwork: An anthropological reader*. Oxford: Blackwell.

Rogoff, Barbara, and Jean Lave, eds. 1984. *Everyday cognition: Its development in social context.* Cambridge: Harvard University Press.

Rouse, Joseph. 1987. *Knowledge and power: Towards a political philosophy of science.* Ithaca: Cornell University Press.

Säljö, Roger, and Jan Wyndhamn. 1993. Solving everyday problems in the formal setting: An empirical study of the school as context for thought. In *Understanding practice: Perspectives on activity and context,* ed. Seth Chaiklin and Jean Lave, 327–42. Cambridge: Cambridge University Press.

Scribner, Sylvia, and Michael Cole. 1973. The cognitive consequences of formal and informal education. *Science* 182 (4112): 553–59.

———. 1981. *The psychology of literacy.* Cambridge: Harvard University Press.

Serpell, Robert. 1969. Cultural differences in attentional preference for colour over form. *International Journal of Psychology* 4:1–8.

Sharp, Donald W., Michael Cole, and Charles Lave. 1979. *Education and cognitive development: The evidence from experimental research.* Monographs of the Society for Research in Child Development 44 (1–2), no. 178.

Simon, Herbert. 1980. How to win at 20 questions with nature. In *Perception and production of fluent speech,* ed. R.A. Cole, 535–48. Hillsdale, NJ: Erlbaum.

Singleton, John. 1998. *Learning in likely places: Varieties of apprenticeship in Japan.* Cambridge: Cambridge University Press.

Smutylo, Terence S. 1973. Apprenticeship in wayside workshops of an Accra neighbourhood. MA thesis, Institute of African Studies, University of Ghana.

Snow, David A., Calvin Morrill, and Leon Anderson. 2003. Elaborating analytic ethnography: Linking fieldwork and theory. *Ethnography* 4:181–200.

Spier, Leslie. 1924. Zuñi weaving technique. *American Anthropologist* 26:64–85.

Stallybrass, Peter, and Allon White. 1986. *The politics and poetics of transgression.* Ithaca: Cornell University Press.

Strathern, Marilyn. 1990. Out of context: The persuasive fictions of anthropology. With comments by I. C. Jarvie and Stephen A. Tyler and George E. Marcus. In *Modernist anthropology: From fieldwork to text,* ed. Marc Manganaro, 80–130. Princeton: Princeton University Press.

Tamari, Tal. 1991. The development of caste systems in West Africa. *Journal of African History* 32 (2): 221–50.

Terrio, Susan J. 2000. *Crafting the culture and history of French chocolate.* Berkeley and Los Angeles: University of California Press.

Thomasson, Gordon Conrad. 1987. Indigenous knowledge systems, sciences, and technologies: Ethnographic and ethnohistorical perspectives on the educational foundations for development in Kpelle culture. PhD diss., Cornell University.

Tyler, Stephen A., and George E. Marcus. 1990. Comments on "Out of context: The persuasive fictions of anthropology." In *Modernist anthropology: From fieldwork to text,* ed. Marc Manganaro, 125–30. Princeton University Press.

Van Maanen, John. 1990. Great moments in ethnography: An editor's introduction. *Journal of Contemporary Ethnography* 19:3–7.

Verdon, Michael. 1979. African apprenticeship workshops: A case of ethnocentric reductionism. *American Ethnologist* 6 (4): 531–42.

Verran, Helen. 2001. *Science and an African logic.* Chicago: University of Chicago Press.

Wacquant, Loïc. 2003. Ethnografeast: A progress report on the practice and promise of ethnography. *Ethnography* 4 (1): 5–14.

Wagner, Daniel A. 1974. The development of short-term and incidental memory: Cross-cultural study. *Child Development* 45:389–96.

———. 1978. Memories of Morocco: The influence of age, schooling and environment on memory. *Cognitive Psychology* 10:1–28.

Wax, R. 1971. *Doing fieldwork: Warnings and advice.* Chicago: University of Chicago Press.

Weber, F. 2001. Settings, interactions, and things: A plea for multi-integrative ethnography. *Ethnography* 2:475–99.

Westbrook, David. 2008. *Navigators of the contemporary: Why ethnography matters.* Chicago: University of Chicago Press.

Williams, Raymond. 1983. *Keywords: A vocabulary of culture and society.* Rev. ed. New York: Oxford University Press. First edition published 1976.

Willis, Paul. 1980. Notes on method. In *Culture, media, language: Working papers in cultural studies, 1972–1979,* ed. Stuart Hall, Dorothy Hobson, Andrew Lowe, and Paul Willis, 88–95. London: Hutchinson.

Willis, Paul, and Mats Trondman. 2000. Manifesto for ethnography. *Ethnography* 1 (1): 5–16.

Wolf, Margery. 1992. *A thrice told tale: Feminism, postmodernism and ethnographic responsibility.* Stanford: Stanford University Press.

INDEX

paradoxes of, 154; as way of being, 12; Western ethnocentrism, as counter of, 9. *See also* critical ethnographic practice; critical ethnography; ethnography

ethnography, 3, 6, 162–63n21; awkward scale, 9; crisis of representation, 4–5; culture, centrality of, 8; ethnographic research, 4, 61–62; ethnographic research, as iterative, 149; genres of, 4; knowledge economy, 14; as seeing and believing, 9; sense of location, 9; as social research, 8; theory, role of, 8. *See also* critical ethnographic practice; critical ethnography; ethnographic practice

Faubion, James D., 161n16
Favret-Saada, Jeanne, 13, 145
fieldwork, 3–4, 8, 12–13, 33, 36; as empirical, 2; minimization of, 5; and monographs, 5; socialization and training, as core of, 9
formal education, 19, 58, 90; informal education, divide between, 16, 20, 22, 24, 32, 37, 41, 59, 61, 91–92, 143–45, 148, 164n23, 164–66n25; general knowledge, 143; teaching by demonstration v. explanation of principles, 20; theory of power of, 19
Fortes, Meyer, 16–18, 158–59n5; bracketing practices of, 21–22; transmitting culture, 21
Foucault, Michel, 174n10

garment inventory, 51, 53–54, 68, 70–71
Geertz, Clifford, 4
Ginsburg, Herbert, 108
Gladwin, Hugh, 180n4
Gola people, 29, 31; secret societies, 30; Vai, differences with, 30. *See also* Vai and Gola peoples
Goody, Esther, 155, 164–66n25
Goody, Jack, 166n27
Gramsci, Antonio, 161–62n18
Greenfield, Patricia Marks, 174–76n1
Gupta, Akhil, and James Ferguson, 7–8, 160–61n12

Guyer, Jane, 176–77n4, 180n1

Hall, Stuart, 161–62n18
Hansen, Karen, 169n2, 171n9
Happy Corner, 2, 15, 25, 27, 35, 37–39, 41, 47–49, 54, 65, 80, 82, 84–85, 89, 91, 98, 118, 133, 145, 150; apprenticeship in, 44, 57; construction of, 43; garment styles, and social differentiation, 56; master tailors in, 44; sewing-machine tax in, 43; tailors in, as mediators, 56; tailors in, rural background of, 42; tailors' income of, as erratic, 44; tailors' livelihood of, as threatened, 43; trousers, and style innovations, 56. *See also* Monrovia; Vai and Gola tailors
Hart, Gillian, 161–62n18; constitution, processes of, 154
Hedegaard, Mariane, 161–62n18
Hlophe, Stephen, 168n36
Hobsbawm, Eric, 166n28, 166–67n29
Holland, Dorothy, 161–62n18

informal economy: and tailors, 41
informal education, 16, 18–19, 21, 23, 58, 90, 148; as concrete, 60; and form, 61; in nonliterate cultures, 22; particular knowledge, 143; of tailors, 41
Islam, 29–30

James, William, 161–62n18
Jenks, Chris, and Herbert Simon, 163–64n22
Judd, Charles, 92, 106; and Judd/Thorndike debate, 176n2

knowledge, 14, 90; and knowing, 14; and knowledgeability, 153; and knowledge economy, 14; knowledge production, and ordinary people, 60; knowledge transmission, 16; knowledge transmission, and acquisition, 116; nature of, 150; non-school situations, 116; and practice, 166–67n29; and praxis, 153; and schooling, 19
Krader, Lawrence, 161–62n18
Kvale, Steinar, 14–15, 151, 164–66n25